WAR STORIES

ORAL HISTORIES OF THOSE WHO SERVED

By Jeffrey L. Meek

Copyright © 2023 by Jeffrey L. Meek

ISBN 9798378491728

On the Cover: *Pilot Don Francke sits in his Corsair at Peleiu. (Photo courtesy of Don Francke)*

No part of this book may be reproduced or transmitted in any form or by any means, electronic, photographic, or mechanical, including photocopying, recording, or by any information storage and retrieval system, except as agreed upon by the author and the publisher. All rights remain with the author except for repeated publications of this book.

Raven's Inn Press
806 Rhoden Rd.
Judsonia, AR 72081

Table of Contents

Foreword .... Page 1

Introduction .... Page 3

Chapter I: World War II Veterans .... Page 7

Chapter II: Korean War Veterans .... Page 81

Chapter III: Vietnam War Veterans .... Page 124

Chapter IV: Cold War Veterans ......,............. Page 279

Chapter V: War on Terror Veterans .... Page 342

Photo section .... Page 359

Conclusion .... Page 363

Also by Jeffrey L. Meek
They Answered the Call: World War II Veterans Share Their Stories
Lee Harvey Oswald - A Lone Gunman?
The Manipulation of Lee Harvey Oswald and the Cover – Up That Followed

War Stories

Foreword by Senator John Boozman

My dad, U.S. Air Force Master Sergeant Fay Boozman, flew on B-17 bombers in World War II and honorably served in uniform for 23 years. As was common with so many of the selfless heroes called to defend freedom during this time, he didn't talk much about his military service. My father, like so many other Greatest Generation veterans, passed away before I could encourage him to reflect on his experiences openly and share memories with his loved ones. This important part of family history, as well as our nation's past, will never be recovered.

Fortunately, people like Jeff Meek are tirelessly working to save the stories of our veterans.

The Library of Congress Veterans History Project, launched in 2000 with the goal to collect and retain the oral histories of our nation's veterans, has been successful in this effort due in part to Jeff's relentless pursuit of capturing these memories.

I have been honored to expand efforts in Arkansas to encourage and teach folks about the importance of preserving stories in the VHP. Through this work, I was introduced to Jeff who has demonstrated his passionate advocacy for veterans through countless hours of collecting their testimonials and sharing them so we can all learn

Jeffrey L. Meek

about the selfless sacrifice of the men and women who wear our nation's uniform.

He has certainly set an example for all to follow in collecting these interviews. In this book, Jeff continues to demonstrate his dedication to our veterans by highlighting the unique situations they faced and the dangerous conditions in which they served with firsthand accounts of their service in answering the call to defend our nation.

This is a link to history and reminder to future generations of the courageous individuals who have shaped our country thanks to their selfless service in uniform.

War Stories

Introduction
"War Stories: Oral Histories of Those Who Served"

Little did I know that back in 2003 my meeting and interviewing America's veterans, would change my life. Our son, Jeffrey Alan Meek, joined the United States Marine Corps in 1996 and soon after that I became interested in learning more about World War II. I wanted to know what my father, PFC Clarence R. Meek, U. S. Army, serial number 46027776, did in World War II, so I contacted the National Personnel Records Center in St. Louis, Mo., and learned that many millions of veteran's records were burned when a fire broke out at the facility on July 12, 1973. That fire burned an estimated 17 million official military personnel files. One of them was my dad's.

All I had at that time was a copy of his Honorable Discharge paper (DD-214) and a certificate saying he had graduated on Nov. 3, 1945, as a rifleman (745) from Replacement School Command, Camp Hood, Texas. As time when on I realized that dad would have very likely been a part of the invasion of Japan had that horrendous battle ever taken place. Thankfully it did not.

I also had approximately a dozen photos, but very little in those photos gave me any clues, until I met a man who collected uniforms and knew others that might be able to identify something in those photos. That happened when he and I went to a militaria show where a friend of his noticed an insignia on my father's garrison cap. "Your dad was in Italy, wasn't he?" the man asked. I replied that I wasn't sure where he was. He then told me the pin on the cap represented the 350th Infantry Regiment. From there I

Jeffrey L. Meek

learned the 350th was part of the 88th Infantry Division, called "The Blue Devil" Division because instead of ties, they wore blue scarves around their neck. Sure enough, there was dad with that scarf on.

Shortly after moving to Hot Springs Village, I received a large envelope from a friend of dad's that was at Camp Hood with him. Inside that envelope were five letters my dad wrote to him. They were dated and also noted where dad was when he wrote them. Eureka! Now I knew where in Italy dad had been.

A few years later I stumbled across a rare book about the 350th Infantry Division in occupation in Italy. I bought it and sure enough, the information in that book followed along the path I could tell my dad traveled according to those precious letters.

I began to read extensively about the war and those words on those pages hit me like a freight train. I was absolutely amazed at what they lived through, what they saw firsthand and what their thoughts were about their experiences. While still living in Illinois, from 2003 to 2005, I began filming veteran oral histories as a way to say, "thank you for your service." Just saying "thanks" wasn't good enough for me so I began doing those oral histories.

Then in June 2005 we moved to Hot Springs Village, Ark. In the fall of 2006, my wife Jeanne and I traveled to Europe, walked the invasion beaches of Normandy, experienced Dachau, the American cemeteries, stood in the remnants of the "Band of Brothers" foxholes outside of Foy, Belgium, and even had a meal at Hitler's Eagles Nest in Berchtesgaden. These experiences added to my appreciation of what World War II veterans experienced

War Stories

and soon thereafter I began doing oral histories in the Village.

In 2007, those stories began appearing in the Hot Springs Village Voice newspaper and continue to do so to this day. To date, I've done about 390 of them. In my first veteran-related book, published in 2011, titled, "They Answered the Call: World War II Veterans Share Their Stories," I included 75 World War II stories, many of them told for the first time.

In this book, I have included 85 stories covering World War II, Korea, the Vietnam era, the Cold War era, and the War on Terror. Some of the veterans mentioned here had their time in service overlap some of those eras but will be shown in only one of those eras.

I thank Hot Springs Village Voice owner/publisher Jennifer Allen for letting me share them here with you again in a book format. And to my publisher, Del Garrett, thanks for your work on this book. As usual, you did a fine job.

I also thank the many veterans who have shared photographs with me, nearly 1,000, taken during their time in service. Several of them are in this book.

And to Senator John Boozman for providing a foreword and to Anita Deason, retired U.S. Army Colonel and former military and veteran's affairs liaison to Senator John Boozman's office for her comments. Both are staunch veteran supporters.

I will forever remember the brave men and women in this book, many who have died since the interview took place. Sitting down with them just a few feet away from me and my video camera, watching some of them breakdown, was chilling and I will always cherish those times together.

Jeffrey L. Meek

At the end of some of those interviews we hugged and wiped away tears, both of us. As I said, the experiences changed my life.

Once on a "Wounded Warrior Project" site I saw this: "The greatest casualty is being forgotten." This book is my attempt at getting their stories out to as many people as possible so that we do not forget their courage, devotion, and commitment to our country.

These stories appeared as columns and were previously in the Hot Springs Village Voice newspaper and are used with the express permission of J. Allen, LLC, which retains the rights to the columns.

War Stories

Chapter I: World War II Veterans

Bill Armstrong served on LST 808 in World War II

Among the many U.S. Navy vessels of World War II was the LST or landing ship, tank. Or as several World War II veterans have told me the LST should stand for "large slow target."

No matter what you call it the ship was one of the real work horses of the period and not a comfortable ride in the calmest of conditions.

LST plans were developed by the company Gibbs & Cox and over 1,150 were ordered by the Navy for use in the war. LSTs carried smaller craft topside and had a tunnel-like hold usually filled with tanks or vehicles, guns, or cargo and of course troops wherever they could fit. On LST 808 was Bill Armstrong who served on the ship in several capacities.

Armstrong grew up in Detroit, Mich., and told me his interest in joining the Navy came from watching war movies, citing "Guadalcanal Diary" as an example. In 1944, still just 17 years old, he got his father to sign the necessary paperwork for him to become a sailor. "I was anxious to get away for some reason," said Armstrong who already had two brothers in uniform.

His first stop, in June, was at the base at Great Lakes outside of Chicago and then to Ames, Iowa to learn diesel mechanics. Next, he went to Gulfport, Miss., for assignment to LST 808 recently arrived from Illinois. Soon he would find himself working in the auxiliary engine area as a Fireman Second Class.

Jeffrey L. Meek

The area had three engines which produced the electrical needs of the ship. Two would be on-line running generators while a third engine ran, but at rest. "The job was to keep things running normally. Basically, you watched two dials so things wouldn't overload," Armstrong said of his job.

LST 808 went to Hawaii for amphibious training which included beach landings and firing at targets. His battle station was as a second loader for a 40 mm gun. Armstrong would hand the rounds to another sailor who would put them in the gun.

After completing the training, the 808 sailed off with a convoy bound for the Feb. 19, 1945 invasion of Iwo Jima. On board were Marines which were taken ashore near the base of the only tall feature on the island – Mt. Suribachi.

The ship hit the beach, unloaded their "Devil Dogs" and had other crewmen help get half-tracks on matting so they could climb the beach's steep bank just ahead. Then on Feb. 23 while parked there on the beach, Armstrong witnessed both flag raisings atop Suribachi.

"I saw both of them. I saw the first one go up, saw it come down and the second one go up," he said of one of the most historic military events of the Pacific war. "I was in an ideal spot looking right up at Suribachi." With the flag-raising came cheering and a brief ship celebration.

Following the completion of the mission at Iwo, Armstrong heard they were sailing to Australia, but instead they went to the Philippines – Tacloban briefly, then Leyte – where the ship was reloaded and prepped for the next big invasion which would be Okinawa.

War Stories

On the way to the April 1, 1945 invasion the convoy hit a typhoon. The crew was sent to their battle stations, which for Armstrong was his gun tub. From that location he had a good look at his ship as it actually twisted left and right as it plowed through the storm.

At Okinawa the ship took Army troops and vehicles ashore. It was here Armstrong, and the U.S. Navy took a historical beating by Japanese kamikazes. "There were kamikazes every day," Armstrong remembers. The term kamikaze is derived from the Japanese words "kami" (God) and "kaze" (wind).

Next the LST was ordered to Ie Shima with more Army troops. Here the 808 and other Navy ships were pounded by "The Divine Wind," another term for suicidal aerial missions.

Up to three times per day, waves of deadly assaults came in, sinking ships and killing America's finest. It was also at Ie Shima Armstrong got a different job. At dusk he and others would load into a Higgins Boat and lay fog all night to cloak U.S. vessels from enemy attack.

Once the island was somewhat secured Armstrong went ashore. He was at a movie one evening when he learned the beloved war correspondent Ernie Pyle had been killed there on the island.

Armstrong also worked to empty oil from tanks. While doing such work one-day LST 808 was hit.

General quarters sounded, so Armstrong quickly went to a shower area to get some of the oil off his body. There he asked another sailor to scrub his back. The man said no, he had to get to the engine room. "Just take a second," Armstrong said to his shipmate. So, the man did

Jeffrey L. Meek

take the time to scrub, which delayed his trip to the engine room which seconds later was hit by the torpedo. Delaying the trip to the engine room by just those very few moments probably saved the man's life.

The crew was soon told to abandon ship, did so and was taken to Ie Shima where they were put into work parties doing different jobs as needed. Near Armstrong's work area was a large ditch which the men used to take cover during the daily Japanese air raids.

One day, he and others decided to stay put in their tents during one such raid. Incoming U.S. Navy gunfire aimed at the planes came in on the area of tents. "I rolled out of my sack onto the ground and as I hit the ground the fella behind me yelled 'I'm hit'," said Armstrong. After the firing stopped the men checked out their wounded comrade and found he had been hit in the foot. Then Armstrong saw where the shell came into his tent. Pointing at his forehead he added, "That's where the shell would have hit me had I stayed there (in the bunk)."

From Ie Shima, Armstrong sailed back to the U.S. and landed in San Francisco. It was here he learned of the Japanese surrender. After a 30-day leave, he was assigned to the USS Saratoga which was now being used as a troop ship bringing men home from war. Armstrong made two such trips to Hawaii. His job was working in the freshwater hold. "We pumped the fresh water to the tanks and boiler room," he said.

Next Armstrong was assigned to the USS General Bliss for a trip to Japan. On the Bliss he worked in the boiler room and wasn't told what was on board the ship or why they were going to Japan. Later the ship returned, and he

War Stories

was discharged on June 16, 1946. As a civilian Armstrong spent 36 years as a Detroit firefighter retiring in 1986.

That same year he and wife Dollie moved to Hot Springs Village, Ark. They have four children: Claudia, Denise, David, and Mark.

Reflecting back on his service and the interview, Armstrong said he had wanted to do the interview for a long time but wasn't sure his story was good enough.

"I'm glad I did it," he said of going through with the process.

Jeffrey L. Meek

LeRoy Baird served on USS Hornet during Doolittle Raid

Every once in a while, a story comes my way that is too good not to share. Such is the case of World War II Navy veteran LeRoy Baird. I met Baird during one of four Honor Flights I experienced. He had a hat on that said USS Hornet. After confirming this, I asked Baird if he witnessed the April 18, 1942 Doolittle raid on Tokyo. "I saw all 16 of them (B-25 bombers) take off," Baird said.

After not being able to get the significance of this man's story off my mind I finally decided to drive to northwest Arkansas to interview him in depth on his experiences aboard the Hornet, which, though serving briefly (it was sunk in the Oct. 26, 1942 in the Battle of Santa Cruz), were many.

Baird had been working in a Civilian Conservation Corps (CCC) camp for 15 months when he decided to join the U.S. Navy. After a training stop at Great Lakes in Illinois he reported to a new aircraft carrier – the USS Hornet – in Norfolk, Va. on Oct. 20, 1941.

As a deck hand his job was to maintain a section of the fantail. His battle station was as a lookout up in a tower on the ship's superstructure.

On Dec. 7, 1941, Baird was on his way to breakfast in Norfolk when he learned of the Japanese attack at Pearl Harbor. He immediately caught a cab and rushed back to the Hornet. Upon his arrival he and others began to load bombs and other munitions on board. While doing so an operator mishandled a loading, Baird stepped in to help and

War Stories

injured his shoulder. He would have the shoulder in a sling for several weeks.

Later, on Feb. 2, 1942, the crew witnessed something rather strange when two B-25 Mitchell bombers were loaded onto the ship's deck. Soon they were loaded with sandbags and the carrier headed for open water where the bombers did a practice takeoff. "They took off like there was nothing to it," said Baird.

Hornet returned to Norfolk where she and the USS Missouri did a shakedown cruise. Then the Hornet, through the Panama Canal, made her way to San Diego, Calif., where U.S. Marine pilots used the ship to practice takeoffs and landings. Baird said two weeks later they sailed to San Francisco where they anchored out in the bay until dark.

The ship then went into nearby Goat Island and loaded 16 B-25s on their deck. The crew thought they would be transporting the planes to Honolulu. Little did they know they were about to embark on one of the most historic missions of World War II, the famous Doolittle raid, a retaliatory air strike on Tokyo, Japan.

The next day the Hornet left America. Later a dirigible appeared overhead and dropped a package on the carrier's red deck. Soon Captain Marc Mitscher announced to the crew they were not headed to Hawaii. They were going to bomb Tokyo.

About 10 days later, near Midway Island, the ship linked up with Task Force 16 and began continuing on toward the Japanese mainland. Baird's battle station was as a lookout high up on the ship's superstructure. They were to proceed to within 400 miles of Japan and launch the B-25s at that point.

Jeffrey L. Meek

On April 18, Baird said he was in the lookout nest when the sailor on his left spotted a Japanese boat, the Nitto Maru. The cruiser USS Nashville opened fire, eventually sinking the vessel.

Fearing the Nitto Maru may have radioed back to Japan, the decision was made to launch the bombers even though they were still 600 miles from their target instead of the planned 400 miles. This meant the planes and their crew would not have enough fuel to return. They'd have to find somewhere to land in China.

Through 30-foot waves the Hornet sailed on and successfully launched all 16 B-25s, then set a course for Hawaii. As they did so, Baird said he spotted another Japanese boat which was attacked and sunk by Hornet-carried airplanes.

About a week later the carrier arrived in Pearl Harbor, was fitted with improved radar, and set out for the Battle of Coral Sea. Before they got there the fight was over, so she again returned to Hawaii. After a brief stay, she was ordered to Midway Island on May 28.

On June 4, planes from the carriers Hornet, Yorktown and Enterprise engaged the oncoming Japan attack ships. The air attack resulted in many losses, but three Japanese carriers were hit.

On June 6, further carrier-based attacks followed which caused the Japanese task force to retreat, thus saving Midway Island and marking a definite turning point in the Pacific war. During the fighting near Midway, Baird told of an incident when a U.S. plane came in for a landing.

War Stories

The plane's right side landing gear collapsed as it hit the Hornet's deck, which caused the plane to pivot to the right toward the superstructure. Then the plane's machine guns began firing which killed five men.

Baird narrowly missed being hit. A friend, also in the lookout nest, pointed to a bullet hole where Baird had been standing. "About two feet above where I was, was a round hole," said Baird. After helping to save Midway the ship returned to Hawaii, got new radar and on Aug. 17 sailed for Guadalcanal to provide naval support.

In October Baird and the Hornet sailed off for the Battle of Santa Cruz. During the Oct. 26 fighting she was struck by bombs, torpedoes, and a dive bomber. Baird said the Japanese had been searching for "the red-topped" carrier, knowing it was involved in the Doolittle Raid.

As matters grew worse aboard the ship the captain gave the order to abandon her. "Everybody started getting into the water as fast as they could. By the time I got down there (from the lookout tower) they (the life rafts) were kind of skimpy," said Baird.

A friend and he began to climb aboard one life raft and were "kicked off" as he described it, because there was no more room on board. Eventually Baird climbed down a knotted rope line to the water's surface. He estimates he was in the water for three to four hours before being rescued by the destroyer USS Morris. As he swam for the Morris, the ship fired rounds around him to keep sharks at bay. Asked if he saw any sharks Baird said, "I didn't know if there were any sharks around or not. I wasn't looking for them. I was wanting to get over there (to the Morris)."

Jeffrey L. Meek

As he reached the destroyer, he attempted to climb onto the guard over the propeller but was too weak to pull himself up. "A couple of men stepped down and grabbed us and pulled us up on deck," said Baird. Early the following morning the Hornet was finished off by Japanese warships and sunk.

The Morris took the survivors to a nearby island where they recovered.

Baird was given a new assignment. He was to be put aboard the USS Crescent City and would drive landing craft onto beaches. "I would take a 34-foot boat and make landings," said Baird. He did so at several islands including Vella Lavella near the Solomon Islands.

He was on Manus Island when he heard of the Japanese surrender and was later taken back to the states on a hospital ship. In San Diego he was put into a hospital. Asked why, Baird said, "They thought I was crazy." Six months later he was discharged.

In civilian life Baird was a welder for General Motors and at a specialty shop, mostly with aircraft. He retired in 1985. That same year, at a Doolittle Raider reunion in Albuquerque, N.M., he got to meet Jimmy and Mrs. Doolittle and some of the other raiders like the captain of plane number five, David Jones. Baird has one child, a daughter Diane.

Baird is one of a few men to have witnessed several significant aspects of World War II and live through it. He said he had never been interviewed before our meeting.

War Stories

Howard Baldwin served with 346th Bomb Group in World War II

The 346th Bombardment Group (Heavy) was activated on Sept. 7, 1942, and assigned to the Second Air Force. With its B-17s and B-24s, the Second served as a training outfit and later as a replacement unit.

Redesignated in Aug. 1944, the 346th prepared for combat with B-29s and moved into the Pacific Theater in June 1945, but the war ended before the unit began combat missions. Within the 346th BG was the 462nd Bomb Squadron and in that squadron was Howard Baldwin who worked as a mechanic.

The Portland, Ore., native was playing softball in the backyard when he heard of the Dec. 7, 1941, Japanese attack on our fleet at Pearl Harbor, Hawaii. "We were just dumbfounded," said Baldwin of the shock of the news.

Baldwin always had an interest in flying and when he became a senior in high school, he decided to enlist in the U.S. Army Air Force (USAAF) in spring 1943. Until graduation he was in the enlisted reserves. Within one month of graduating, he got a letter calling him to service. "I remember looking in the mailbox and seeing this red printed letter and I knew I was on my way," said Baldwin of the letter and envelope he still has to this day.

He was first sent to Fort Lewis, Wash., for indoctrination and on Dec. 4, 1943, he went to Buckley Field in Colorado for basic training. Next was a ride to Salt Lake City, Utah, and assignment to the Second Air Force.

In March he was ordered to Dalhart, Texas to work as an aircraft and engine mechanic. The job surprised him

Jeffrey L. Meek

because he thought he would be sent to gunnery school. At Dalhart, Baldwin did flightline work on the B-17 Flying Fortress, a 74-foot-long bomber with four 1,200 horsepower Wright GR-1820-97 Cyclone radial engines. The plane could fly up to 300 miles per hour, held a crew of 10 and could cover a distance of 1,850 miles. The 55,000-pound beast was armed to the teeth with 13 50-caliber machine guns and could carry up to 17,600 pounds of bombs. The pilots of the B-17s were replacements bound for the air war in Europe.

On a typical day Baldwin and others would use a checklist of required maintenance items, pre-flight the planes, refuel them, and have everything ready for service the next day. They would also stay with the bombers on standby until the crews arrived. "We started the engines, loaded the props and that would be a normal day," Baldwin said.

Maintenance would also take place at 25, 50 and 100 hours of use. The mechanics would, as needed, change spark plugs, magnetos, batteries, cylinders and fix numerous oil leaks in the engines. Prop maintenance was also necessary at times when the props would be dented. These props were reversible by the pilots to 180 degrees so they could better control the aircraft and provide better fuel efficiency.

Months later Baldwin was put with the 346th BG at Pratt, Kan., to now work on the huge B-29 Superfortress. This meant double the workload because that plane's engines had 18 cylinders instead of nine like on the B-17 and it was higher off the ground due to its immense size.

War Stories

This giant had four 2,200 horsepower Wright R-3350-23 Cyclone radial engines that could fly the Superfortress at speeds up to 350 miles per hour. At 99 feet long and a wingspan of just over 141 feet this super bomber would be the first to have the capability to reach the Japanese homeland with a large bomb load and return to an island base. It was the B-29 that would later be used in the August 1945 atomic bombings of Hiroshima and Nagasaki. It was also the first pressurized bomber in the U.S. air fleet.

But the plane also had a recurring problem – engine fires – which were many and sent many of the B-29s and their crews to an early grave. If fact the first one Baldwin ever saw was while he was at Dalhart and this Superfortress crash landed.

Baldwin said the B-29 had a lot of oil leaks which would fuel the fires. He said the leaks likely occurred because of vibration which would loosen clamps and hoses and cause the oil to leak. And sometimes the cylinders would blow and spew oil.

To make an engine change the mechanics would take an entire day to complete the job. In fact, during temporary duty in Puerto Rico the mechanics changed out 31 engines in 30 days. In August 1945 the war ended, and Baldwin was sent to Fort Lawton, Wash. A few weeks later they were put on a train headed for San Francisco, but the train was stopped in Chico, Calif.

"They didn't know what to do with us," said Baldwin of the situation. They stayed there for approximately three months, kept in shape, played sports, and helped fight a forest fire. "I learned then that I never wanted to be a fire

Jeffrey L. Meek

fighter," said Baldwin. Finally, he was ordered to Salina, Kan., in Nov. 1945 for work at Smokey Hill airfield doing B-29 maintenance so pilots could still get their flight time and pay.

Baldwin said it was there they also got a different version of the B-29 engine, one that had an advanced fuel delivery system that also provided cooling for the engines. "That helped a lot with the serve-ability of the engines and the operation was a lot smoother. It stopped a lot of those fires," he said.

As we were near the end of our interview Baldwin remembered an interesting occurrence while in Puerto Rico when Vice President Harry Truman was at the base. Touring the facility, Truman made his way to the area where Baldwin was working. "He came through and shook my hand out on the line and said I needed to get my hands treated," said Baldwin, whose hands were covered with cuts.

Baldwin was later sent to Fort Lewis for separation on April 4, 1946. From there he returned to Portland and that fall attended Oregon State University on the GI Bill. "That was a great thing we had," Baldwin said of the GI Bill. He graduated four years later with a major in accounting and a minor in industrial engineering.

Baldwin then went to work for Crown Zellerbach, a paper products manufacturer, for the next 22 years, then moved to Crossett, Ark., for work with Georgia Pacific for 19 years. Thereafter he became a consultant, retiring in 1991. That same year he moved to Hot Springs Village, Ark., from Crossett. He has three children: Tom, Laura, and Wendy.

War Stories

Looking back on his days in uniform Baldwin said serving in the USAAF had a tremendous impact on his life. "I think it set up my life forever," said Baldwin who cherishes the memories of the people he served with.

Jeffrey L. Meek

George Bell served aboard a destroyer in World War II

The destroyer USS Flusser was out to sea with the aircraft carrier USS Lexington when the Japanese attacked Pearl Harbor on Dec. 7, 1941. On December 12, she returned to the devastated harbor. Thereafter, she sailed as a convoy escort and patrol ship throughout 1942-1943. As Allied forces began retaking Pacific islands, Flusser conducted shore bombardment and fire support to provide cover for many invasions. Later she participated in actions in the Philippines, Okinawa and finished the war on occupation duty in Japan. George Bell served on the Flusser and this is his story.

Born in Brownsville, Texas, Bell was outside playing football with friends when his father came out on the porch and told the boys of the Pearl Harbor attack. "I told dad we should go join up," remembers Bell. He and his father went to the recruiting station the next day.

After signing up, Bell was sent to Great Lakes Naval Station in Illinois. From there he was off to San Francisco where he and others were divided into groups of 20 for training purposes. Bell's group was assigned to submarine duty. Just as he was about to board the sub he was pulled out of the group. He was told he couldn't be a sub mariner because he was colorblind. Instead, he was assigned to the destroyer USS Flusser.

With no destroyer-related training, Bell went aboard. As a deckhand, he did some painting, and the ship underwent some repair and did a trial run. Once completed, Flusser sailed to Hawaii. The ship then joined five other destroyers and made its way to Guadalcanal. From there

War Stories

they went to New Guinea as part of "MacArthur's Navy" as the men called it. Actually, it was the 7th Fleet. The ship was involved with pre-invasion bombardment and fire support to cover many assaults.

Bell and his shipmates then went to Australia for an overhaul and also participated in the sinking of two Japanese submarines. He worked on a five-inch gun crew carrying shells and gunpowder. He was later chosen to become a torpedo man. His job was to man torpedo tubes on the destroyer and to prepare torpedoes for firing.

Bell recalls two instances when the ship was hit during combat. In September 1944, after a stop at Pearl Harbor, the ship was patrolling the Marshall Islands. She sustained damage from a Japanese shore battery while cruising near the island of Wotje. Nine men were wounded, including Bell. "We had 244 holes in the ship," said Bell.

The ship left the area immediately. That night they heard Tokyo Rose announce that the USS Flusser had been sunk. After repairs, they sailed to the Philippines escorting reinforcement convoys to Leyte.

During this time the ship was attacked. "Two betty bombers came in from our fantail," said Bell. Both bombers dropped 500 pounders but missed direct hits. "The ship lifted up right out of the water," Bell recalled. Damage was sustained below deck, but the ship was able to carry on. Bell hurt his back.

At times, when he was not needed as a torpedo man, Bell worked in the ship's repair shop. He and others would also do maintenance on large tanks containing smoke for use in evasion tactics.

Jeffrey L. Meek

Bell and the Flusser made stops at many islands as they escorted convoys and helped cover landings of troops. In December 1944, while in the Philippines, the ship received damage from a near miss of kamikazes. "One of them hit close enough the pilot came out, bounced off our deck and into the water," said Bell.

Later the ship was assigned picket duty during the invasion of Okinawa. After the war ended, the ship made a quick stop at Nagasaki, Japan to look at the damage done by the atomic bomb. From there, Flusser went to Sasebo, Japan. Shortly thereafter, Bell was told he was going home. He made his way to San Francisco and then to Galveston, Texas for discharge in October 1945. His father, who worked for the FBI, was there to meet him.

An executive officer asked Bell to reenlist for three years, but Bell said no. He was one of the lucky ones. Of the nine ships in his squadron, five had been sunk. He also lost a good friend, a fellow-torpedo man, who was killed in action. The man was buried at sea.

After the war, Bell attended the University of Houston for a time, but was lured away with a job offer in the appliance business. He spent the rest of his career in the appliance business and ran his own place for 43 years. From his first marriage to Betty Lou, he had two children: Donna and Lou Ann. With his second wife, Muriel, he had another Donna.

War Stories

Keith Brown served as Navy instructor during World War II

Keith Brown grew up in Illinois, played football – offensive guard and linebacker – at Wheaton High School in the Little Seven Conference. Brown's father was a World War I Navy veteran that made 19 trips from the U.S. to the war zone. That partially prompted him, while still in high school, to take a Navy exam for placement at Annapolis. Sixty students tested, 30 of them were college students. Brown came in as second alternate to the appointment. "In those days a Congressman could appoint one (person) to Annapolis and then there was a first alternate, second alternate and third alternate. I was the second alternate," said Brown.

The Navy also had a V-12 program for college students. The V-12 program was to supplement the force of commissioned officers during World War II. The program's goal was to provide officers, and to assign them to several different specialties. Tens of thousands of students took the competitive exam, as did Brown in April 1943 while still in high school.

He was selected for the V-12 program and on July 1 reported to the University of Wisconsin – Madison for mechanical engineering school, along with approximately 500 other young men. Brown hoped to be an aeronautical engineer but accepted his post and began his studies.

Initially, now in Wisconsin, Brown was glad to be there, despite the tight quarters in a men's dormitory. Each morning began with exercises, breakfast, then off to learn.

Jeffrey L. Meek

Brown said the classes equaled a 40-hour work week, plus many more hours of study.

The Navy's rule was lights out at 10 p.m. "So we studied under the covers and in closets in order to stay with it," said Brown. The program taught a lot of math and science, plus some physics and other courses.

Every Saturday, for about three months, Brown participated in a boxing program. He talked about his boxing partner, a senior. When the two boxed, Brown said they sort of "friendly boxed." The instructor said to step it up and start hitting more seriously. Suddenly, Brown said, "I was on the ground. What I learned was Willy (his partner) had tried out for the boxing team and he sure knew a lot more about boxing than I did," chuckled Brown. Boxing was just one of the many programs the Navy had in place for the men to participate in on the weekends.

The men would hit the town of Madison on Friday and Saturday nights but would have to be back in the dorm by midnight. Brown said with so many men in the war, the girls outnumbered the guys 10 to one.

Also, during his schooling, he participated on Wisconsin's varsity track team for two seasons. He lettered both years. "I ran hurdles, low and high hurdles," remembered Brown.

By March 1, 1946, he completed eight semesters, got his mechanical engineering degree, then took a month off. Once back, he asked for and was assigned to Glenview Naval Air Station outside of Chicago. The job he was given was to teach a new ground school program. With the war over, many were leaving the service, but still more came on board. It was these men, mostly right out of high school,

War Stories

that Brown taught such things as naval organization, ranks, ratings and about the different Navy ships, all in an effort to learn "the Navy way."

Sometimes, in the afternoons when he wasn't teaching, Brown would go down on the air station's flight deck. There he got to know some of the guys and one in particular was mentioned by Brown. A pilot friend offered him a ride in one of their planes. A week later Brown took him up on the offer and hopped on an old biplane with two engines, Brown in the front seat, the pilot in the back seat. "We went out and flew around and it was very nice," said Brown. Miles away was a training field where the pilot would touch down and takeoff again. "We got a little further away from Glenview and he said 'want to do a few loops and other things?' And I said sure, why not. So, we did a loop and that was an interesting experience," said Brown with a smile.

Later, the pilot told him to grab the control stick to get a feel of the plane. A few minutes later the pilot had Brown actually fly the plane. "So, I flew it and moved it a little bit, but not very far. But I actually flew it for maybe 10 minutes," said Brown of the experience.

On July 4, 1946, Brown was discharged from the Navy at Great Lakes Training Center. As a civilian he went back to school, taught at the University of Wisconsin at Madison, then worked for Shell Oil Company in the engineering department.

Later he went to work for the Kohler Company as a sales engineer, then off to Mobil Oil for 30 years, becoming a commercial sales manager. In December 1983, Brown retired and with wife Jean moved to Hot Springs Village,

Jeffrey L. Meek

Ark., from Fairfax, Va. They have five children: Kevin, Craig, Nancy and twins Martha and Marjorie.

Looking back on his days in the Navy, Brown said he was disappointed he did not see any action, but also felt being in the Navy was a great experience. He added, "Technically I'm a veteran, but never saw combat, but we did what we signed up to do."

War Stories

Milton Crenchaw trains Tuskegee Airmen

It all began in January 1941 when the U.S. War Department announced the establishment of a black flying unit. By July an airfield was under construction in Tuskegee, Ala. Later that month the first class of cadets arrived for training. There to train those cadets was Little Rock native Milton Crenchaw who would work as a primary flight instructor for what would soon be known as The Tuskegee Airmen. Eventually these African-American pilots would form the 332nd Fighter Group – 99th, 100th, 301st, 302nd Fighter Squadrons – which would be led by Col. Benjamin O. Davis, Jr.

From July 19, 1943, to June 28, 1946, 2,483 pilots trained at Moton Field and Tuskegee Army Airfield. Of those, 996 graduated and 352 would deploy to Europe. Eighty-four of them would be killed in action as they completed 1,578 combat missions bringing down 112 enemy aircraft. To distinguish their planes from others it was decided they would paint the tails of the fighters with red paint and thus become known as the Red Tails.

After graduation from high school Crenchaw got interested in becoming an auto mechanic. In 1939 he had an opportunity to attend the Tuskegee Institute where he would take mechanical engineering classes. While at the Institute he decided to join a civilian pilot training program in which he learned to fly a Piper Cub airplane. The training took place at a nearby airfield close to Auburn University. As the training phases developed, chief C. Alfred Anderson of Howard University brought with him Waco biplanes to accommodate training needs.

Jeffrey L. Meek

In March 1941, Eleanor Roosevelt visited nearby Kennedy Field. The First Lady had helped obtain the funding for the construction of Moton Field at Tuskegee and while there, wanted one of the pilots to take her for a ride.

Anderson was the outfit's chief instructor pilot, so it was he that took her up. "She was down there because she was a trustee and it just happened that she came out on the field. I buckled her down in that Piper Cub," said Crenchaw. He added that the rear seat's control stick had to be moved to accommodate Mrs. Roosevelt because she was wearing a skirt. "Off they went over to look at the Institute," added Crenchaw.

On Dec. 7, 1941, Crenchaw said he was in Birmingham, Ala. having hitchhiked there to receive his instructor's rating qualification flight. On Dec. 8, he learned of the attack and was also told he needed to provide his own airplane for the flight. "He (the instructor) asked me where my airplane was. I said I didn't have an airplane," said Crenchaw of the experience.

Not owning a plane, he had to locate one for rent, which he did at Birmingham Airport. After returning to the other airfield for the flight he was asked where his parachute was. Again, he had no chute, so he had to return to the Birmingham airfield, rent a parachute and return again. So, with a rented airplane and parachute, Crenchaw took to the air, passed the test and was officially certified as a primary flight instructor.

Now on the payroll as a primary flight instructor Crenchaw would take the cadets up for one hour training flights, many of which were pretty scary due to the inexperience of the cadets. "All the flights were (scary) until

War Stories

you could calm them down," said Crenchaw of the Piper Cub flights. As time went on more and more black cadets arrived as he continued the job of training the young men until the war ended. "I worked my tail off," said Crenchaw of the job.

He left Tuskegee when the unit was disbanded, returned to Little Rock, and started a flight instruction school at Philander Smith College. In 1953 he left the college and became a crop duster near Scott, Ark.

Later he returned to flight instruction at several Air Force locations, retiring as a civilian flight instructor in 1983. That year he received a Department of the Army certificate of service recognizing 30 years of Federal Service. The certificate was signed by Major General Bobby J. Maddox. Crenchaw has four children: Milton, Jr., Dolores, Ervin, and Countess.

Reflecting on his service Crenchaw said, "I have lived the perfect life. God has been good to me." In 2007, Crenchaw was elected to the Arkansas Black Hall of Fame and spoke following the Jan. 20, 2012, premiere of the movie Red Tails in Little Rock at the Rave Theater. He has been recognized by President Bill Clinton, Congressmen Vic Snyder and Mark Pryor and Governor Mike Beebe.

Jeffrey L. Meek

Don Dahl served as ball turret gunner on a B-17

Perched beneath the B-17 Flying Fortress heavy bomber was a 43-inch diameter steel ball with .50 caliber machine guns sighted through a Sperry gun sight. Commonly known as the ball turret, it was a location on the bomber that saw plenty of action as gunners fired on approaching enemy aircraft.

It was a tight fit for most men assigned there, which included Don Dahl who served as a ball turret gunner with the 8th Army Air Force (AAF), 379th Bomb Group, 526th Bomb Squadron in England from Jan. 22, 1945, to April 25, 1945. The 379th would later be known as one of the top two most accurate bomb groups in England, dropping over 26,400 tons of bombs on its targets.

Dahl was attending a party when he heard of the Japanese attack on Pearl Harbor. "I wasn't too happy with the Japanese," he said of hearing what had happened. Dahl had deferments because of his farm work, but in December 1943 he and a cousin decided to join the AAF. The night before they were leaving to sign up, a blizzard swept through the area. He rode a horse to his cousin's house and then the two walked to the train station for the ride to the enlistment center Kimble, Minn.

Once there, Dahl underwent tests and told the recruiter he had polio two years ago. "My leg was still a little weak. They flunked me out right now," said Dahl. He went back home and checked the mailbox. In it was a draft notice, so he went to a different center, did not tell them about the polio and was accepted. Dahl then went to the AAF desk,

War Stories

passed a test, and was sent to Amarillo, Texas for basic training.

After basic, Dahl went to Salt Lake City in January 1944 for assignment. From there he traveled to Dyersburg, Tenn., where he was put to work on the flight line repairing airplanes.

One day he saw a notice saying gunners were needed, so he volunteered and was shipped to Las Vegas on June 1, 1944, for training. There he learned about .30 and .50 caliber machine guns and shot them from a turret on the ground.

Next, in the air, the would-be gunners fired at targets. "I was just barely able to squeeze in beside the two .50 caliber machine guns," said Dahl of the tight fit in the ball turret. "Your knees are up in your chest."

After completing the training, he was shipped to Lincoln, Neb., where his B-17 crew formed up. More training followed in Alexandria, La., and later in November he went back to Lincoln, picked up a new B-17, which flew the crew to Grenier Field, NH., Goose Bay, Labrador, Reykjavic, Iceland, and finally to Preswick, Scotland on Dec. 30, 1944.

Shortly thereafter he was put with 379th Bomb Group, 526th Bomb Squadron in Kimbolton. The base, which was in the middle of a farm field, had four squadrons, one in each corner of the field.

A few weeks later Dahl flew his first mission when the outfit, through heavy flak, to bomb the oil plant in Sterkrade, Germany. Upon their return they noticed they had four holes in their B-17. Most of his 16 missions were flown in the B-17 called "Wishbone."

Jeffrey L. Meek

On days off he would occasionally go to London. Dahl got to know one British family who lived in and owned a pub not far from the city. On one visit to London one of the German V-1 buzz bombs struck the city so close to him that it blew him out of bed.

The worst mission he flew was his last mission – April 25, 1945 – on an armament factory in Pilzen, Czechoslovakia. At the morning briefing he and the others were told the AAF had let the Germans know they were coming so they'd remove the Czech workers from the plant. "So, there will be enemy anti-aircraft fire," Dahl was told. Because of this the fliers were told not to make any second bomb runs on the target.

Dahl was in the lead squadron whose bomb run was off target. So, against their orders they swung around and tried again. "By that time, they (the Germans) opened up with everything. I saw two of our planes go down and I understand two others went down," said Dahl of the flight.

Talking about flying through the heavy flak (which is short for the German word fliegerabwehrkanonen – anti-aircraft artillery) Dahl said "I guess you're kind of numb and say well is it going to get me? And I guess you do a lot of praying too."

Of Dahl's 16 missions, 12 were in the ball turret. Because of a B-17 modification he flew the other four as a waist gunner. This modification saved his life. Because on his first mission in the waist the ball turret on the B-17 was hit and partially blown off.

Because his missions took place in 1945, he didn't see many German fighter aircraft, but on one occasion he did see the ME-262 jet fighter streak through their

War Stories

formation. Flying at altitudes of up to 30,000 feet the men were exposed to extremely cold temperatures. According to Donald Miller's book, Masters of the Air, more men were lost to frostbite than to combat-related wounds in the first year of 8th AAF operations. Anything over 12,000 feet meant the fliers would need to wear their oxygen masks. Dahl said ice would form on the bottom of the mask.

The ball turret was so small he could not be in his turret with a parachute. To get to his chute he'd need to exit the turret and get his chute stowed in another part of the bomber. Again, because it was so uncomfortable in the turret, Dahl did not get in until over enemy territory. Looking over a list of his missions one sees he participated in the famous and controversial Feb. 14, 1945, bombing of Dresden which ignited a firestorm.

While Dahl was at Kimbolton the war ended in Europe. Celebrations broke out everywhere. On V-E Day Dahl went to the pub owned by his British friends, who were also in a big celebratory mood. He (the owner/friend) said, "Don I've got three bottles of scotch. One for each of my daughters when they get married and one for V-E Day so let's go at it," laughed Dahl.

After a few stops in England, he was put aboard the Queen Mary on Sept. 5, 1945, his 21st birthday and was later discharged in California. As a civilian he went to college, became a mechanic, and later worked for General Motors, ending his career 30 years later as a zone service manager in Omaha, Neb.

Dahl retired in 1987 and moved to Hot Springs Village, Ark in 1990. He has two children: Kevin and Lee Ann.

Jeffrey L. Meek

Mike Disabato served in WWII Quartermaster Corps

The U.S. 8th Army was sent to the Pacific in the summer of 1944. Their early missions were to seize control of New Guinea, New Britain, the Admiralties and Morotai. Later they moved on to the Philippines before finishing up as part of the occupying forces in Japan. With the 8th Army was Mike Disabato who served in the 189th Quartermaster Corps.

Disabato grew up in the Chicago area and was at work in his brother's garage when they learned of the Dec. 7, 1941, attack at Pearl Harbor. After high school graduation he had some trouble finding a job and was eventually drafted in February 1944. His first training stop would be Fort Lee, Va., where he also did some technical automotive work.

After a leave back home, he was ordered to California, was put on a troopship jammed with 4,500 men, and headed for the Pacific and a fate as yet unknown. The voyage was not without incident.

Disabato said about two days out, while in convoy, during the night, the ship was struck by a plane. He said the men never did learn what kind of plane or any other information about the matter. To this day he's not sure what really happened that day.

Now damaged, the troopship had to drop out of the convoy and get to the Marshall Islands for repair. Approximately one month later the ship was repaired and off they went. At sea they learned they were going to Luzon in the Philippines.

War Stories

As they approached the secured beachhead the troopers were put on an LST and taken ashore. Soon they were all assigned to different units and Disabato's was the 189th Quartermaster Corps. Their job was to set up a gasoline distribution point.

They began organizing the depot, fighting the hellish mosquitoes, and prepared to get 55-gallon drums filled with fuel to wherever they were ordered. The gasoline came to them in large tanker trucks. Disabato and others would use hoses to get the gas from truck to drum and then, with a crane, stack them in preparation for travel. Smoking was done by most servicemen back in these days, but not at Disabato's depot. The job was dangerous enough without asking for troubles arising from smoking.

Besides the handling of the gas, he would also at times be called upon to drive a tanker to some destination. The roads were narrow, curvy, and rough which caused many mechanical breakdowns, usually axles.

And the roads weren't the only menace along those jungle roads. Diehard Japanese soldiers also sniped at the trucks and drivers as the snaked their way down the "roads." On one occasion Disabato's good buddy was driving the truck in front of him when suddenly the truck was hit and erupted into a blaze. His friend was badly burned and sent home for recovery. Disabato was more fortunate. He and the trucks he drove were never hit by enemy gunfire.

With all the mechanical problems that took place, a maintenance crew was formed. It included Disabato who, as the reader may remember, got some automotive-like training back in bootcamp.

Jeffrey L. Meek

The work was tough, the truck parts few in number, and there were times when the repairs had to be made out on those dangerous roads. Sometimes the men had to cannibalize one truck of its parts to fix another. And a shortage of lubricants also contributed to the mechanical breakdowns. As time went on the men got the parts and lubricants, they needed to get the job done.

Then one day the 189th got the word they had prayed for. Japan had surrendered. The war was over, but not for Disabato and his fellow soldiers. They would be going to Japan as part of the occupation forces. Sure enough, they boarded the ship that took them to Tokyo where they did similar work hauling gas and fixing trucks. Disabato said he didn't leave the base too often but when he did his experiences with the Japanese people were pleasant. He also recalled sending home a lot of silk.

As the calendar changed to 1946, Disabato finally had earned enough points to get back to the good ole USA. Before leaving he helped newer soldiers learn the ropes and also built doors for some jeeps that were used in the cold winter months. By teaching the newer guys how to do their job he took on an officer-like supervisory role which brought up an incident that still troubles him even today.

Back when Disabato was in his early training days he had scored well on several tests and wanted to attend Officer's Candidate School (OCS). After completing the requirements, he met with three captains for a review. It was then he learned he had not been approved for OCS. Not because of his test scores, but solely because of his height. "That hit me hard, but I went on," Disabato said of the big disappointment. Now fast forward to his time of discharge.

War Stories

In May 1946 he arrived back in the U.S. From Seattle and by troop train he went to Camp McCoy, Wis. for discharge. Now a Sergeant, Disabato received his final paycheck and was asked a question: would he consider attending OCS? "I said you've got to be kidding me and he said no, they'd like to have me attend. I said I was (told) I was too short," said Disabato.

The man asked him who had told him he was too short. "I said two-and-a-half years ago I was told that, and I haven't grown since," he recalled. So, he declined the offer and went home with that bitter taste in his mouth of what could have been back in 1944.

Disabato used the GI Bill to attend the University of Illinois where he graduated with a degree in electrical engineering. He then went to work in the auto industry in sales, then spent 16 years on the Advisory Board with American Motors. He then switched to advertising and spent another 12 years with the company.

After retiring Disabato decided to go back to work and became a realtor. Thirteen years later he retired again and in 1997, with his wife Pat, moved to Hot Springs Village, Ark., from Orland Park, Ill. The couple has three children: Dale, Mark, and Karen.

Looking back on his Army service Disabato said, "It made a man out of me in a hurry. It's (the Army) the greatest discipline in the world." And another thing came out as the interview concluded when Disabato said going ahead with the interview helped him to put the OCS matter behind him.

Jeffrey L. Meek

John Dykstra serves in Pacific war as infantryman

The U.S. Army 24th Infantry Division, known as "The Victory Division," was sent overseas before the Pearl Harbor attack on Dec. 7, 1941. By war's end the division saw 260 days in combat, fighting in the New Guinea, Southern Philippines, and Luzon campaigns. One part of the 24th was the 34th Infantry Regiment and in that regiment by late 1944 was John Dykstra.

Dykstra grew up in Chicago, went to school in Cicero, Ill., just a few blocks away from the Al Capone home. He was still in high school at the time of the Pearl Harbor attack. "Everybody was so devastated that our country got attacked. Patriotism was so high, and everyone wanted to join the military," said Dykstra who remembers his father using a bicycle to get to work because of the rationing of gasoline. "There wasn't enough gas to drive his car," he said. "People were suffering, but they gave up these things (gas, sugar, meat, etc.) because they knew it was for the war effort. We saved our bacon grease because they needed it for munitions. We were glad to help anyway we could," said Dykstra of the World War II home front.

In August 1944 he was drafted, took a physical and reported to Fort Sheridan near Chicago for processing. Next came a train trip to Camp Roberts in California for basic training where he learned to handle an M-1 Garand, a bazooka, mortars, and hand grenades.

After a 10-day furlough Dykstra returned to Camp Roberts and received orders to report to Fort Ord where he boarded a ship called "Sea Fiddler" which took 2,100 men on a zig-zag course to New Guinea. Next was a trip to

War Stories

Mindanao in the Philippines where he was soon placed in Company F, 34th Infantry Regiment as a rifleman.

The men were housed in large tents. Early one morning he awoke to the sounds of gunfire, took cover, and stayed low as bullets whizzed through their tent. A Japanese patrol had attacked the camp, but Dykstra and the others in the tent could not return fire. They had their rifles, but no ammunition.

Shortly thereafter they loaded into trucks and headed for the jungle to carry out patrols. The company searched for the Japanese, spent nights in a three-man foxhole, then continued the patrol each day.

About four days into the patrol, they contacted dug-in Japanese troops. Dykstra and the others were told to spread out and fix bayonets. A firefight ensued. Finally, the shooting stopped, and the searching began again.

Asked to try to describe what being in combat is like, Dykstra said, "Adrenaline flows and it seems like you do things automatically. You don't think about much other than to keep from being shot, keeping your head down, keeping yourself safe. It's an experience I don't want to go through again. After it's over you feel good that you made it. It's hard to explain, but it's something you had to do. You don't ask why; you just do it." Some of his buddies were slightly wounded in the fight, but Dykstra made it through without being hit.

The patrol ended up on a plateau near an airstrip near a pineapple farm. The men made pineapple wine that Dykstra said, with a smile, wasn't any good. Soon the troopers loaded into planes, then trucks took them back to their unit camp.

Jeffrey L. Meek

After a time, his unit and others were taken by ship to Palau to invade the island. After naval bombardment the men climbed down the ship's nets and headed for the beach. "We got to the beach and there wasn't a shot fired at us. It was as calm and quiet as could be," Dykstra said. The men moved up, went out on patrols, and before long took control of the island. Here, too, Dykstra came under fire for a short time but made it through once again.

Ships took the men back to Mindanao where they soon heard of the dropping of an atomic bomb on Japan. "Then came a second one and after that we heard about the surrender and that was like music to our ears. We all cheered (and thought) this is the end of the war, now we could go home. But then we learned the 24th Infantry Division was going to be first in occupation," Dykstra recalled.

He and his outfit ended up in Nagasaki, the site of the Aug. 9, 1945, atomic bomb attack. Here they came ashore carrying as much ammo as they could. They formed up in lines and marched into the city. "It was amazing to see the whole city. There was nothing left of it. Everything was destroyed. Most of the buildings were gone, just rubble all over," said Dykstra of the scene.

The unit's objective was to load all Japanese rifles into trucks so they could be hauled off and dumped in the ocean. While doing the work the men were told they could take one rifle as a souvenir, which he did, boxing it up and sending it home.

During his time in Japan he met friendly Japanese people, including a pilot. The men did some sight-seeing

War Stories

and continued their occupation duties as they waited to accumulate enough points to come home.

Finally, that day came as Dykstra boarded the SS Milford Victory which took the men to San Francisco where a band and cheering people gave them a warm welcome home. From there he went to Fort Ord, then Fort Sheridan where he was discharged on Oct. 17, 1946.

As a civilian he eventually became an auto mechanic at a dealership, then later worked in waste management for 35 years, retiring in 1989. He and wife Lois moved to Hot Springs Village, Ark., from Westmont, Illinois the following year. They have four children: John, Sandra, Karen, and Kenneth.

Looking back on his time in World War II Dykstra said it was an experience he never expected. Being raised in a Christian home he always felt he was protected by his God. "I always had the feeling that He would take care of me in whatever situation I was in," Dykstra said. He added that he saw his entire life being directed by his Creator.

Jeffrey L. Meek

Don Francke served in the Pacific with the USMC

It was arguably the most powerful naval aircraft of World War II accounting for over 2,000 enemy kills in the Pacific theater. The F4U Corsair, known as "Whistling Death," by the Japanese, was powered by a 2,450-horsepower engine, could reach a speed of 446 miles an hour and climb to 41,000 feet. One of the men piloting these fighter airplanes was Don Francke who served in World War II from 1942 to 1945.

He was at the Waukegan, Ill., airport where he took flying lessons when he heard of the Japanese attack at Pearl Harbor. "Everybody, right then, said let's go enlist," Francke recalled. Shortly thereafter his brother and two friends did enlist. "My mother didn't want us both to go so she held me back a year. I went in the Marine Corps in September 1942."

Originally enlisting in the Navy's V-5 program he attended Navy flight training and eventually graduated on Sept. 28, 1943. "Tyrone Power pinned my wings on," smiled Francke. That day would be memorable for other reasons as well. That same day Francke was told his brother, a P-38 pilot, was missing in action and later that afternoon he would be the best man in a friend's wedding. "It was an up and down day," Francke said. His brother was never found and was listed as killed in action a year later.

He requested assignment to the Marine Corps and was sent for operational training to Lee Field, Jacksonville, Fla., with the F4U Corsair. "The Corsair was a great airplane. It was strong and it was fast. It was the best prop plane they had in World War II," said Francke.

War Stories

Next, he was ordered to El Toro, Calif., in early 1944 for further training for overseas duty. Coming back to the base one day, one of his good friends was killed in an accident. Francke accompanied the body back home to Minnesota.

After completing the training, he and others were designated as replacement pilots, boarded the USS Savo Island on March 23, 1944, and left for the fight in the Pacific. Their first stop was Espiritu Santo in the New Hebrides Islands where they were transferred to Quoin Hill on the island of Efate for more training in overwater navigation and combat tactics. While there another friend was killed in a landing accident.

Francke was then assigned to the Marine Fighter Squadron 114. The squadron, which contained 24 planes and 40 pilots, was told they'd be a part of the next invasion. That turned out to be Peleliu.

When the time came for the squadron to fly to Peleliu they moved from Guadalcanal to Bougainville and then Emirau where they waited for the airstrip to be secured. On the way in they made a stop at Owi where a Seabee saw his last name and said they had a Francke in their outfit. Turns out it was cousin Walter, who Francke had not seen in many years. Walter gave him many cans of food because he knew there was little food on Peleliu.

Finally, they were off to Peleliu and had to come in under 100 feet because of the enemy fire coming in over the airstrip. Landing on the island he saw a lot of damage. "It was really torn up from the artillery and bombing. There were a few Japanese items around the airfield – an old tank and a couple of airplanes and not much else," Francke said of the area around the runway.

On the island his base camp would occasionally come under sniper fire from the nearby hills. "They also blew up an ammo dump alongside the airfield that shot a lot of shrapnel over into us and one of my good buddies got hit," Francke said.

As soon as they arrived the squadron was put to work. Their job was to bomb the hills alongside the runway. "We had the shortest bombing run in history. We wouldn't even pull up our wheels. We'd just load up with bombs and napalm, take off, turn, and go right alongside the runway and drop the bombs and napalm. Then we'd come in and land and they'd reload us, and we take off, leave our wheels down, drop again and come around and land," said Francke of his early Peleliu missions.

Later the missions moved farther inland as the Corsairs strafed the hills. Missions also included combat air patrols and barge sweeps looking for Japanese movement on the barges as they went from island to island.

Francke and others also learned how to "skip bomb," which was skipping the bombs across the surface of the water and into a target. During one such mission the squadron was sent out to sink a Japanese troopship. Four Corsairs, one at a time, come down on the vessel. The first three missed and Francke was number four. "I laid it (the bomb) right in the middle of the ship and blew it up. They gave me the Distinguished Flying Cross for that," Francke said.

War Stories

He flew several other types of missions which included air cover at Ulithi for the assembled fleet of U.S. ships, and a P-38 photo recon mission. Francke was also a part of a large flight at Koror Island in which the entire Squadron napalmed an area to drive out the enemy. During the mission they flew through heavy anti-aircraft fire which downed the skipper. His body was never recovered.

And there were times when he came close to going down himself. Like when he flew so low, he took out a few coconut tree tops and another incident when he was hit in a wing tank.

On one strafing mission, Francke got hit in his oil cooler. The plane was smoking and losing oil as he climbed out of the attack run. He flew the Corsair for another 25 minutes to the base, lowered his flaps, cut the engine and the prop stopped. "I landed with a dead engine. The fire trucks were coming up behind me. Somebody jumped up on the wing and said are you okay. I said yeah and it turned out to be an old high school buddy I didn't even know was there," laughed Francke.

His squadron was being prepped for the invasion of Okinawa when he got word he was going home. Back in the U.S., based out of Floyd Bennett Field in New York, he ferried planes across the country from manufacturers to airfields.

After the war Francke had inactive reserve status, applied for regular Marine Corps duty, and served one tour in Korea flying F9F2 Panther jets. Later he did a tour with the Air Force, flying Saber jets.

Francke also served at a test pilot school, a naval ordinance test station at China Lake and ended his 24-year

Jeffrey L. Meek

military career in 1966 as commanding officer of a C-130 transport squadron at Cherry Point, N.C. In civilian life he worked with data processing and later as Executive Director of the Air Traffic Control Association until 1971. Following this he worked as a flight instructor and as a consultant for the Air Traffic Control Association until 1984.

That same year he and wife Darlene, also a U.S. Marine, moved to Hot Springs Village, Ark. They have one child, Donna.

War Stories

Darlene Francke served in Marine Corps during World War II

Darlene Francke grew up in Illinois. She was living in Waukegan when she learned of the Japanese attack at Pearl Harbor, Hawaii. "I was at home, and we were all upset," she said of that moment when she got the news. After graduating from high school, she and two friends got jobs with the Illinois Bell Telephone Company. Francke worked as a telephone operator.

Later, in 1943, the three girls decided to spread their wings, as she put it, and moved to Houston, Texas, rented an apartment and went to work for a telephone company there.

As time went on the three thought more and more about the war and what they could do. One night they sat down and had a serious discussion. "We decided we should do something for the war effort," Francke said of what was about to be a turning point in her life.

Her two friends joined the Navy and Francke joined the Marine Corps. "I decided I wanted to be a Marine. I had a favorite cousin that was one of the first lady Marines and she came home once in her uniform and I was so impressed with it that it clicked for me," said Francke.

She returned to Illinois, spoke with her parents about her decision, got their blessing and went to an enlistment center in Chicago. She took the necessary tests, passed and was on her way to becoming a U.S. Marine.

Francke said she was treated well along the way and ended up at Camp Lejeune, N.C., in April 1944. At Lejeune she was put with 10 women for boot camp. "They would

Jeffrey L. Meek

wake us up at the crack of dawn and we would jog to the mess hall, then back to the barracks," she recalled.

In a location separate from the men, the days were filled with marching and lots of exercising. "We were busy the whole time we were there. They had you moving all the time," she said of her male drill instructors.

Following boot camp, she was chosen for work in Camp Lejeune's communications center, probably because of her prior work with telephone companies. "I worked the teletype machine sending and receiving messages," Francke said of the work. Each day at the center she would check in with a female lieutenant and get to work. Besides working with the teletype machines, she would also make phone calls to various base locations to get things where they were needed.

She'll never forget one message that came in when she was on duty. "On the teletype machine I was the first one to know the war was over because I was working the machine at that point. I took the message up to the commanding general of the base. That was exciting and of course there was a lot of shouting and carrying on all day and all evening," said Francke of the thrilling notification of the end of World War II.

On occasion she and others would get a pass to go into nearby towns. Francke said she wasn't teased about being a female in the Marine Corps. "We were treated just like one of them," she said.

On April 3, 1946, she received her honorable discharge and returned to Waukegan by train. She was anxious to get back home. During an earlier visit she started dating a fellow Marine named Don, who is also in this book.

War Stories

He was then flying out of nearby Glenview Naval Air Station with the inactive reserve. After returning home they resumed dating and were married in September. The two moved 18 times over the next 20 years as he continued his military service. "It was a wild 20 years," said Francke.

After discharge she worked at the nearby Great Lakes Training Center. Much of her time was spent mapping the routes discharged veterans would take to return home.

Looking back on her service as a Marine, Francke said she is very proud to have served. "Once a Marine always a Marine. We even have it on our license plate," she said with pride.

Jeffrey L. Meek

Claude Griffin served in World War II and Korea

The 88th Infantry Division did much of the fighting in World War II Italy as they participated in the Rome-Arno, North Apennines, and Po Valley campaigns. Known as "The Blue Devils," the men spent more than 300 days in combat.

Following the war's end, the 88th was chosen for occupation duty in northeastern Italy and was given the job of patrolling the Morgan Line which was a temporary border between Italy, Austria and Yugoslavia as the higher-ups worked to determine a permanent border. Claude Griffin served with the 88th, 350th Infantry Regiment, "E" Company along the Morgan Line during this time, then later served with the 376th Engineer Construction Battalion in Pusan, Korea.

Griffin was playing football with neighborhood friends against players from Annapolis on Dec. 7, 1941, when he heard the Japanese had attacked Pearl Harbor. After graduating from high school he attended Virginia Tech from September 1943 until being drafted by the Army in July 1944. After induction he went to Ft. Meade, then Camp Wheeler for 17 weeks of infantry training.

Following this Griffin was ordered to the University of Illinois for a sanitary engineering course. That course was to lead to attending medical administrative Officer Candidate School to be part of the Sanitary Corps, but by the time he completed the course the Corps was closed. Instead, Griffin went to Ft. Belvoir, Va., to become an engineer.

After finishing the training, he was put in a replacement depot and in January 1946 shipped out to

War Stories

Italy, landing in Naples later that month. Surprisingly he was not given an engineer assignment. "I was made an infantry platoon leader," said Griffin.

A truck took him through rubble-filled Naples to a barracks. Then by train he was taken north where he joined the 88th Infantry Division, 350th Regiment, "E" Company and assigned to an outpost near the Morgan Line. Griffin remembers the outpost being located in the town of Cave del Predil, which is in the Province of Udine.

The job there for the 350th was to monitor traffic. "We stopped all traffic, pedestrians, bicycles, carts, automobiles and trucks and inspected them to see that nothing (contraband-wise) was going in either direction along the border," said Griffin of the work in the cold mountainous terrain.

The company headquarters was near Udine. When in Udine Griffin stayed with a local family in their home.

His duties included administratively handling the outpost, keeping the men in shape, and supervising three shifts of guards on the Morgan Line. Griffin said there was, to his knowledge, only one time when an incident occurred on the Line when a man refused to stop when told to do so. "He was on a bicycle and one of my sentries fired a round over his head. He immediately stopped and came back," said Griffin who added that once searched no contraband was found.

As Griffin's overseas duty wound down, he made his way back to Naples through towns like Livorno (aka Leghorn) and eventually returned to the U.S. Along the way the ship made a stop in Morocco to pick up G.I. dependents of those who had married during the war. Then later the

Jeffrey L. Meek

ship made a necessary stop in the Azores for repair, then four days later sailed for New York. After arriving he was sent to Ft. Dix, then to Ft. Meade and was separated and sent home.

Griffin decided he'd join the reserves and in July 1950, just a month after the Korean War began, he was put on active duty. As a Second Lieutenant he first helped find needed equipment for transport.

Thereafter he went to Ft. Carson in Colorado Springs, Colo., where he was told to inspect the old WWII base at Camp Hale to assess the condition of the camp's water, sanitation, and sewage treatment systems. "To my knowledge the camp was never reopened," said Griffin.

As part of the 376th Engineer Construction Battalion he took a 98-car train to Oakland Army Base then on Dec. 30, 1950, shipped out with the equipment on the SS Pittston Victory (and old WWII Victory Ship) to Yokohama, Japan. After arriving, the heavy equipment was transshipped to Pusan, South Korea. En route the ships were hit by a typhoon and some of the EQ was lost overboard. Griffin spent the next six weeks searching for replacement equipment to fill the void.

In March 1951 he was sent to Pusan and re-joined the 376th. In Pusan the Battalion maintained roads and, Griffin said, set a new record for venereal disease cases in the theater.

In late 1951 integration caused the unit to be disbanded and Griffin was put with a different outfit, the 409th Construction Brigade at Headquarters in Pusan where he became the Building Design Officer until his departure from Korea in May 1952.

War Stories

After arriving back in the states, he was discharged. Then as a civilian he returned to Virginia Tech where he earned a Civil Engineering degree, then went to Yale and obtained a master's degree in Structural Engineering.

Griffin later worked for a consulting engineer in the Baltimore area and also designed and supervised construction projects like roads, ports, and transportation systems until retiring in 1994. That same year he and wife Eleanor moved to Hot Springs Village from Tucson, Ariz.

Griffin has three children: Nelson, Shelley, and Virginia.

Jeffrey L. Meek

John Hornecker served with 89th Infantry Division in WW II

The 89th Infantry Division fought in the Rhineland and Central European campaigns during World War II. After arriving in Europe in January 1945 they officially fought 57 combat days against the German Army. John "Jack" Hornecker served with the 89th Division, as part of the 914th Field Artillery unit. He worked in the communications section and also did time as a driver and forward observer.

Hornecker was attending college at The Citadel in late 1941 and had just returned home from church when, on the radio, he heard of the Japanese attack at Pearl Harbor. The next day a recruiting station was set up on campus and he and many other cadets enlisted. "On December 8 I became a reservist in the Coast Artillery Reserve," said Hornecker. He was later called into active duty in March 1943. From Jefferson Barracks, Missouri, he was sent to California where he learned to handle 40 mm anti-aircraft guns.

Because he had two years of training at The Citadel, he was soon made acting Sergeant. Later he became the gun captain of a five-man 40mm gun crew. Next, Hornecker attended ASTP at Compton Jr. College and then UCLA.

Soon ASTP was closed down and he was placed with the 89th Infantry Division at Camp Robertson near San Francisco. "The division was mule pack at that time. We had mules instead of jeeps," Hornecker said of the animals used to carry the heavy 75 mm gun barrel. Later the division got jeeps to replace the mules. The men were then transferred to Camp Butner, North, Carolina and trained until

War Stories

December 1944. In December they traveled to LeHarve, France aboard a captured German vessel.

From there they were taken to an area and told to build a camp. "It would become Camp Lucky Strike. We built it from scratch. It was nothing but a muddy field when we got there," Hornecker recalled.

From the camp the men moved to Dieppe and then to Luxembourg City. "We traveled at night with no lights," Hornecker said. The unit entered combat at the Moselle River, crossing at Alf. As they approached, they were fired on by German 20 mm cannons.

Headquarters was later set up in a butcher shop in Alf, and Hornecker had to drive an officer to a nighttime meeting there. After waiting out in the dark for two hours he learned they would be part of a task force whose mission was to secure the bridge at Mainz. They traveled at night and got to within sight of the bridge when the Germans blew it up.

The mission wasn't a total loss. "We did succeed in capturing quite a few Germans. By the time we got to Mainz we had so many Germans we had to put them out in a field and have them take off their shoes and pants and stationed a 40 mm gun at each corner of the field," Hornecker said.

Later, after their Rhine River crossing, the men were given a day off. They bathed in cold creek water and got new uniforms. The old uniforms were so bad they were burned.

The division went from town-to-town meeting sporadic resistance along the way. Then they came to Ordruf and witnessed the horror of the concentration camp there. "We were driving down the road and we saw this fortress-like stockade. That's when we said what is that odor?"

They stopped at the fence and Hornecker walked inside the compound. There were dead bodies lying everywhere. He then left and reported what he had seen to headquarters. "It was pretty horrible to see that mess," Hornecker said. He added that he can still see it today.

The division continued their advance through Jena and on to Chemnitz where they were told to halt and wait for the Russian forces coming from the east. While waiting, German forces in the area would occasionally lob artillery shells into the 89th's position. Hornecker narrowly missed one round that exploded 15 feet away by getting under his jeep.

As events began to quiet down the men began searching for some real food – eggs, ham, chicken – anything but a "K" ration. They were able to purchase items with what would soon be worthless German Marks. The German people would only accept the Marks and not invasion money.

Hornecker was manning a radio when a call came in that troops had found a warehouse full of liquor. He was to immediately send a truck. "We had German liquor, French liquor, and scotch," Hornecker said.

The truck was secured until the next morning – VE Day – May 8, 1945. "We each got about six bottles," he said. "We were smart enough to not drink it all at once."

From Chemnitz he was ordered to Ebenzee, Austria where they guarded an SS prison for three months. Hornecker was then shipped back to LeHarve and soon thereafter the United States.

War Stories

He knew a WGN Chicago radio personality named Ann Calvert. When he returned home to Chicago, she gave him a call and asked if he'd like to see Louie Armstrong. Hornecker quickly said yes. He picked Calvert up that evening, and they went in through a back door. They were then escorted to Armstrong's table. "I met Satchmo. It was quite a deal," smiled Hornecker.

After completing college at Washington University in St. Louis, he joined the active reserves and made 2nd Lieutenant. Later he became Battalion Adjutant of the 381st Field Artillery, 101st Division.

As a civilian, Hornecker worked for several companies including the Brown Shoe Company, Equitable Life and Address-o-Graph Multigraph Corporation.

He retired in 1988 and with wife Margaret moved to Hot Springs Village, Ark., in 1991. The couple has three children: Leslie, Linda, and John.

The unit then moved on toward Cassel. "On that trip I got to meet General George Patton. My captain was a senior officer and was called up to see Patton. I was his driver," Hornecker smiled.

Jeffrey L. Meek

Leroy Jonsson served with 80th Infantry in World War II

They were known as the Blue Ridge Division and were one of several divisions who saw heavy fighting in Europe during World War II. Officially they were the U.S. Army's 80th Infantry Division which went overseas in July 1944, suffered over 3,000 killed in action and over 17,000 casualties as they fought their way through France and Germany as part of Gen. George S. Patton's Third Army. In places like Argentan and Bastogne the men of the 80th fought to defeat the German Army and restore peace in Europe. With them was Leroy Jonsson who served as a rifleman.

He grew up in Chicago and was on his way to a pool hall on Damen Ave. when he learned the Japanese had attacked the U.S. fleet at Pearl Harbor. Knowing he'd soon be drafted, he and a friend decided they wanted to volunteer for the Army Air Force, but instead were put in the infantry.

Their first stop was at Camp Grant, near Rockford, Ill., then they were off to Camp Robinson, Ark., for basic training. "That's where we learned most of Arkansas was rock and when it came to digging a foxhole you couldn't dig," said Jonsson of the state's hard ground.

Eventually he was placed with the 80th Division, 317th Regiment, "G" Company and trained in various U.S. locations, including camping out on a frozen lake at one point. Next, he was prepped for oversea, no letters or phone calls home as the division's departure was to remain hush – hush.

War Stories

On the Queen Mary, with no escort, the division sailed out of New York Harbor in July 1944. Five days later Jonsson said they arrived in Scotland, trained, and soon left for France.

After crossing a Normandy beach his outfit moved inland and fought near Falaise, helping to create the famous Falaise Pocket, the near encirclement of retreating German forces. As a rifleman, Jonsson was under fire repeatedly as nearby tanks fired on each other as U.S. forces moved forward. "I was scared to death," Jonsson said of his combat experience.

Once near a town his squad was fired on by a German tank and retreated. The tank fired over their head as he and others ran for better cover. Jonsson and two others made it to a nearby orchard and saw a fence ahead of them. As the three men kept running a German machine gun sprayed gun fire all around them and a tank fired a flare to better illuminate the area.

"I was taught in my training that when they shot a flare (I was) to hit the ground. So, I hit the ground, but the other two guys with me were trying to get over the fence so they (the Germans) shot 'em," Jonsson recalled. Later Jonsson got over the fence and ran for cover.

"Your heart was beating so hard you couldn't know anything but fear. I was fortunate I didn't try to climb that fence, or they would have got me. I hit the ground and stayed on the ground," said Jonsson. Thereafter his unit, with help from another unit, took the town.

Next, in mid-November, near Metz, the men approached the Moselle River, crossed in boats, and waited as engineers put up a pontoon bridge. Jonsson said this drew German shelling which damaged the bridge more than once. As the men advanced, they were told to attack a hill, all the while under enemy fire. "Somebody was always shooting at you," Jonsson said.

Once while moving down a road to advance as silently as possible, the men pushed, not drove, a supply-filled jeep along the road and down a hill, all in an effort to avoid notice and the subsequent German shelling.

Then in mid-December the German Army mounted a huge counterattack. We Americans know it as the Battle of the Bulge because it pushed our troops back, creating a bulge in the front lines.

Things looked grim for a time and Supreme Allied Commander Gen. Dwight Eisenhower met with his other generals to see who could quickly join the fight to halt the German attack. The history books say he directly asked General Patton how soon he could get some of his Third Army up from the south and in the fight. Patton said he'd get three divisions in immediately – the 4th Armored and the 26th and 80th Infantry. Jonsson and thousands of others were headed into the bulge.

He said he remembered walking through snow up to his hips as the divisions moved nearly 100 miles north. The cold was bitter, the snow deep and many were lost to frostbite. Some sources say more men were out of the fight from frostbite than from wounds. Jonsson got frostbite on his left foot but was able to remain with his unit. As they fought, the men used abandoned German foxholes for protection, a good sign the Allied fighters were pushing the Nazi troops back.

War Stories

By the end of January 1945, the German assault was not only stopped, but the bulge removed, as forces now pressed into Germany. Along the southern flank Jonsson said the 80th took villages and towns, advancing steadily.

Near one town the men found a respite in the drudgery of war when they came upon a champagne factory. "So, every guy got two bottles of champagne. Patton found out about it and cut it off. All the champagne was down the sewer," said Jonsson.

As the war concluded he found himself in Austria. While in the area, he and others met Russian troopers going along a road in a jeep. By December 1945 Jonsson had enough points to go home and returned to the U.S. on a Victory Ship. Along the way they saw a storm-damaged aircraft carrier.

After landing in New York, he traveled to Camp Grant where he was discharged on Dec. 29, 1945. By train and cab he came home, walking the final two blocks. At 1 a.m. he entered his home to the surprise of his family.

As a civilian, Jonsson worked several jobs and later got into the printing business where he stayed for 27 years. He retired in 1984 and moved to Hot Springs Village, Ark., with wife Marjorie in 1997 from Glenview, Illinois.

About his time in uniform Jonsson summed it up quite simply when he concluded the interview by saying, "War is hell."

Jeffrey L. Meek

Gilbert "Gib" Miller served with Graves Registration unit in Philippines

The U.S. Army Quartermaster Corps had several responsibilities during World War II. One of them was graves registration, the care of deceased military personnel. Unit training for these companies began in April 1943 when several units were officially formed. One of them, the 609th Quartermaster Graves Registration Company, was activated at Fort Warren, Wyo. Later in 1946, Gilbert "Gib" Miller was assigned to the 609th for duty in the Philippines.

Miller grew up in Olney, Ill., and was attending the University of Illinois when drafted in March 1946. He reported to Fort Sheridan, Ill., before being sent to Camp Robinson, Ark., for basic training. There he learned to march, shoot weapons, and had bayonet practice even though the war had ended six months earlier. After a brief furlough at home, Miller went to Fort Dix, and on July 27, 1946, boarded the Army transport ship Tufts Victory, AP 771, and sailed off past the Statue of Liberty.

But the ship then headed south. They weren't going to Europe. Miller had no idea where he was heading or what his military job would be. Instead, the ship went to Panama, through the canal and on to Hawaii. In Hawaii they made a brief stop for fuel and provisions, then sailed on into Manila Bay, Philippines, on August 28. Once there he was put with the 609th as a medical technician. "To this day I don't know how I ended up in graves registration," said Miller.

Now in the Philippines, Miller said there were a few hostilities still going on in the outskirts of Manila as he and the 609th moved out to a camp on the north side of Manila.

War Stories

Near the camp was a large cemetery with at least 5,000 gravesites and Japanese prisoners-of-war doing maintenance work, mowing, trimming and other manual labor.

The camp also had two licensed morticians to handle bodies and crews that brought bodies, bones and other remains to the camp where Miller and others worked to identify the remains and prepare them for shipment back to the United States. Several Filipinos also helped Miller with the gruesome work.

The process involved recovering bodies which would then be physically cleaned up, embalmed, if possible, placed in a casket and stored until enough were prepared for shipment back home.

Miller many times supervised the work and told me it was seldom that a body came in with dog tags. Sometimes he'd get only a bag of bones or teeth to work with in the identification process.

Of the camp, Miller said it ran like its own little city with a motor pool, cooks, drivers and more, all living in tents or Quonset huts. Miller said remains would come in sporadically and some would be recent deaths, like a few men who had just drown in Manila Bay.

While on the job he said there were a few incidents involving Japanese "hold outs" who would not surrender. At the motor pool there was once some shooting going on that he thought was hold out-related.

In 1947, Miller got some good news. He was going home. He arrived back in the states on April 1, 1947, at Camp Stoneman, Calif., where he was discharged on April

Jeffrey L. Meek

27. He returned home and went back to the University of Illinois for a medical degree. After graduation he attended medical school in Chicago.

When his education was completed, he practiced medicine in Illinois for several years and then made an interesting decision. While practicing in Lawrenceville he was looking at an AMA publication that said join the U.S. Air Force (USAF) and see the world. His wife was receptive of the idea, so he joined in July 1976.

He first went to Webb AFB, Texas and was put to work in a small hospital there. Asked why, after nearly 25 years in practice, did he decide to re-enter the military Miller said with a laugh, "Just crazy I guess."

He also worked in an outpatient clinic with two other physicians taking care of retirees and active-duty personnel. Dealing with blood pressure issues, heart problems, infections, arthritis and other maladies, the work was very similar to his work in private practice.

One year later he was sent to Williams AFB, Ariz., where he worked for another five years in a clinic at the Air Training Command base. Next, he was ordered to Keesler AFB, Miss., for more clinic work. After three years there he left the Air Force, discharged on July 2, 1985.

But Miller wasn't ready to retire. In Biloxi, Miss., he went to work for the Veterans Administration in a long-term care unit checking charts and keeping watch on patients, monitoring their condition and progress.

Miller retired in 1996 and came to Hot Springs Village that same year from Ocean Springs, Miss. He has six children: Jeffrey, Nathan, Dale, Janice, Christopher, and Brian.

War Stories

Speaking of family, it is interesting to note he has an uncle, Christian Schilt, who is a Medal of Honor recipient in 1928 for demonstrated heroism in Nicaragua where two U.S. Marine patrols were ambushed. Schilt made several flights evacuating casualties in his Corsair biplane.

Looking back on his time in uniform Miller said if there was anything good that came from World War II it was the GI Bill.

Jeffrey L. Meek

Sam Padfield served in World War II as tank driver

U.S. Armored divisions in World War II were involved in many campaigns and provided infantry support in both the European and Pacific theaters of war. Near the end of the war the 787th Tank Battalion served with the 86th Infantry Division as they went through southern Germany. The 787th's main weapon was the M-4 Sherman tank. A Chrysler engine powered the 32-ton machine which was armed with a 75 mm gun and .50 caliber Browning machine gun. Driving one of those tanks was Sam Padfield.

Padfield was attending college in Greeley, Colo., when in the spring of 1943 he was drafted into the Army. Soon he was off to Camp Chaffee, Ark., for basic training.

Following this he was ordered into the tank corps, which was quite a surprise for him. "I said tank corps. I've never even seen one," said Padfield of the assignment. Upon giving some thought he decided it was certainly better than the infantry because now he wouldn't have to walk everywhere.

At Fort Benning, Ga., he became a part of a new outfit – the 787th Tank Battalion. "They gave us new tanks and you had to put a name on it. Our tank commander, who was a buck sergeant, said he couldn't think of a name. Sam, can you help me? I said let's name it Carol Ann," said Padfield of naming the tank after his first niece.

The Sherman tank had a crew of five – a tank commander, an assistant driver called a BOG, a driver, gun loader and a gunner. Each man carried a revolver, which later would prove valuable to Padfield. Each man had to know the other men's jobs in case someone was killed or

War Stories

hurt. Driving the tank involved moving levers to turn it and pedals for speed and stopping.

After completing his tank training, he was shipped to New York and then on to LaHarve, France, on a convoy of ships. "That ship took 13 days to get to LeHarve and I was sick every day," said Padfield of the long journey. Behind Padfield's convoy was another convoy carrying the 787th's tanks.

In France the men were put in Camp Lucky Strike to await the tanks. This took longer than expected because the other convoy had hit a rough storm and sailed back to the U.S., but a week later the tanks arrived. In the meantime, the lull gave Padfield and others an opportunity to make a quick visit to Paris to see the sites.

Padfield's records show he arrived in France in March 1945, and it was then the unit was ordered to southern Germany. Along the way they would pass through towns and rural areas. On one occasion going through the countryside a young girl ran across a field toward them with a basket in her hand. The tank commander said not to stop; she could have a bomb in the basket.

"The girl got right in front of my tank, so I stopped anyway. I didn't want to hurt her. She had a basket of strawberries," said Padfield in a tender moment.

As they made their way through southern Germany, south of Munich, the unit came upon and freed a concentration camp. "When they (the prisoners) came out they looked so filthy and dirty. None of them could speak English," Padfield remembers. Some of the prisoners climbed aboard the tanks and hugged their liberators.

Jeffrey L. Meek

The 787th reached the Danube River late one night and crossed on a steel bridge built by the Corps of Engineers. Halfway across they were hit by rifle fire. "Immediately we buttoned up, closed the hatches and I had to finish driving across the Danube at midnight using a periscope," said Padfield of the attack. The gunfire was coming from a nearby house which was soon taken out.

The men made their way toward Austria where rumors said the hardcore SS units may hole up in redoubts for a final battle. While stopped for a break near a tree line Padfield had an experience he'll never forget.

"We got out of our tanks, and I had my back toward the trees when my BOG yelled 'Look out Sam.' I turned around and here's a young Nazi coming at me with a dagger. He was about 10 yards away and he kept yelling 'Heil Hitler, Heil Hitler' when he was coming at me to kill me with this knife. I kept yelling no, no, stop, stop, stop, and put my hands up to stop him and he wouldn't stop. He kept coming so I took out my revolver and shot him. A medic came down and hauled him off," said Padfield.

During the last month of the war the unit received orders from General George Patton – take no prisoners. "That's what we were told by our commandeering officer of the battalion," Padfield said. With the mission accomplished and the war in Europe over, the men were sent back to LaHarve. From there they would return to the U.S. and prepare for action in the Pacific.

Padfield arrived in New York on June 28, 1945, and went home to Colorado for a two week leave when he got a phone call. President Truman had dropped the atomic bomb and he was to report to Fort Jackson, S.C. Upon his

War Stories

arrival he was made director of all athletic programs for the battalion. Padfield organized activities and games which the men were required to participate in. Several months later he was sent back to Colorado for discharge.

After the war Padfield went back to college and became an educator and basketball coach in Arvada, just outside of Denver. Later he became an assistant principal. Padfield then left education and spent 33 years working for General Mills, retiring in 1987. That same year he moved to Hot Springs Village. Padfield has three children: Mary, Gary, and Lindy.

Looking back on his service he said, "I felt I was called to serve and proud to do so. I grew up immensely as an individual from an 18-year-old boy to an adult when I came out. I'm sure it helped me in my college environment with my studies because I approached everything as more of an adult. I grew up in a hurry."

Jeffrey L. Meek

George Shaw served at Fort Leavenworth during World War II

Fort Leavenworth, Kan., has served as a post for the U.S. Army for over 175 years. It is the home of the Military Corrections Complex which includes the U.S. Disciplinary Barracks (USDB). Part of the USDB in World War II was the First Guard Company in which George Shaw served in several capacities.

Shaw grew up in Lincoln, Neb., and said he couldn't believe what he was hearing on the radio on Dec. 7, 1941, as the broadcaster announced the Japanese attack on the U.S. Fleet at Pearl Harbor. After graduating high school Shaw attended the University of Nebraska working on a major in English and Journalism. Just a year later he was drafted and entered the Army in June 1943.

As a young child, just five years old, Shaw was involved in a car accident in which glass cut his right eyeball. The mishap caused him to permanently lose sight in that eye. When he reported for his physical, he was told he would not be accepted for service. "They said I don't think we need you," Shaw remembers. "I said wait a minute, I've come this far, everyone else is gone. I can't go home. I gotta get in," Shaw responded.

He explained how the eye has not been a problem in his life and thus he should be allowed into the Army. Eventually the man relented, and Shaw was sent to Fort Leavenworth in what was called "Limited Service."

After training to become a guard, he was put with the First Guard Company at the USDB. Once the training

War Stories

was completed, he began his guard duties, several times in a tall guard tower affixed to the walls surrounding the prison inside the fort. Shaw said the fort housed men that had been court marshaled for various reasons. It also held German prisoners of war.

Shaw was told the Germans were there because they had raped and killed some women, but another source, unbeknownst to Shaw, said it was because the German POWs were there to be executed for killing other Germans that had cooperated with U.S. military authorities. "They sent them there for us to hang," Shaw said of their fate.

In January 1945, the 14 Germans were hung for their offenses. Shaw said he was grateful he wasn't chosen for the duty of witnessing their executions, but a few of his buddies were chosen and had to see the ordeal. Of the Germans, Shaw said they were watched very closely "because we knew they were violent." He added that they wore blue jeans-like clothes with POW on front and back. Occasionally there would be prisoners out on a work detail that would try to escape. "Then we'd all have to go out and try and round them up and bring them back," Shaw said. All the guards were told not to fraternize with prisoners so there was little communication between guard and prisoner.

Work shifts were four hours on and four hours off and the rest of the time the guards were on call. Shaw said there were many times he was in the search party but he himself never was the one to find the escaped prisoner. When the incarcerated men finished their sentence, they would be dishonorably discharged and sent home.

Jeffrey L. Meek

Shaw lived in a two-man squad room when off duty. His roommate was a high school classmate. The living quarters consisted of two bunks, lockers, a table, desk, and chairs.

After 18 months of guard duty his job changed when he was sent to the mail room where he censored incoming and outgoing mail. "Most of it was dull (reading)," Shaw said of the work. Then later he had another job change when he was sent to the company clerk's office where he typed rosters, morning reports and other administrative paperwork.

In February 1946, now a Sergeant, Shaw was discharged, went home, and resumed his education at the University of Nebraska. With a journalism degree he first went to work as a city hall reporter in Beatrice, Neb. Later he moved to Bloomington, Ill., covering the same beat.

Then it was back to school, this time at Kansas University, for a public administration degree which led to him becoming a city manager in Michigan and later in Carpentersville, Ill., from 1965 to 1985.

Next, he moved to North Little Rock, Ark., and got into real estate. In August 1997, he and wife Dorothy moved to Hot Springs Village where he continued to work for Century 21 until retiring in December 2008. The couple has five children: John, Jill, Jane, Deege and Cathy.

Reflecting back on his military service Shaw said the experience helped him to grow up, to mature and he's glad he got the opportunity to serve.

War Stories

Miles Stepal served on World War II minesweeper in Alaska

World War II era minesweepers were an integral part of the U.S. Navy. One hundred and thirty-six feet in length and powered by two 500 horsepower diesel engines spinning two propellers, the ships cleared sea lanes and harbors to make travel of other ships safer. Aboard Yard Mine sweeper (YMS) – 125 was Miles Stepel.

He hails from Illinois, was drafted by the Army in September 1943, and reported for his physical examination to a Chicago armory in early October. "We formed a straight line, and they asked every fourth person to take a step forward. I happened to be the fourth person. I took a step forward and we made a left face and were grouped together. Where this was taking us, we had no idea whatsoever," Stepal said. Just a few minutes later he learned he was not going to be in the Army. He was going into the Navy.

By bus and train he and others were sent to Farragut, Idaho for training. During four weeks of boot camp Stepal was with the 101243 Company, he said. He told me they learned four things: respect, neatness, honor, and "to straighten up and fly right."

During an interview Stepal mentioned he had worked in his uncle's meat store for a few years. So, the Navy assigned him to cook and baker school in Bremerton, Wash., for training. For the next many weeks, he learned how to construct a menu and feed hundreds at a time, "which I thought was impossible," Stepal said.

Jeffrey L. Meek

He explained that 20 to 30 pounds of bacon would be put in a deep fryer and many cooks with small skillets would fix the eggs. They would form a long line of cooks that cracked eggs and shuttled pans down the line. "You had to see it to believe it," he added.

Stepal then went to Astoria, Ore., to await his next assignment. A few days later he learned he was going to Adak, Alaska. They flew to Kodiak Island to refuel and on to Adak, arriving on March 20, 1944.

At first, he worked in a commissary and was also put in a LORAN school. LORAN (Long Range Navigation) was a radio navigation system which allowed a receiver to determine its position by listening to low frequency radio signals that were transmitted by fixed based radio beacons. He worked as the cook for 18 enlisted men and officers at a high-tech radar station.

Then, eight months later, Stepal was assigned to YMS (Yard Mine Sweeper) 125 as a cook. The ship had 28 enlisted men and four officers. While a mess cook took care of the officers, Stepal handled other cooking duties. Every day for 13 months Stepal planned the menu and fed the sailors, with one exception, when the ship was in rough water.

"Everyone got sick except for two people, and they had free reign of the galley. The rest were too sick to want to eat," Stepal said. In those rough waters, he told me, the ship would be tossed so violently there were times he wondered if YMS-125 would stay afloat. Comparatively speaking the ship was small and the rough seas put everyone in a very precarious situation. But they made it

War Stories

through these times and kept up with their duties of sweeping for mines and other matters.

The ship traveled to Attu, Dutch Harbor, Kodiak Island and wherever else the Navy sent her to look for mines. YMS-125 had a wooden hull and thus wasn't a magnet for mines. As mines were dislodged, they floated to the surface and men onboard the ship shot them, thus safely exploding the deadly weapons.

The crew also patrolled the icy waters in case aircraft had to ditch. Their job was to find and rescue any downed pilots, but Stepal said this situation never occurred.

He was still on YMS-125 when the Japanese announced their decision to surrender. "We all had a drink, which was a no-no," Stepal said.

Now back in port and tied up to the dock, Stepal said they were told the ship was going to be decommissioned. They then sailed to Bremerton. Before being let off then ship the men were warned about bringing with them any contraband. Soon Stepal flew to Chicago, Illinois, for his May 25, 1946, discharge, thus ending his World War II experience.

As a civilian he worked as a meat cutter, retiring on Aug. 25, 1987. He recently moved to the Village from Green Bay, Wisc. Stepal has two children: Laura and John.

Looking back on his military service, Stepal said it made him a better man. He felt he became much more knowledgeable and saw it as a good experience. "I had second thoughts about staying in the service," he added as we closed our interview. "I was tempted, but then it didn't materialize."

Jeffrey L. Meek

Walter Wilson served in USAAF in World War II

I was especially anxious to do this oral history. This veteran had the same job as my uncle Walter Meek. Uncle Walt never talked about his service during WW II. It was years after his death when I was given his service records, I learned that besides being an airplane mechanic he was also a Link trainer. Named after the creator of the device, Edwin Link, a Link trainer was the first flight simulator used to teach pilots to use their instrumentation in bad weather. Walter Wilson was also a Link trainer, and this is his story.

Wilson recalls being in Phoenix, Ariz., when the Japanese attacked Pearl Harbor. He had driven down from Maryland and was visiting family. "I immediately planned on going back to Maryland to enlist because I was, like most of the young folks, really energized by this vicious attack," said Wilson. "The country and the people reacted angrily, and you couldn't not want to sign up."

He enlisted in the Army Air Force and became a cadet. But there were so many cadets ahead of him that he had to wait six months for his official call-up. In August 1942, it was Wilson's turn to begin training. Eventually he was sent to Nashville, Tenn., for classification as a pilot, navigator, or bombardier. After three weeks at the base, Wilson was classified for pilot training and sent to Maxwell Field in Alabama. At Maxwell he received 13 weeks of pre-flight training learning airplane recognition, navigation skills and Morse code.

Wilson was then sent to Ocala, Fla., for primary flight training in November 1942. He was put into class 43-E. This signified a possible graduation in May 1943.

War Stories

He trained in a PT-17 which was a biplane. After seven hours of flight time, he and 40 percent of the class were washed out and dropped from the program. "It was very disheartening. It was around Christmas time, and I'll never forget it," Wilson said.

He was made a private, put on a cattle car and sent to Valdosta, Ga., for reassignment. His first job was cutting down trees to create more space for the base. Wilson learned he could get assigned as an air tower operator and jumped at the chance.

While learning the job he was reassigned to an advanced flight training base at George Field in Illinois. After arriving he was put in a crew that washed airplanes with kerosene. It was not what he had in mind for a military career.

Once again, Wilson found out about another possibility, this time as a Link trainer. He signed up and eventually became an instructor. Every pilot had to take Link training every month, no matter their rank. "It helped them learn instrument flying in bad weather," said Wilson.

The pilot would climb into the wooden airplane-like box with stubby wings and at his desk Wilson would record every move the pilot made as he reacted to certain procedures. The trainer was mounted on an air-controlled system so it could move like an airplane.

Later, Wilson and a friend were asked to go on temporary duty in Boca Raton, Fla. In Florida they continued Link training for PBY pilots on submarine patrol duty. On days off, Wilson would fly with the PBYs on their missions.

Six weeks later Wilson was briefly sent back to George Field and then asked to go to Randolph Field in

Jeffrey L. Meek

Texas for advanced Link trainer school. The advanced training was mostly due to an upgrade in electronic equipment.

Randolph Field was a prime base for assignment and Wilson was given a chance to make it his home base instead of George Field in Illinois. He was told that if he could rank in the top 10 percent on testing he could stay at Randolph. "I loved the place. That was the only incentive I needed," said Wilson. He scored in the top 10 percent and made Randolph his home from 1943 until the end of his service in December 1945.

In civilian life, Wilson spent a career in the insurance industry eventually retiring from Met Life in 1982. He moved to Hot Springs Village, Ark., from Woodlands, Texas in 1997 and has three children Arthur, Janet, and Wanda.

In looking back at his military service Wilson wanted to mention an interesting and sobering thought. As mentioned earlier in this story, Wilson was briefly a part of class 43-E but washed out with many others. He told me what later happened to the graduates of 43-E. They were assigned to B-26 crews for low level missions over France. Wilson said, "They were just decimated and so many were lost over France. I always think, why me? I was blessed."

War Stories

Chapter II: Korean War Veterans

John Atherton served as Marine Corps wireman, chaplain assistant

Although they may have spent much of their time back behind the front lines, many times wiremen would have to go out and repair communication lines that had been cut by enemy forces. The enemy many times would then lay in wait for the wiremen to show up and ambush them as they attempted to repair the line.

In most cases the wiremen would not have any additional infantry support. It would be a two- or three-man group who'd have to protect themselves from a potential enemy attack. John Atherton served in the United States Marine Corps from 1952 until 1955, mostly as a wireman and later a chaplain's assistant.

He grew up in Wichita, Kan., and graduated high school in 1951. Back during World War II, he attended a Marine Corps demonstration set up in Wichita at Lawrence Stadium where the Corps had built a mock Japanese village that was then attacked. "I was approximately nine or 10 years old at the time and after that I knew I was going to go in the United States Marine Corps," said Atherton of the experience that made a big impression on him.

The Korean War began in June 1950 and Atherton wanted to join the reserves, but his parents wouldn't allow it. Later, one week after turning 18 years old, he joined the Corps on Feb. 5, 1952. During the interim he helped Marine Corps recruiters sign up new Devil Dogs. "I was that excited about it," said Atherton.

Jeffrey L. Meek

A crowded troop train took him to Marine Corps Recruit Depot (MCRD) in San Diego for boot camp. Next came an assignment to a field wire school to learn about telephones, how to lay out wire, splice it and repair it, how to climb poles and run a switchboard. After graduating he was ordered to Camp Lejeune, N.C., where he was put with the Second Marine Division in a communications unit.

Months later he applied for and received an assignment to an electronics school at Great Lakes, Ill. He attended a nearby Methodist Church in Waukegan where he met Marilyn, the woman he would later marry. In fact, he took her to her senior prom in his eye-catching Marine Corps dress blue uniform.

Atherton decided he didn't care much for electronic school, opted out and reported to Camp Pendleton, where the entire Third Marine Division was about to sail for Korea. Atherton remembers they even tore apart walls for the wood needed to make crates in hold their equipment.

He was assigned to the 9th Marine Regiment as a field wireman and headed for Korea. Days later the men received new orders. An armistice had been signed so the men were now to report to Japan.

They were some of the first troops back to the islands that were still littered with the remnants of World War II. Helmets, rifles, vehicles and even an old navy dive bomber were still

In Nagoya, he and others in his outfit were put up in the morgue of an old Japanese hospital. He then participated in several maneuvers on Mt. Fuji, and the islands of Okinawa and Iwo Jima.

War Stories

there rusting away. To make things safer for the men on maneuvers, demolition units came in and blew up any old WW II munitions.

During the war games Atherton was put in charge of communications supplies that would be needed. He oversaw the assigning of the equipment and the loading of it. "We would come in behind the first waves to set up communications," said Atherton of their work. The wiremen would string wire to headquarters and then man the switchboard for messages.

Once when he had to go out to repair broken wires he was ambushed and "killed" twice in one day. Those that were "dead," gathered on a hill to await their next replacement job.

Atherton also talked about what life was like in Japan at the time. The men were allowed to interact with the locals, but World War II was never discussed. He said prostitutes were numerous and they aggressively sought out American servicemen.

At his base in Gifu, Japanese locals took care of the garbage. "They would eat out of our garbage cans. They were hurting for food at that time, still recovering from the aftereffects of the war," Atherton said.

This was also a time when integration was occurring, and Atherton said there were a few minor riots on the base when blacks and whites would clash. "It was still a tremendous issue bringing the two together into the military," he said of that time period.

Atherton spent his days cleaning and repairing equipment, organizing it and participating in the ever-present PT – physical training. He remembers an old World

Jeffrey L. Meek

War II veteran in the unit who was an alcoholic and a mental wreck who would have to be taken to medics to be sedated during the time of inspections. And there was another chapter in his time in Japan that he hasn't forgotten.

One night in the barracks a man who had fought at Chosin Reservoir during the recently concluded Korean War went berserk thinking he was in hand-to-hand combat against the Chinese. "I can't remember how many of us it took to get close enough to him to take him down, get the bayonet out of his hand and hold him until he passed through that experience. It made me aware of what combat does to a person who has fought extensively," said Atherton.

"Marines can do crazy things," said Atherton as he began to tell of how some of the men would throw the KBAR knives at people's feet to see how close they could come. On at least one occasion one Marine threw his KBAR and hit another Marine's foot. After being treated, the Marine with the injured foot was made to participate in maneuvers while on crutches.

Atherton served 13 months in Japan, returned to the U.S. in September 1954, was put with a casualty company of short-timers, and then assigned as a chaplain's assistant at Camp Pendleton. He was later discharged on Feb. 4, 1955. As a civilian Atherton worked on the assembly line at Boeing and Beech aircraft companies, then later attended seminary in Evanston, Illinois.

He wanted to be a Navy chaplain, but back surgery changed his life's plan. Instead, he became a Methodist Church pastor at churches in Illinois. He retired in 1996 and

War Stories

moved to the Village that same year from Walnut, Ill. The Atherton's have two children: Jonalyn and Cale Pete.

He has spent some time organizing letters he wrote and received during his years in the Corps and, for the Voice, reflected back on his Marine Corps service. Atherton said it was a defining period of his life. It taught him discipline and commitment to his country. "Once a Marine, always, always a Marine," Atherton said.

In Hot Springs Village, Atherton had the honor of hoisting the Marine Corps flag at the Village's Veteran's Memorial dedication back in 2004 and has served as an interim pastor at Christ of the Hills United Methodist Church while senior pastor Dr. Walter "Bubba" Smith completed his service in Iraq.

Jeffrey L. Meek

Dave Chaphe served as aerial observer during Korean War

Some books on the Korean War refer to artillery as the "King of Battle." The U.S. deployed 54 battalions of field artillery to Korea which used 105 mm howitzers and 155 mm heavy guns also known as "Long Toms." Later in the war, huge 240 mm howitzers were used to throw out devastating barrages of firepower.

Another aspect of these battalions was the observation required to determine target coordinates. This was done both on the ground at forward locations and in the air using small L-19 observation planes. Flying in one of those L-19s was Dave Chaphe who was with the 937th Field Artillery Battalion in Korea.

Chaphe spent some time traveling around the U.S. which included St. Louis where he and his buddy got a job selling soda at St. Louis Cardinal baseball games. After a while they moved on to New York, then to Chicago and it was there in Illinois in 1950 he learned he was about to be drafted.

Chaphe returned home to California, was drafted by the Army and reported to Fort Ord for basic training. He was then sent on to Fort Benning, Ga., for artillery fire control training with the 105 mm guns. Chaphe did well, was soon chosen for Officer Candidate School (OCS) and put with the 82nd "All-American" Airborne Division. He attended leadership school in South Carolina, then transferred to Fort Sill to begin his OCS schooling.

After graduating, Chaphe asked to be assigned to the Fourth Infantry Division at Camp Cook where he then

War Stories

became a Second Lieutenant. Once again, he moved up the ladder quickly and was made Battery Commander of the Headquarters Artillery Battalion. As such he was responsible for the outfit's jeeps, trucks, guns, and planes.

Then Chaphe was called up by the Far East Command for assignment to Korea. After a stop at Camp Stoneman, he was flown to Japan and stationed at Camp Drake near Tokyo where men were deployed as needed. Chaphe was ordered to Korea and put with the 937th Field Artillery Battalion which had the "Long Toms." He arrived at Pusan and was soon sent north by train to a forward observation post on the frontline. The fighting there was static, but while there in support of the South Korean Army he got quite a scare.

When the men of the 937th awoke one morning they found the South Korean unit had completely pulled out. "That was the shock of all shocks," said Chaphe of the feeling of being out on the frontline without support. His unit then also pulled back.

It was around this time of his deployment that a call came out for volunteers to become aerial observers. "I thought that sounded like a lot of fun," said Chaphe who soon signed up. Each battalion had two different L-19s which were overhead wing planes made by Cessna. By the time Chaphe completed his time in Korea he would fly an astounding 250 combat missions in the L-19s, pulling multiple flights in a single day because of the shortage of aerial observers.

In the plane he would be seated behind the pilot as they flew over North Korean and Chinese frontlines. There

Jeffrey L. Meek

were even a few times the pilot let him fly the plane in case he had to do so if the pilot became injured.

The targets included troops, tanks, vehicles, and tunnel openings. Many times, while observing these targets they would come under enemy fire. The tunnels were an especially important target because they were used to conceal artillery that would roll out, fire, and retract back inside. Chaphe would call in the coordinates for the needed air or artillery strikes. He flew so many missions in the north the U.S. Air Force requested that he accompany them on a B-25 mission, using his information and experience as a needed source of intelligence.

There were also times when his flights threw out propaganda leaflets urging North Korean and Chinese troops to surrender. "That's as close as I got to bombing someone, throwing out the leaflets," Chaphe joked.

Finally, he had earned enough points to return home and did so on a Navy troopship. About this same time many American prisoners of war were released. So as not to arrive back in the states before the released POWs, his ship sailed for 30 days before landing in the U.S. The men killed time mostly by playing bridge and enjoying the good food. Chaphe said the men attacked the fine tasting food "like there was no tomorrow." Butter, ice cream and other good eats were enjoyed for the first time in a long time. Once arriving in California, he was soon discharged in August 1953.

As a civilian Chaphe got into sales and marketing for paint-related companies, traveling all over the world. Later he worked in the coil coating business. In 1995 he and wife

War Stories

Sally moved to Hot Springs Village, Ark., from Riverside, Calif.

The Chaphes had two children: Dewey and Bradford. Unfortunately, Bradford was killed in 1984 while serving in the Tank Corps in Germany. Since the time of this interview Chaphe has since moved to Washington State to be with Dewey.

"It was quite an experience," said Chaphe of his Korean War experiences. "I was offered a regular Army commission because of circumstances and my record, and I thought seriously about that. But I went to work in sales instead," he said summing up his military career.

Jeffrey L. Meek

Floyd Garrot served in Korea with 417th Engineer Aviation Group

During the Korean War U.S. Army engineers served in many capacities with many units. Some were put in U.S. Air Force aviation groups. When the war began in June 1950, the Fifth Air Force had only the 930th Engineer Aviation Group, but by 1952 they added the 417th Engineer Aviation Brigade to supervise airfield construction. With the 417th in Taegu, Korea was Floyd Garrot who served with their headquarters unit.

After graduating high school, he attended LSU year-round, graduating in just three years, earning a degree as a mechanical engineer. He went to work for Humble Oil Company in August 1949 in Texas. Later in January 1951 he got a draft notice. Uncle Sam had called him to service in the U.S. Army.

At Baton Rouge, La., he boarded a train for Fort Sam Houston, Texas, for induction. Basic training was at Fort Bragg where members of the 82nd Airborne Division conducted the training. "The idea was to influence a lot of people to go into the airborne," said Garrot who was really impressed with the training.

He considered becoming a paratrooper until he watched an airborne drop go bad when parachutes attached to equipment exiting the plane did not open. "That discouraged me a little bit," he said.

Back at Fort Sam Houston he had taken several tests, did well and was sent to leadership school at Fort Jackson, S.C., in August 1951. Next came Engineer Officer Candidate School at Fort Belvoir, Va. Garrot called the OCS

War Stories

school the greatest experience he ever had, great training with great officers in charge.

He finished second in his class and received a commission on June 3, 1952. Garrot then was placed with the 40th Engineer Pipeline Company at Fort Leonard Wood, Mo., as Company Commander. Once there he had to sign off on all the property books which would then make him responsible for all the unit's equipment. But his predecessor had apparently not run too tight a ship and Garrot found many things unaccounted for. Eventually matters were sorted out, Garrot signed the books and moved on with his duties.

Thereafter he got orders to report to Korea. After a 30-day leave, he went to San Francisco and boarded a troopship headed for Japan, arriving in late December 1952. "It was cold," said Garrot of the area. He then flew to Korea in a cargo plane. "I think that was as cold as I've ever been in my life. It was just cold air blowing through that plane," he recalled. After landing in Taegu he reported to the 417th compound which was surrounded by concertina wire.

There he became Company Commander for most of the 10 months he served with the unit. "What we did there was we took care of all the brass in that Brigade," Garrot said of the duties.

I asked him to describe a typical day. With a big smile and a laugh Garrot said, "A typical day for me was getting chewed out by the Executive Officer because of something that didn't go quite right in our little compound." Taking care of the officers meant making sure they were comfortable. "We had a very excellent mess hall, and we had good provisions," Garrot said. The compound also had

Jeffrey L. Meek

a motor pool, officer's club, nice barracks, and a cadre of Koreans that helped the unit.

Garrot said he had a lot of interaction with the Koreans inside the compound. He remembers paying them with stacks of money because of the hyper-inflation in the country at that time. He also remembers dealing with the head of the Korean helpers who later turned out to be a crook.

He had let other Koreans inside the compound to steal things. "We had to let him go," said Garrot. "They were extremely poor people and would steal stuff to try to stay alive. They had nothing."

Garrot said Taegu was in terrible shape, one of the worst places he'd ever seen. "We saw roofs of houses that were made out of beer cans. I couldn't believe the poverty," he said.

Ten months later he was due to go home. The armistice had been signed and the men were asked who wanted to be separated. Garrot was selected and in a few days flown back to the U.S. via Alaska. From there he went back to Fort Sam Houston and was discharged on Oct. 30, 1953.

He went right back to work for Humble Oil in Texas as a junior petroleum engineer, a career he stayed with until retiring in 1986. Two years later he and wife Pat moved to Hot Springs Village from New Orleans. The couple has five children: Lynn, Mike, Carol, Sherry, and Bill.

Reflecting on his time in service he again said it was a very interesting experience. Garrot said he grew up in a sheltered environment as a kid on a sugar plantation and

War Stories

did not have much exposure to the real world. Responsibility and discipline were the two traits he learned that helped him move forward with his life.

Jeffrey L. Meek

Lyle Grooters served with USAF in Korea

Helicopter rescue squadrons played a vital role during the Korean War helping to bring home downed pilots. Serving with such a unit was Lyle Grooters who served with the United States Air Force from 1951 to 1955.

Grooters, born on April Fools Day, grew up in Cedar Falls, Iowa. While in high school he was active in sports programs, playing both football and track. He graduated from high school in 1950, just as the Korean War broke out. Several of his friends soon went into the Army and were quickly sent to the fighting in Korea. Grooters decided he'd join the fight as well and in 1951 he enlisted in the U.S. Air Force.

His first stop was in San Antonio, Texas, for basic training. Then he was ordered to Scott Air Force Base in Illinois. At Scott he was put in an electronics program. Most of the course work had to do with radios. Grooters learned radio basics, trouble shooting and radio repair. "If something was wrong, we had to figure out what it was," said Grooters of those early days in the Air Force. He also learned to specialize in fixing communications gear related to helicopters. Upon completion of the 10-month training course Grooters was made an instructor.

Next, he was ordered overseas and sent to Morocco, Japan and finally Korea. Along the way he continued his work with radio repair and other communications gear. Grooters said his stay in Japan was brief, barely a stopover on the way to Korea. Upon his arrival in 1953 he was put with the USAF 2157th Air Rescue

War Stories

Squadron at Kimpo Air Base, near Seoul. The unit's motto was "That Others May Live."

His first impressions of Korea were not good. Dirty and smelly is how he remembers it. He and the others lived in a tent with six beds and a wooden floor. Grooters spent most of his time maintaining the communications gear after the aircraft returned from their many missions. Grooters said each day a sergeant-in-charge would assign him and the other men to certain choppers for communications repair.

Doing so put him in close proximity with some of the pilots who would speak of their dangerous flights to pick up downed airmen. "Getting shot at was not their favorite occupation," Grooters remembers of the conversations. Some of these scary flights took place in North Korea. It was also at this time Grooters bumped into a high school friend. Neither knew the other was serving in Korea, let alone the same area.

Day after day he worked on the radios. Many times, they were removed from the helicopter and taken to their repair shop where all the testing gear was located. Grooters said the radios used vacuum tubes and could many times be easily fixed by replacing the bad tube. Resistors, capacitors, and other parts would also go bad at times.

Microphones and wiring would also break down. Because this equipment was needed as soon as possible, the bad microphones and wires would be thrown out and new ones installed. They did not take time to repair them. If a radio had been struck by bullets, they too, would be thrown out and not repaired. The 2157th had

Jeffrey L. Meek

approximately 10 helicopters in the squadron ready and awaiting missions.

Once, Grooters got to go up on a flight. "That was quite a view," said Grooters of his ride. While in the air Grooters would test the radio to see if all was working as it should.

On a day off he would occasionally get a pass to go to Seoul. "It was pretty beat up," Grooters said of the South Korean capital. The men would also get three day passes to travel to Japan. Grooters made one such trip. In Japan he watched USO shows with U.S. entertainers. One show featured Marilyn Monroe.

He said the trip to Japan was very educational and the Japanese people treated him well. During his travels he could see battle damage from World War II which had ended 10 years before his visit.

Preparing to return to Korea the weather turned bad, and the men ended up stuck in Japan. "We had spent all our money, so I hocked my wristwatch," Grooters said. However, he still has that watch today. A friend of his later had a three-day pass to Japan and got the watch out of the pawn shop for him.

In 1955, Grooters was sent home and assigned to a base in Columbia, S.C., where he was soon discharged. Looking back on his military days, Grooters said he is still grateful for the GI Bill which helped him attend college.

He first got a degree at Iowa State Teachers College, then a master's degree at Long Beach State College, followed by a doctorate at the University of Oklahoma and finally a master's in library science at the University of Wisconsin - Madison.

War Stories

As a civilian he taught college electronics and math courses in Cedar Rapids, Iowa, then at the University of Wisconsin – Whitewater, and finally at Kansas University. He retired in 2000 and moved to Hot Springs Village, Ark., that same year. He has two children: Rebecca and Matthew.

Jeffrey L. Meek

Lee Jablonski served in U.S. Air Force in Korea

The 54th Fighter Interceptor Squadron served from 1953 to 1960 as part of the Aerospace Defense Command or ADC. The ADC's mission was planning for and executing the air defense of the United States. Possible scenarios included a Russian attack coming from Canadian airspace. Lee Jablonski served with the 54th.

Born in Grand Island, Neb., he recalls coming home from church on Dec. 7, 1941, and hearing the news of our fleet being attacked at Pearl Harbor. "My mom cried, we all cried," he remembers. His big brother Lawrence immediately joined the Marine Corps.

Troop trains began coming through Grand Island and Jablonski who had a shoeshine stand at the railroad station, saw thousands of GI's coming through on their way to training camps or units.

Years later, the Korean War broke out and Jablonski enlisted in the United States Air Force in June 1951. He was sent to Parks Air Force Base in California for boot camp and lots of tests. Jablonski chose to become a mechanic and was sent to Amarillo, Texas, for further training. He chose work related to fighter planes, but eventually worked on all sorts of aircraft.

His next stop was at Ellsworth Air Force Base in Rapid City, S.D., home of the 54th Fighter Interceptor Squadron. The base was considered part of the Strategic Air Command or SAC. He remembers getting up at 4 a.m. in the bitter cold to prepare engines and planes for flying later in the day. The squadron was later told to prepare to take F-84 fighter planes to England, but the action was called off.

War Stories

Instead, Jablonski became involved with evacuating the wounded from Korea. He made six such flights. These flights would made stops in Guam and Japan as necessary.

Jablonski later served in Greenland. It was so cold they never turned off the airplane engines. After a flight, the plane would taxi to their hanger, which was a carved-out glacier. Occasionally an engine would shut down. "It was so cold you would need 600 volts to get an engine started," said Jablonski.

He was later sent back to South Dakota and shortly thereafter, he was called in to his commanding officer's office and offered an opportunity to become a pilot. It was a dream come true, but there was a problem. His enlistment was up and his mother was at home ill with cancer. He felt the need to go home and take care of her. So, he turned down the offer and was honorably discharged in 1956.

Jablonski went home, tried to attend college, but ended up working for the Union Pacific railroad. He became a machinist and worked for the company until 1997. That same year he moved to Hot Springs Village, Ark.

"I really liked the Air Force, in fact, I fell in love with it," Jablonski said. Had his mother not been ill and needed attention, he feels he would have made a career out of it, but "mother came first," he said. "Life's been good to me," Jablonski said.

Several times during our talk, he referred to his brother, Lawrence. You can tell he respected him greatly. Brother Lawrence served in the Marine Corps with the 1st Marine Division in World War II and Korea. He fought throughout the Pacific at Guadalcanal, Iwo Jima and Okinawa and later died in 1989.

Jeffrey L. Meek

Dick Jester served with 7th Army Division in Korean War

It has many times been called the "forgotten war." Sandwiched between World War II and the Vietnam War, the Korean War was at a time in the early 1950s when thousands of U.S. troops risked their lives to halt a North Korean advance into South Korea.

The South Koreans managed to put up a good enough fight to buy some time for the United Nations to respond. The U.S. was the first to do so when, on June 27, 1950, our naval and air forces were ordered into action. Dick Jester fought and was wounded while serving in Korea as part of the U.S. Army's 7th Division, 49th Field Artillery Battalion as a forward observer, or FO.

Jester was attending the University of Illinois when he was drafted in September 1951. His first training stop was Camp Chaffee, Ark. He was later assigned to an artillery unit and learned all about the 105 mm Howitzer. Jester learned how to set up the big gun, load it, aim it and, as he says, "to put the shell where you want to put it."

As an FO, Jester would go out on patrols with infantry units with a large radio and communicate back to the gun battery as to where to drop their shells. He would also go out atop a hill and stay for up to two weeks to observe enemy movements.

His first patrol was to Hill 404. During the fight, a friend of his was badly hit by shrapnel and Jester's radio was shot. He finished the radio off with a grenade so it would be of no use to the enemy. "That was a long, nervous night," said Jester.

War Stories

Repeatedly he and the others would fight their way to the top of a hill, only to be driven back; and then repeat the process. He recalled a time when he was digging a foxhole and came across a dead enemy body. "The smell was just unbelievably bad," remembers Jester.

The men would receive the 105 mm Howitzer artillery shells two to a crate. They would then use the wood from the crate to make flooring in their tents. The men lived on "C" and "K" rations during the fighting.

Jester also fought at Triangle Hill, and it was there he earned the Purple Heart. Speaking of the battle he said, "That was a messy one." As Jester was making his way up the hill there was an enemy round that exploded behind him. "Then a bullet caught me in the leg and the next thing I knew I was back down below," Jester recalled. He was wounded in the knee and had shrapnel in his arm. The knee would require hospitalization. He didn't tell his parents he was wounded, but they would find out anyway.

On Dec. 30, 1952, Jester was visited at the 25th Evacuation Hospital by Cardinal Francis Spellman, Archbishop of New York at the time. During the visit a photographer snapped a picture. The picture and a caption eventually ended up in his hometown newspaper.

Jester spent two weeks in the hospital in a full cast on his leg. After the cast was removed, he got around on crutches for about two days and was then sent back to his unit for more of the same duty. There were other hills and other fights, but Jester made it through them all.

Along the way he earned a Bronze Star for Valor which was presented to him by General Matthew Ridgeway. Eventually he earned enough points and came

Jeffrey L. Meek

back to the U.S. in March of 1953. After a two week leave, Jester was ordered to Camp Crowder, Mo., where he served as an instructor to new recruits. He would teach them the dos and don'ts of military life before they shipped out for basic training.

In July 1953 Jester was discharged. "I was so glad to get out in one piece," Jester said. Looking back on his combat experiences he said, "It was pretty hectic, and I didn't think I'd make it. You just try to stay alive and do your job. And hope the other guys do too."

As a civilian, Jester worked in the record industry. He first spent 10 years as a buyer for a retail record store and then 26 years with Columbia Records in Chicago. At various times he worked in sales, promotion, and credit.

Jester retired in 1989 and moved to Hot Springs Village, Ark., that same year. He and his wife Patricia have four children: Richard, JoAnne, Judith, and Joseph.

War Stories

David McClure served in the U.S. Army In Korea

Organized in October 1917 on the World War I battlefields of France, the U.S. Army's Second Infantry Division fought in six campaigns in World War I and another six in World War II. In July 1950, the division sailed for Korea to help defend against the onslaught of Communist forces invading the South.

Fighting at Kunu-ri, Hongchon, the Hwachon Reservoir, and elsewhere, the division earned a U.S. Presidential Unit Citation and two Republic of Korea Presidential Unit Citations. Eighteen members of the division earned the Medal of Honor as the division suffered approximately 25,000 casualties including 7,094 killed. Part of the Second Infantry Division included David McClure who fought with the division's 9th Regiment, "E" Company.

After his 1947 high school graduation McClure decided to enlist in the Army. His basic training took place at Fort Jackson, S.C.. McClure loved playing in the band in school and continued his playing by attending Army Band School. He was then assigned to the 62nd Army Band at Fort Bliss, Texas. A year later he was discharged at the end of his 18-month enlistment.

In January 1949, he re-enlisted and was put with an Army-Navy band in Hot Springs, Ark. About a year later McClure requested and was chosen to play with a band in Japan.

In June 1950, he was in Seattle awaiting the trip to Japan when the Korean War broke out. He and 5,000 others were sent to Fort Lewis to prepare for duty in Korea. Instead

Jeffrey L. Meek

of being a band member, McClure was now a rifleman with the Army's Second Infantry Division and headed for war.

On July 17, 1950, he sailed for Korea aboard the USNS M.M. Patrick. Their destination was Pusan. On the Patrick the men were taught marksmanship and other infantry-related skills. On July 31 the men arrived at Pusan. McClure said the first night was spent at a rat-infested wharf. The next morning a train took them inland. For six days the division continued to arrive and amass their forces.

Trucks then took them to the Naktong River along the frontlines. "The first thing we saw after we got off the trucks and were lined up on each side of the road was a big Army truck loaded with dead soldiers," said McClure.

He and the others were placed in the nearby mountains overlooking the river. The next day they attacked an enemy position along a ridge, took the ridge and held it. His company was chosen to cross the river, but instead was put in reserve. The company was then reinforced with additional medics, mortars, and machine guns. On September 1, they returned to the river. McClure was made a squad leader and told to be ready to cross the next morning.

That night a huge enemy bombardment occurred along the river and the crossing was called off. Platoons were split up. McClure's group went to the right. The men that went to the left found themselves surrounded the next morning. His unit moved on and joined up with other elements of the division. From the ridgeline he and others went out on patrols to keep the area secure.

On September 15, Operation Chromite, the surprise amphibious invasion of Inchon on Korea's west coast, took place. Designed by Army General Douglas MacArthur it

War Stories

ranks as one of the most daring military moves in history. The attack took place in the rear of the advancing enemy forces and caused them to immediately pull back. This allowed the Second to move forward. Within 10 days, resistance stopped in McClure's area along the Naktong.

The division moved forward through Seoul and eventually to the North Korean capital. Along the way there was little resistance. McClure and others thought the war may soon be over. It was not to be.

In mid-October Chinese Communist Forces (CCF) secretly began to infiltrate large units into North Korea. By the end of the month several hundred thousand CCF fighters crossed the Yalu River and confronted the Eighth U.S. Army.

U.S. forces were overrun and pulled back. In November, McClure's unit was hit by the Chinese. The morning of the attack saw heavy losses in his unit. They pulled back several miles and regrouped. The weather conditions were brutally cold. Temperatures dropped to far below zero and McClure, and many others, got a case of frostbite. On November 28 he was taken to an aid station and then driven nine hours south to a hospital near Kunu-ri. All along the way the road was filled with retreating U.S. forces.

McClure described the frostbite. "All of the flesh on the bottom of the souls of my feet was totally off. I could see raw meat. I could not walk. We had not been able to change our socks or clean our feet for several days as we had moved," said McClure.In December, in Japan, he received treatment, medication and rehabilitation. In

Jeffrey L. Meek

February 1951, he was sent back to Korea and rejoined his unit.

A week later, Operation Killer was launched. The operation was an Allied counteroffensive to drive CCF and the North Korean People's Army (NKPA) out of the south. Each day McClure and the other men attacked the enemy and patrolled.

In April, McClure was chosen to join the X Corps Honor Guard. He moved back to Corps headquarters in South Korea. For several months he served on guard duty at the headquarters. In June he was notified he'd be going home and arrived in Seattle on July 4, 1951.

McClure was then placed with the First Armored Division band and served with them for about a year. In June 1952 he was discharged.

Looking back on his combat experiences in Korea, McClure remembers the devastating losses. He said of the 182 men in his company only 39 returned without a scratch. "For some reason I survived. I know I was very fortunate to survive," said McClure.

He is also haunted by an experience in which a close friend was wounded three times. "All three times I was within a hundred yards of him. Why him and not me," McClure wondered.

As a civilian McClure earned a law degree in 1959. He worked as a real estate manager for Mobile Corporation obtaining service station locations. He retired in 1986 and with his wife Nancy moved to Hot Springs Village, Ark., from Fairfax, Va., in 1989. He had two children: David and Laura.

War Stories

Don Van Scotter served in a medical unit in Korea

Medical care of the wounded during the Korean War was much improved over that of World War II. Statistics show 28 percent of all WW II wounded died from their wounds. In Korean that number dropped to 22 percent. Much of this can be attributed to the use of peripheral vascular surgery and the use of helicopters and other aircraft in transporting the wounded to facilities equipped to handle the wounds. In January 1951, the U.S. Army began their own air ambulance service. With one of those medical units was Don Van Scotter.

Van Scotter grew up in Wisconsin. In school he played basketball, baseball and was a kicker on the football team. He also remembers a time back in those days when youngsters collected money to aid the war effort during WW II. Van Scotter said they ended up with enough money to purchase two jeeps for use by U.S. military services.

After high school graduation he went to work for a year, then decided to attend college in Milwaukee. A year later he enrolled briefly in pharmacy school at the University of Wisconsin – Madison. But he ran out of money, so he decided to join the Army in January 1951, which was approximately seven months after the Korean War began.

He was sent to Fort McCoy in Wisconsin where it was 45 degrees below zero when he and others arrived. "I was put in an artillery group from Iowa. That's who gave me my basic training," said Van Scotter. While in boot camp he also attended a radio school and became radio operator for the commanding officer at McCoy.

Jeffrey L. Meek

Later, he was transferred to a medical battalion in summer 1951. During that time, he also applied for Officer Candidate School (OCS), passed the tests, but was put to work at the battalion's headquarters.

Thereafter he got word he'd been accepted into OCS and for Van Scotter that meant a trip to Fort Riley in Kansas. This led to him being placed into the Medical Service Corps as a Second Lieutenant in July 1952.

Van Scotter then took leave, went home and on July 20, married Jean, his high school sweetheart. The couple then traveled to Fort Sam Houston, Texas where he received more medical training at a medical field service school. That training included learning how to manage a medical unit which entailed field work, deskwork, and office work, all of which Van Scotter found interesting.

In October 1952 he reported to Camp Cooke in California where he joined the 44th Medical Battalion, 44th Infantry Division. A few weeks later the base closed and the 44th was transferred to Fort Lewis in Washington State. It was soon thereafter he received his orders. Van Scotter was being sent to Korea.

On a ship he went from San Francisco to Okinawa to Yokohama, Japan. After filling out some paperwork he boarded another ship and sailed off to Inchon Harbor in Korea. Van Scotter talked about Inchon as he saw it in late 1952. "That was quite an experience. There wasn't much left of the city. It had been retaken and retaken and retaken a number of times, so it was devastated," he said.

Van Scotter was sent to the 121st Evaluation Hospital for a short time, then ordered to the 25th Infantry Division up north near the frontlines. He got a ride to the

War Stories

base in a jeep and was assigned to Headquarters Company as an operations officer.

During the first few weeks the unit was sent out to replace the First Marine Division on the frontline. Van Scotter was given a hand drawn map and told to lead a convoy up to the front. In the dark, Van Scotter began the journey using only blackout lights on the vehicles. On the way the convoy came to a fork in the road and Van Scotter wasn't sure where they were on the map.

He then noticed some lights up ahead, so he went off to see what was there. He found an Australian unit, showed them the map he had been given and asked if the Aussies could help. No sir, they had no idea where on the map they were now located. So, around 1 a.m., Van Scotter chose a fork in the road and got the convey moving again. About 4 a.m. they reached the correct location. It had been a slow, uncertain trip for all.

After arrival his medical unit began setting up their facilities. "They were expecting casualties by noon, which we did receive," Van Scotter said. Their facility was close enough to the front the men could hear the exchange of gunfire.

Van Scotter was put in charge of all the enlisted men working in the unit. He added that they were very much like a MASH unit but did not have nurses like the television show "MASH." "We took care of the wounded we could handle," said Van Scotter. If his unit wasn't able to treat as necessary, the men would be taken by helicopter or ambulance to the 121st Hospital.

"We saw a lot of casualties and we also got cases of hemorrhagic fever," Van Scotter said. In an effort to find out why the men were getting the fever, a sanitation unit was brought in. Some thought it may be coming from the rats running around the area that were carrying an organism that was spreading the disease. Van Scotter said he only saw two rats while there, but after the sanitation unit set out traps and poison, he was amazed at what was learned. "There were thousands of them," Van Scotter said. Just 24 hours after arriving, the sanitation unit left with a truckload of dead rats.

Van Scotter stayed with this unit until the armistice was signed on July 27, 1953. He took an opportunity to travel with a friend to Panmunjom where the armistice had just been signed. While there they got to see the building where the peace talks had taken place and, maybe even more important, got to have a nice steak dinner while there. This day was also special in another way for Van Scotter. It was the day he was promoted to First Lieutenant.

Although the fighting stopped, the casualties kept coming in. Once the wounded were stabilized, they were moved to hospitals in Japan. Van Scotter said there were times when the outfit was short on doctors, so he'd help as needed giving shots, administering anesthesia and whatever else he could do to be helpful. All this work heightened his interest in medicine.

In late 1953, he took a 19-day ride on a ship back to San Francisco, then traveled by train to Fort Sheridan, Ill., where he was discharged on Dec. 10, 1953. He then joined a Reserve unit and was eventually made a Captain in the U.S. Army Dental Corps, Reserves.

As a civilian Van Scotter went into dental medicine, first at the University of Wisconsin – Stevens Point, then at Marquette University for his D.D.S. degree. In June 1958, he

War Stories

worked for the U.S. Public Health Services Hospital in Boston, Mass. He then did a residency in periodontics at Wood Veteran Administration Center in Milwaukee.

In July 1959 he attended graduate school at Marquette where he earned a M.S. degree in periodontics.

Van Scotter also taught dentistry for many years and retired in 1988. In 1993 he and wife Jean moved to Hot Springs Village, Ark., from Elkhorn, Wisc. They have four children: Donald, Peggy, Linda, and Laura.

Reflecting back on his Army days, Van Scotter said he was surprised that so many people back home had no idea what was going on in Korea. "They had no idea how serious it was in Korea," Van Scotter said. Of his experiences he added, "It was the greatest experience I ever had. Just going through leadership training, the command training, and the workload I had, which aged me a little bit, I learned so much. Everything I've done in life, in some way or another, had some bearing on (serving) in the military."

Jeffrey L. Meek

Nap Videan, Jr. served on the USS Essex during Korean War

The aircraft carrier USS Essex earned several battle stars for her participation in the Korean War and also received the Navy Unit Commendation Award during tours in Far Eastern waters. The ship launched airplanes for many attacks against North Korean targets including the Yalu River. Aboard the Essex was Nap Videan, Jr. who served the U.S. Navy from 1951 to 1953.

Born in Chillicothe, Ohio, Videan's family later moved to Bellevue, Ohio, where he played basketball and football in high school until he experienced a serious auto accident. "That pretty much ended my athletic career," said Videan.

He was on his way to a movie on Dec. 7, 1941, when he first heard of the Japanese attack at Pearl Harbor. He immediately returned home. "My Dad said it would be over in six months. He missed it a little," Videan said with a smile.

After high school he attended Heidelberg College in Tiffin, Ohio, and joined the Naval Reserves in March 1948. Then in June 1950 the Korean War began and Videan was called to active duty. But he was allowed to finish his senior year, then in 1951 reported for duty at Bambridge, Md., for basic training, much of which was redundant because of his time in the reserves.

Because he was a college graduate, he was in line for Officer Candidate School (OCS). He passed the tests but failed the minimum height requirement. "They said don't worry about that. Then two or three days later they came back and said sorry, we can't take you. You don't meet the minimum height requirement," Videan said.

War Stories

Because he did very well on his tests, he got to choose his next assignment. For him that would be Jacksonville, Fla., for preparation for aviation school. There in Jacksonville he attended aviation storekeeper school, learning about several aviation-related jobs. His favorite was storekeeper work, at which he did well. But Videan wanted more so he requested other duty and was placed on the USS Essex. To board her he first went to Treasure Island in California, then was put on the troopship USS General J.C. Breckinridge (AP-176) which took him to Okinawa, then Yokosuska, Japan where the ship was currently docked. Videan was assigned to the S-1 Division, Aviation Supply Division that had all sorts of aircraft needs, even including the big items like wings.

The Essex soon sailed off for duty along the Korean coast. Most of his work was in a storeroom and life on the Essex was pretty much routine, Videan said. He worked on aircraft parts and would spend some of his free time up on deck where he needed several layers of clothing to ward off the bitterly cold temperatures. On deck he would stand in a gun tub and watch planes take-off and land, mostly Corsairs and F-9F Sabre jets. Videan also witnessed a few crash landings during rough seas, one of which he'll never forget.

A plane and pilot had gone over the side one day as Videan looked on. "I looked down and I could see the pilot scratching at the canopy trying to get his canopy open and the plane immediately sank out of sight," he said of the sad scene. "The water was so frigid the choppers wouldn't even get a chance to take-off because they knew the pilot was dead in something like seven seconds."

Jeffrey L. Meek

Videan also had a few weeks of mess duty. "That was pretty bad because we worked around the clock," he said. And there was a time when the workers found lice in some of the bread.

Back in Japan he interacted with a lot with the Japanese people. "They were very friendly. I never felt threatened in Yokosuka," Videan said. However, there were incidents when 'GIs' robbed other American personnel.

Only once, in Yokohama, did Videan come across some bad feelings. "There was a Japanese military band playing and they were all horribly disabled and disfigured from World War II, all twisted up, eyes gone and just mangled. We stopped and looked at them and a Japanese gentleman came over and said 'I know you don't mean anything by it, but I wouldn't stick around. Feelings are still kind of strong.' And this was seven years after World War II, so we just left the area," Videan recalled.

He also talked about riding on trains and that many Japanese would smile and bow to him. "But I'd also see someone at the other end of the (train) car staring at me with just hate in his eyes. I knew from his age he was a World War II vet and that they didn't take to us much."

On the Essex his battle station was as a telephone talker with the Marines manning six-inch guns. Sometimes that duty would last up to 14 hours.

Then word came that the ship was going home, or so they thought. In spring of 1953 he was told by a young Japanese girl that no, the ship's not going home. "She said you're not going home, mark my words," said Videan. Sure enough the Essex sailed north to check out reports of Russian airplanes flying in Japanese airspace.

War Stories

The Essex headed for Vladivostok, Russia, for patrol duty. There they cut the ship's power so no sonar could pick them up. "We just drifted for two weeks off the coast of Vladivostok. At the end of two weeks no planes had come out so the captain said we might as well go home," Videan said.

He got back to California the day after July 27, 1953, the Korean War armistice was signed. NBC Newsman John Cameron Swayze had a crew there when the ship docked, and several photos were taken. Videan later learned folks back home saw him on the news broadcast coming off the ship. "I guess a dozen people had called my folks," said Videan about being seen on TV. He later joined the U.S. Coast Guard Reserves in the 1970s.

As a civilian he got into the insurance business as a claims adjuster and manager. Sixteen years later he went to work for the Federal Government in Baltimore, then later in Dallas as a special agent ending up with 30 years of service.

In January 1999 he retired and moved with wife Betsy to Hot Springs Village, Ark., in 2003 from Mesquite, Texas. They have two children: Nap IV and Beth.

Reflecting back on his navy service, Videan said he was surprised that "people all over the world are just like us," he said of their basic nature.

Jeffrey L. Meek

Bob Whipple served with the Navy at Inchon, Korea

Operation Chromite, better known as the Inchon invasion of Sept. 15, 1950, was a daring, strategic attack behind enemy lines designed by Gen. Douglas MacArthur. Troops from the First Battalion, Fifth Marines breached the sea wall at Inchon's Red Beach and were soon reinforced by elements of the Second Battalion, Fifth Marines, and the First Marine Regiment.

Within hours initial objectives were achieved and by September 18 nearby Kimpo airfield was retaken. On September 26, other U.S. forces linked up with the invasion forces near Osan as the North Korean Army stronghold on the peninsula was cut in half causing enemy forces to retreat north and U.S./U.N. troops to advance up the peninsula after having been almost pushed to the sea near Pusan. Later serving at Inchon with the U.S. Navy was Bob Whipple who served as a diesel engineman.

The Wisconsin native was working in a machine shop after high school graduation, thought he'd be drafted and decided to join the Navy as an enlisted volunteer for a one-year active-duty stint followed by four years in the reserves. He signed the papers on Dec. 9, 1948. Whipple first went for basic training to Great Lakes near Chicago, Ill., "in the slush and snow," Whipple said of the cold.

Next, he was assigned to a destroyer, the USS Robert H. McCard (DD822). With the 7th Fleet the ship patrolled the Mediterranean for many months, then returned home to Boston to replace some guns.

War Stories

About this time Whipple was released from active duty and began his time in the reserves. But the Korean War had broken out and he was soon called back for active duty, taken to Treasure Island, Calif., where he boarded a troop transport and sailed to Yokuska, Japan, where he was assigned to the air facility at Opoma Naval Air Facility. Here Whipple was put with a boat pool that was ready for sea rescue when needed.

"We were out there standing by when any of the PBM bombers took off to fly to Korea. We'd standby every time they'd take off in case they had a problem, which we never did all the time I was there," said Whipple. With them on board was a corpsman just in case of an injury following a crash landing. Whipple and two other men were in charge of the engines on board the ship.

In Japan he visited Mt. Fuji for a few days and remembers the beauty of the area. "You could see it from 50 miles away," Whipple recalled. A year later he was shipped to Korea, first landing at Pusan. Then a train took him to Seoul followed by a trip to Inchon on a weapons carrier.

At Inchon, Whipple was put with a maintenance crew in a boat pool which was active evacuating casualties with LCM's to hospital ships in the bay. Whipple worked with supply and as a mechanic.

The boats in the pool kept blowing head gaskets until the guys figured out the engine blocks were warped. Whipple ordered four new engines and with the others installed them. That was the end of the gasket problems. Swapping out the engines was a big job which included removing the rear deck of the boat, removing the engine,

Jeffrey L. Meek

setting it on the beach and putting the new engine in place. These engines were six cylinders, 671 cubic inch that were started by using ether in cold weather situations. They also had a flame starter which would, with a sprayer, ignite and heat the engines to get them fired up in the cold.

Whipple lived in a hotel in Inchon and used a shower and outhouse across the street. He said the city had little battle damage where he was, and that Koreans would take GI brass that was left lying around. The men used young Korean houseboys to clean the area. He said the Koreans wore snowsuits in the winter and baggy pants in the summer.

Also, while in Inchon the men mounted machine guns and GMC truck engines in small Korean boats. "We made pirates out of them," Whipple said. What those boats and the men on them did was never discussed. He has no idea what they did.

And there was one time when an enemy air raid struck near Inchon, but not close to his location. It was the only such raid taking place during Whipple's tour of duty.

After a year in Korea, Whipple went back to the U.S. The trip included a stop in Hawaii where they stayed a week awaiting a plane to fly them to Treasure Island. A few days after returning to the U.S. he was discharged and visited his parents who had moved from Wisconsin to California. After the visit he completed his journey to his home in Madison, Wisc.

As a civilian Whipple worked at auto dealerships and rose to become assistant body shop manager, then went into the insurance business with GMAC for 19 years. Then he moved to Texas, became a claim supervisor with the

War Stories

Texas Credit Union League before taking a similar position with CNA.

He retired in 1993 and with wife Eyvonne moved to Hot Springs Village, Ark., a year later. The Whipples have three children: Diane and twins Paula and David.

Looking back on his military service Whipple said, "I learned how to grow up. You learned to get along by yourself, make friends and be self-sufficient."

Jeffrey L. Meek

Roger Witcraft served on Navy destroyer during Korean War

The USS Boyd was commissioned in May 1943 and participated in numerous operations during World War II including Iwo Jima and Okinawa. The 2,000-ton ship also saw action during the Korean War during which she earned five battle stars. Aboard the Boyd was Roger Witcraft who served as a gunner's mate.

Witcraft grew up in the Black Hills in Lead, S.D. After graduating he enlisted in the Navy in December 1951 and was sent to San Diego, Calif., for basic. From there many of his friends were assigned to aircraft carriers, but Witcraft received orders for duty aboard the Fletcher-class destroyer USS Boyd (DD544). The 376-foot-long ship was in Long Beach, Calif., when Witcraft walked aboard to begin his duties. "You're just a deckhand at that time," he said of his first job on the vessel which included chipping paint and re-painting.

The USS Boyd traveled to Hawaii, Midway Island to refuel, then went on to Japan and Korea, landing at Wonsan Harbor, about 110 air miles north of the 38th parallel, where they spent much of their time.

On one mission the ship had the task of moving along the coast of North Korea close to shore to draw enemy fire so the gun locations could be pinpointed. Then the battleship USS Iowa would pound the enemy with their 16-inch guns. As this was going on, the Boyd would contribute by firing their five-inch guns.

Witcraft said there were times when MIG jet fighters would engage U.S. Navy Corsairs which were prop-

War Stories

driven World War II era fighters. On occasion they would shoot down the Corsairs and the Boyd would rescue the pilot. The men and their ship would patrol Korea for nine months, return to the U.S. for three months to partake in exercises and then go back to Korea for more patrolling.

During his second tour in Korea, Witcraft was called home to attend gunnery school. Here he learned more about the five-inch guns on the ship. As gunners' mate, he would learn how to maintain the gun, ammunition, and be sure the gun was always ready for action. The gunners would consist of a gun mount captain, which Witcraft became, and five others that would operate all aspects of the gun and the 54-pound projectile.

"The powder is shoved up through a hole and the powder man grabs it and puts it in a tray. Then the projectile man takes the projectile out of a hoist and puts it in," said Witcraft of gun operation. "The projectile has a timer on it, so it goes off at a certain time. We used it (the five-inch gun) mostly for shore bombardment," Witcraft said, then added that the gun would also fire star shells to light up an area if needed. Besides the enemy fire was the dangerous weather the ship had to endure, like typhoons and extreme cold.

After sailing to Japan, the Boyd was told of an approaching typhoon so they quickly headed back to Korea. On the way the storm struck. Of the typhoon Witcraft said, "The big thing is, on a small ship like a destroyer, they really bounce. In your bunk you have to hang on or get thrown out." The waves were so tall the ship's propellers would come out of the water as she crashed through the raging sea. Those who slept aft had to go along the outside of the ship to get to the mess hall. As they would make their way, they took hold of a cable so as not to be washed overboard.

The conditions were so bad the Boyd had to maintain the same north heading for three days because it was too dangerous to try and turn the ship. Witcraft said the guns had 10 inches of ice on them as did most of the other areas on the ship, but they never lost a man overboard. Other vessels were not so lucky. Witcraft and the Boyd continued their duty cruising the Korean coast until the war ceased in July 1953.

From here the ship went to the Formosa Straits for patrol duty, again through rough water most of the time. The cruise also included stops in Hong Kong for R & R, one Christmas in Bangkok and patrols to and from Japan. Witcraft returned to the United States in 1955.

After arriving, the ship was on maneuvers off the California coast with dozens of other warships, some practicing the landing of Marines on a beach. That night a Japanese freighter had somehow sailed into the task force on their way to a California port and struck the Boyd broadside.

"We were dead in the water, didn't have any power or anything," remembers Witcraft of the collision. "It hit about 20 feet in back of us," said Witcraft who was in a gun mount at the time.

"He (the Japanese ship) just backed out and took off." The next morning a tug towed the Boyd into San Diego. Witcraft was discharged there the following week on Dec. 10, 1955.

As a civilian he worked as a maintenance welder at a gold mine in the Black Hills, then taught welding at

War Stories

Hennepin Technical College in Eden Prairie, Minn. Witcraft also spent three years in Saudi Arabia with the U.S. Dept. of Labor organizing welding programs, then returned to teaching until retiring in 1994. He and wife Mary Ann moved to Hot Springs Village, Ark., that same year from Eden Prairie.

Reflecting on his military service, Witcraft said the friendships made were very special. He recalled a time when he got together with a buddy that he had not seen in 42 years, and it was like they had never been apart. He added that the service transforms youngsters into men by giving them responsibilities.

At this point Witcraft told another part of his story while aboard the USS Boyd.

Interestingly, he had also spent time on the ship as its helmsman, including a time when he had to steer the vessel alongside a tanker. He also took the Boyd into San Diego Harbor with the help of a few tugboats. "That's an experience you never forget," said Witcraft. Concluding, he said of his service, "I have no regrets. I didn't know what to expect, but I enjoyed it."

Jeffrey L. Meek

Chapter III: Vietnam War Veterans

U. S. Army Major General Tom Arwood served 34 years in U.S. Army

This the story of U.S. Army Major General Tom Arwood. His military service covered 34 years which included moving 21 times. Through it all, was wife Peggy by his side.

Arwood grew up in Ohio in a family that had little. After high school graduation, Arwood was attending Bowling Green University and working the 11 p.m. to 7 a.m. shift on the Baltimore-Ohio, railroad. On campus one day, someone told Arwood about something called ROTC. "Someone said if you join this thing called ROTC they pay you. I saw pay as meaning eat. So, I joined ROTC," said Arwood.

He completed the program and was commissioned a Second Lieutenant in the Army Reserve but had no intention of staying beyond his reserve time. "I was going to be a CPA," said Arwood. On graduation day, he married Peggy, and they were off to Utah where Arwood became a Commissary Officer, which is very similar to being a grocery store manager.

Later, Arwood decided he would apply for the regular Army. He was accepted and received orders to report to Fort Benning in Georgia. After basic training, Arwood next completed Airborne School. Following graduation, he joined the 2nd Infantry Division as a First Lieutenant.

War Stories

He and others then created a brand-new battle group of about 700 men. "We taught them how to be a soldier," remembers Arwood. He was then sent to Virginia Beach where the unit practiced landing on beaches. Toward the end of his two-year tour of duty, he was given a choice to stay with the infantry or return to the Quartermaster Corps. He took the Quartermaster option. Before making the move, Arwood was working in Division Headquarters of the 2nd Infantry.

He received orders to deploy to Oxford, Miss., where federal troops helped secure the admission of James Meredith at the University of Mississippi. About a month later, Arwood returned to Fort Benning. Shortly thereafter, he received a 'red alert.' They were told to prepare to go to Cuba. It was the Cuban Missile Crisis, and the Division was preparing for a possible invasion. The crisis ended with President John F. Kennedy and Soviet Premier Nikita Khrushchev reaching an agreement that averted nuclear war.

His next move was to Bangkok, Thailand. Arwood, now a captain, worked with a unit called Army Security Activity, a rather cryptic name. I asked Arwood what that meant and what they did. His response surprised me. He couldn't say what they did, but he did say that he continued to organize logistics and traveled to places like Japan and Vietnam. About this time, an event occurred that would signal the beginning of major participation of the U.S. in the Vietnam War.

On Aug. 2, 1964, the U.S. destroyer Maddox reported being attacked by North Vietnamese patrol boats in Tonkin Gulf. Two days later, the Turner Joy also reported

Jeffrey L. Meek

being attacked. On August 7, the U.S. Congress passes the Tonkin Gulf Resolution, and the escalation began. In February 1968, the U.S. Senate Foreign Relations Committee began hearings on the events leading to passage of the Tonkin Gulf Resolution amid rumors that no attack actually occurred. I asked Arwood about this dispute over the facts and, again, he could not comment on the issue.

Arwood was later sent to the second tier of officer training – the Career Course. While there, he received the Legion of Merit for his service in Bangkok – service he could not discuss. The medal is for meritorious conduct and is one of only two medals issued as a neck order – the other being the Medal of Honor.

He was then made Company Commander of the Quartermaster school with 375 men in his command. After nine months, he received a promotion to Major and was assigned to a new Battalion – the 262nd Petroleum Battalion. Their job entailed handling fuel and all related issues. The battalion grew to 575 men, and they were told to get everything ready in six months and prepare to deploy to Vietnam. He would have to leave behind his wife and three-month-old son.

Once in Vietnam, they set up shop at Cam Ranh Bay, a natural harbor located in Khanh Hoa Province. It developed into one of the largest seaports in South Vietnam. There, Arwood took charge of all sea going vessels hauling fuel into Vietnam. The operation went on 24/7. They took over large tank farms and built more tanks; 94 percent of what they handled was jet fuel, known as JP4. It would take two days for a single tanker to unload its fuel

War Stories

through eight-inch lines running from ship to inland tank. Arwood also oversaw four companies of tanker trucks which hauled gas into the interior.

He accompanied them into hostile territory on several occasions. One incident he remembers well was when one of the convoys missed a turn and found themselves in a very dangerous area. Soon, the convoy was surrounded. Arwood took a helicopter to the area to check out the situation. All was resolved thanks to naval gun support which allowed the convoy to break out.

He had a close call in 1968 that still lives with him today. An above ground refueling point was getting their tanks and lines shot up so Arwood and a contingent of men went to see what could be done about it. They came under an attack which lasted into the night and continued throughout the night. They were pinned down and Arwood needed his radioman, which was right next to him. Arwood looked and saw the man was dead. He had been hit by shrapnel that missed Arwood. They eventually made it back to safety.

In May, Arwood returned to the U.S. and worked with the Fifth Army Staff at Fort Sheridan in Chicago. He wanted to finish his graduate degree and was sent to the University of Richmond in Virginia where he completed a degree in Business Administration. To put the degree to work, he was sent to West Point to oversee the cadet mess hall.

At West Point, Arwood's organization served up to 12,600 meals per day. They had their own bakery and head baker, a head chef, 282 waiters, 160 kitchen workers and even their own ice cream plant. Two years later he became

Jeffrey L. Meek

a part of the Command and General Staff College at Fort Leavenworth, Kan. This was the top level of officer training.

His next assignment was in Saudi Arabia. In June 1973, he worked with logistics and was a military advisor to the Northern Army of Saudi Arabia at Tubac. He was stationed there when the Arab – Israeli War broke out. After meeting with the Saudi Arabian commanding general, it was agreed that Arwood would not become involved. He waited out the war until it ended several weeks later. It was during this tour of duty that Arwood became a Lieutenant Colonel.

After completing the tour, he and his family reported to Fort Campbell, Ky., where he commanded a support battalion of the 101st Airborne Division. During this time, he served with Colin Powell and the two men became good friends.

Two years later, he became the division G-4; General Staff for logistics. In 1976, he and the 101st went to Germany where they trained for a theoretical Russian invasion of Germany.

Next, Arwood attended the Air War College in Montgomery, Ala., for a year.

He was then assigned to the Pentagon and served in logistics in the Department of the Army.

The job was to deal with war reserves. That meant making sure adequate supply was stockpiled in Europe and the Pacific should any fighting break out. Later, Arwood was promoted to Colonel.

A month later he was sent to Europe to command the 8th Infantry Division Support Command in Kreznach,

War Stories

Germany. The mission was to deploy to the Polar Gap if a Russian attack should ever take place.

Two years later, Arwood was selected to run the V Corps as the G-4 in Frankfort, Germany. Nine months later, he received his first star and became a Brigadier General.

He was sent back to the U.S. and assumed command of the Defense Realization and Marketing Command which had 48 locations around the world. The responsibility was to take charge of all excess generated by the Department of Defense – process it and sell it off. "We put $350 million back in the U.S. Treasury," Arwood said. They sold a submarine, airplanes, parts, typewriters, clothing, and anything else that was in excess.

After three years, Arwood went back to Germany and became commander of the Corps Support Command for two years. Then it was back to the U.S. to lead the Army Material Command in Virginia. They managed all Army depots.

He was later studying at Harvard when, in 1990, Operation Desert Shield began. On Aug. 2, 1990, Iraq attacked their neighbor, Kuwait, with 120,000 troops and 200 tanks. Arwood returned to Washington to put together the logistics.

In 1992, Arwood was playing golf on a Saturday morning when he was notified, he was to immediately take charge of humanitarian relief efforts in Florida as a result of Hurricane Andrew. A total military force of 27,000 arrived on the scene. "We handled all donations. We could have filled the Orange Bowl four times," said Arwood. They also were in charge of all medical support as well.

Jeffrey L. Meek

With the help of the Canadian military, they rebuilt 21 out of 23 destroyed schools in only three weeks. He finished his work and in October 1993 decided that moving 21 times over the last 34 years was enough. He and wife Peggy decided it was time to retire.

At his retirement, Arwood received the very first Humanitarian Relief Medal given out by our government. The Arwoods bought a lot in Hot Springs Village in 1993 and built there in 1997.

As we ended our interview, Arwood expressed how lucky and grateful he was for all the great training he had and leaders he worked with. He also said how fortunate he was to have a wife like Peggy who put up with all the moves and the time away from each other during some of his tours of duty.

So, there it is. The story of a young boy from Ohio, who may have ended up as a factory worker were it not for a friend that mentioned something he had never heard of – ROTC.

Instead of a factory worker, he rose to the rank Major General in the U.S. Army and served our country for 34 years.

War Stories

Doug Beed served with the Big Red One in Vietnam

Doug Beed served in the First Infantry Division, First of the Second Infantry Battalion, First Infantry Brigade in Vietnam. He grew up in Iowa and was transferring to another college when he decided to let his student deferment expire. As expected, he was drafted into the Army and began his service in April 1968. He then decided to enlist in a Warrant Officer Candidate School for helicopter pilots.

He first went to Fort Polk, La., for basic, then to Fort Walters for flight training. After a time, he dropped out and ended up in infantry training. After a leave he went to Oakland, Calif., for processing, then flew to Ton Son Nhut Air Base in Vietnam. Next, he was taken to Bien Hoa and put with the First Infantry Division as a rifleman.

Beed then went to Di An Base Camp about 12 kilometers from Bien Hoa where the division was headquartered and began doing short patrols that returned to the base camp most nights. On the patrols Beed also carried C-4 explosives and extra ammunition.

Then, at Lai Khe he soon became an M-60 machine gunner. The M-60 is the biggest gun in the platoon, provides the most firepower and is therefore a special enemy target for the enemy. Beed's platoon was usually one of three that would be dropped at a landing zone (LZ) and search for enemy trails. At night they'd set up an ambush on what looked like a well-used trail. Their job was to stop infiltration down the Ho Chi Minh Trail.

Jeffrey L. Meek

Beed talked about how an ambush is set up and functions. He said they would pick out a location and right at dark slip into it, lie down without digging in and stay quiet. Claymore mines would be put in place and a machine gun set up on the left and right to create a deadly field of fire and to protect their flanks. The rest of the men would be in three-man teams positioned between the machine guns.

As the enemy would approach, the men would wait until they were in the kill zone, then set off the claymores and rake the area with small arms fire. Beed said the ambush needed to be executed quickly because, in an ambush, there is no defense. "If you don't get it done in the first 30 or 40 seconds or a minute you've got a real problem on your hands because then you are as vulnerable as they are."

Contact with enemy units was made on many occasions. And sometimes the platoon would stumble on an enemy base camp which would result in large, prolonged firefights. On one of Beed's patrols his and two other platoons were suddenly ambushed from a position that included bunkers. The patrol formed up, took casualties, and fought for their lives. "It was a huge base camp, and it took six or seven hours for us to get out of a problem," said Beed.

To make matters worse, smoke grenades and air support fire caused the bamboo forest they were in to catch fire. Beed crawled through the bamboo and was eventually able to get into a position to fire on an enemy bunker that was causing many of the casualties.

War Stories

He dove out into the bunker's field of fire and opened up with his M-60. Seconds later his assistant gunner joined him and began feeding ammo belts into the gun.

Beed kept firing on that bunker opening for an hour so the wounded could be pulled out and to give cover to all as they pulled back. "That was the day I won the Bronze Star with V," said Beed whose machine gun got so hot he had to alternate which finger he used because of the heat. "I had to change my (trigger) fingers because it was burning my fingers," said Beed of his situation.

When the platoon pulled back, choppers arrived to extract the wounded, using jungle penetrators due to the thick surroundings. Beed said close air support kept them from being overrun that first night and it was a full three days until they were able to break all contact with the advancing forces and get back to their base camp at Quan Loi.

The guys got resupplied and bedded down for some much needed sleep when suddenly, in the early morning hours, they were awoken by the sound of gunfire. The enemy had broken through the perimeter and was attacking the camp. Beed's platoon was a blocking force holding the invaders back. A DC-3 nicknamed "Spooky" dropped flares and opened up on the attackers with three mini-guns spewing 3,000 rounds per minute.

The platoon then received orders to attack the Vietnamese that were now holed up inside the base's bunkers. In the end, 36 out of nearly 100 men survived without injury. "After that we were deemed not battle ready," Beed said. He later learned that everyone in their

Jeffrey L. Meek

mortar platoon had been killed except for one survivor. After all this, the rest of the platoon was pulled off the line. Beed was eventually taken off the M-60 and put with a mortar platoon as a Sergeant. A month later he joined the fire direction team.

On Dec. 2, 1969, Beed left Vietnam and was discharged just two days later in California. Back in Iowa he returned to college. He was against the war by the time of his return and said he felt almost "invisible," and was not anxious to talk about the war.

Beed recalls being at the University of Iowa watching student riots. "It was a really strange feeling. I had a lot of demons and I basically stayed drunk for the next two years. Finally, my demons were far enough away I guess, so I slowly started getting back into life. And I met my wife and I fell in love and finished my two years of school and a bachelor's degree and just started living my life again," Beed said.

As a civilian he taught construction management and technology and also worked as a carpenter, and painted water towers and grain elevators. He retired in 2010 and with wife Penny moved to Hot Springs Village in January 2011 from Cedar Rapids, Iowa.

Looking back on his service Beed said, "I wouldn't go through that again for anything and yet it's absolutely one of the most important parts of my life. A lot of who I am today, morally and ethically, is a direct result of the tasks my government asked me to do in those two years. I saw enough to know how bad it can be."

In 2017, Beed wrote a book about his experiences called, "Chasing Understanding in the Jungles of Vietnam: My Year As a 'Black Scarf'." It's a real page-turner.

War Stories

Bill Behan served in United States Marine Corps

Bill Behan hails from Brooklyn, N.Y., attended Public School 102 and an aviation high school that taught mechanics, pre-college, and Federal Aviation Administration-related courses. His interest in aircraft began when a cousin wrote a book on aircraft recognition. "Any time I went to his house I poured through it. I just loved it," Behan remembers.

After graduation he decided he'd joined the Marine Corps and enlisted in May 1961. Parris Island, S.C., was his first stop for 13 weeks of basic training. Next came infantry training at Camp Lejeune. During that time, he also served on guard duty.

Behan had been guaranteed an aviation job but tried instead to get an Embassy duty assignment. After a leave. he reported to Naval Air Station (NAS) Memphis where he went through a screening process, tried to become a C-130 navigator (the school closed), but decided to apply for an air traffic control assignment. He was granted the job and began learning the necessary skills in Olathe, Kan., arriving on Jan. 2, 1962, in the midst of a two-day blizzard that dumped 30 inches of snow on the area.

He then passed a seven-part exam and moved on to NAS Glynco in Georgia where the men reported to a blimp hanger for their instruction. Behan said the Corps tried something new when they sent him straight into radar school which then qualified him in radar and control tower work. After graduation he received orders to report to Buford, S.C., where he was put on mess duty for 30 long days.

Jeffrey L. Meek

The skills learned for the job involved keeping the planes on the appropriate glide path as the aircraft came in for landings. As an air traffic controller with Marine Air Traffic Control (MATC) Unit 63, Behan was also qualified as an official weather observer. The radar equipment included surveillance radar that would reach approximately 40 miles, along with ground and precision approach radar.

Behan was there when the October 1962 Cuban Missile Crisis brewed into becoming a historic, global-reaching event as the U.S. and Russia squared off over the introduction of Soviet missiles in Cuba. He said one day all the squadrons left the base. He and others packed their bags and all their radar equipment and waited for what was to come. He found out later the planes had all gone to Key West, Fla., in case they were needed for attacks.

Behan said the controller-learning process could be overwhelming. "Every time you took a test, if you failed it, you might get one more chance, but if you failed you were sent somewhere else to another school. So going through school was interesting," he said. Tests were also given at each base, so the controllers knew the surrounding area and terrain for 50 miles. Behan stayed in this role for two years, then left the Marines in October 1964, only to re-enlist a month later.

He was sent to Quantico, Va., for similar work, but also assigned to watch presidential helicopters. At Quantico he served until 1966 as a controller, 24 hours on, 24 hours off, plus on stand-by over the weekends.

Later that year he was sent to Japan, but was later, by request, transferred to Vietnam. He landed at Da Nang and was then sent to Dong Ha farther north. Behan said the

War Stories

scariest part of being there was when the B-52s bombed the area. "They would bomb within a thousand feet of us. You'd see the flash, then you'd hear the noise and then the ground rumbled," he said.

In 13 months at Dong Ha the control tower had to be replaced 13 times because of enemy attacks trying to hit C-130s and helicopters. "We were collateral damage," Behan noted of the towers. He was alone in the tower during one attack trying to help a C-130 takeoff. Luckily the runway wasn't hit, and the plane got out unscathed. Behan then left the tower and later returned to find heavy damage where he had been sitting. Shrapnel holes were everywhere.

Following this 13-month assignment he returned to the U.S. for duty at NAS Willow Grove in Pennyslania with MATC Unit 74 where he trained reservists on radar. Nine months later he went back to Japan for control tower work at Iwakuni NAS. There, among other things, he worked with U-2 and other high flying surveillance aircraft. He realized these planes were unique when a pilot once radioed in saying his altitude was 66,000 feet. "I had never worked an aircraft anywhere near that high before," said Behan with a smile.

With talk of the U-2 comes talk of Francis Gary Powers, the U-2 pilot shot down over Russia in 1960 and later swapped for Russian spy Rudolph Ivanovich Abel on Feb. 10, 1962, and is the subject of the hit movie, "Bridge of Spies."

"I knew him," said Behan of Powers. Later when Behan was working for the FAA, Powers was flying a helicopter for an NBC affiliate in Los Angeles. "In the evenings he'd come up in the tower and we'd sit around and talk," said Behan.

Behan was later transferred to El Toro Air Station near Los Angeles. He was made NCO in charge of flight clearances. Because he also had experience in handling presidential choppers, he would also handle President Richard Nixon flights out of San Clemente.

Behan recalled a time when the Nixon chopper took off, then soon disappeared off the radar screen near Newport Beach. Minutes later he learned the helicopter had made a quick stop to pick up Nixon's friend Bebe Rebozo.

On Nov. 6, 1970, Behan was discharged. He then went to work for the Los Angeles Dodgers, in charge of the ballplayers parking lot. Next came a job with the FAA as a controller. With the FAA he later became a senior executive, retiring after 25 years, in 1999. Behan then was employed as an aviation vice president with several companies. He and wife Ann have three children: Dawn, Robyn, and William.

Reflecting on his time in service, Behan said the experiences helped form his future career with the FAA, for which he was obviously thankful. Looking back on those days he remembered another story, this one about President George Herbert Walker Bush.

One day he got a call, and it was Bush who was calling about getting a control tower put in at Aspen, Colo. Behan said he was sorry but doing so met none of the criteria for such a tower. Behan said Bush asked him, "Do you know who you are talking to?" to which Behan replied yes sir, but I have criteria I have to follow. Guess what? Aspen got a control tower.

War Stories

Arnold Black served in the 101st Airborne Division in Vietnam

Arnold Black grew up on a farm in North Dakota. After completing high school, he attended Breckinridge Technical School and went to work at Sears in Mason City, Iowa. On April 2, 1968, he was officially drafted into the U.S. Army. Black had tried to get in the Air Force but couldn't before getting that Army draft notice.

From Fargo, N.D., he took a train to Fort Lewis, Wash., for his basic and advanced infantry training. "It rained every day and if it wasn't raining, it would be in a few minutes," Black said of the conditions. He added that many men washed out and that portions of the terrain were good preparation for going to Vietnam.

In August, he received four weeks leave, then went to Edwards Air Force Base for the flight to Vietnam. After arrival in Saigon he was assigned to the 101st Airborne Division and taken by helicopter to his base about 25 miles away. From there the 101st went to Camp Eagle near the DMZ in northern South Vietnam. "It was a huge camp with all kinds of facilities. Basically, it was the center where all the 101st was deployed from," he said.

The base was under rocket and mortar attack on a frequent basis, which at times caused casualties. From that base Black and his unit would chopper out for patrols for days at a time, sometimes landing in a hot LZ, taking fire from the enemy as chopper gunners fired back. His job was as a radio operator, which made him a priority target for the enemy.

Jeffrey L. Meek

From five to 15 kilometers per day the men made their way through jungles, using trails made by men or animals, watching for booby traps and trip wires. Dogs came along to sniff out the problems. "Sometimes they did a good job, sometimes they didn't," said Black. "We had several get injured." Rice patties were full of snakes so they tried to stay out of them when they could.

In June of 1969, his firebase was overrun. At that time Black was assigned as the radio operator for the Battalion Commander, as the unit sat perched on top of a mountain. They were supposed to get out before dark, but they didn't, and it proved to be a huge mistake.

That morning, at about 3 a.m., the enemy attack began. Sirens went off and flares went up as the enemy units poured inside their base. His outfit worked with South Vietnamese men, so it was hard to distinguish good guy from bad guy, Black told me.

"That's when I got wounded. They came through the barbed wire. I was out at one of the bunkers facing the wire and I heard somebody walking behind me. I turned around and a North Vietnamese was coming into the bunker. When I shot him, it set off a charge he was carrying and it just leveled the bunker. It blew the sides out and it collapsed down on us," said Black. He was severely burned and blinded by the blast. The men were trapped inside the bunker until morning when others finally got them out.

Black was taken to a MASH unit, then flown to the hospital ship "Sanctuary." For six weeks they treated his burns and then medevacked him to Japan, where he underwent eye surgeries to reattach his retinas.

War Stories

He was later flown from Japan to Fitzsimmons Army Hospital in Colorado, for further treatment. There the doctors worked for months to remove tiny pieces of brass that were still in his eyes. Later, as the brass pieces would work their way to the surface of an eye, he'd go back to Fitzsimmons to have them removed. "The brass that was in my eyes would work its way to the surface. So periodically I'd have to go back in and they would pull out a piece that was sticking out, because it would catch on my eyelid," said Black. Sitting there doing the interview with him, I was amazed at how calmly Black spoke of his horrible ordeal. To this day he sees only from his right eye. On Nov. 12, 1969, Black was medically retired from the Army.

As a civilian he worked for Ball Brothers Research as an electronic technician, then for a company where electronic weighing equipment for labs was manufactured. Black later started his own business, helping banks with mergers of acquisitions of data processing centers, retiring in 2013.

He and wife Toni moved to the Village in June of 2015, from Albuquerque, N.M. They have three children: Nicolle, Noelle, and Jared.

Looking back at his years in uniform Black said he did not have any PTSD, so was able to get out of the Army and move on with life, getting a good job right away. "I never looked back," Black said. He told me he sees the military doing the same thing in the Middle East that was done in Vietnam, taking areas over and over again. "We do the same cycle over and over. That's what frustrates me about our military. They have newer technology, but still do the same stupid stuff they were doing in Vietnam, old tactics. They haven't learned."

Jeffrey L. Meek

Boyd Burkholder served with 25th Division in Vietnam during 20-year career

The U.S. Army's 25th Infantry Division served with distinction in both World War II and Korea. In January 1966 the division's Third Brigade arrived in Vietnam for combat duty and elements remained until 1970. During those years the division suffered 34,484 men killed or wounded in action and earned the Vietnamese Civil Action Medal and Vietnamese Cross of Gallantry with Palm. Boyd Burkholder served with the 25th as a platoon leader and later as a company commander.

Burkholder grew up in Glendale, Calif. After finishing high school, he decided to join the Army. He enlisted to become an operating room specialist. Burkholder was first sent to Fort Ord in Monterrey for basic training and then to Fort Sam Houston for medical training. A few months later he applied for Officers Candidate School (OCS) and was accepted into infantry OCS in May 1963 at Fort Benning, Ga.

The school included parachute school and a two-year stint at Fort Polk, La., serving as a company executive officer and company commander. Also, during this time Burkholder attended ranger school.

Following this he was assigned to the 172nd Infantry Brigade at Fort Richardson, Alaska, in December 1965 as a platoon leader of the Fourth Battalion, 23rd Infantry. Burkholder thought it would be a two-year tour of duty there but only three weeks later they were told they were headed for Vietnam. "It was a surprise. The battalion commander got all the officers together for officers' call and

War Stories

said Merry Christmas boys, we're going to Vietnam," Burkholder said.

In January 1966, with the Fourth Battalion, 9th Infantry Brigade, he left for Hawaii where he joined the 25th Infantry Division, First Brigade. Following a promotion to First Lieutenant and three weeks of training they went to Vung Tau, Vietnam, and then by plane to Saigon Airport. He was then loaded onto a truck that took him to his base camp at Cu Chi.

After settling in Burkholder led patrols near the base. There was an extensive network of enemy tunnels in the area and even under their base at Cu Chi so the enemy was never far away. Later the men went out on longer helicopter assault missions and would be gone for several days in the bush.

Burkholder said there were routine missions, the occasional tripping of booby traps and snipers to deal with as they performed their duties. At night they would set up a base camp near a clearing and dig in to form a circle. As platoon leader it was Burkholder's job to choose and place the men where needed. Claymore mines would also be set out to protect the perimeter and thus alert the men if the enemy should advance on them.

Months later Burkholder's outfit was changed to a mechanized infantry battalion with diesel powered personnel carriers. Burkholder said they made plenty of contact with the enemy but one day in January 1967 was quite memorable for him.

He was serving as company executive officer when they made an air assault on a small village with suspected Viet Cong (VC) activity. "In this area there were booby traps

Jeffrey L. Meek

everywhere. The company commander tripped one and I myself got hit in the forearm and hand," said Burkholder of his injuries. "My wounds were really quite insignificant compared to a lot of other men."

In the village, as was usually the case, they found women and children hiding underground and no VC. "That was indeed one of the frustrating things about being there. You really didn't know who was who and there was a real dichotomy there because we went to great lengths to not have unnecessary casualties, but it was difficult to do. Like I'm sure it is in Iraq," Burkholder continued. After a few days at the battalion aid station at Cu Chi he was back on the line.

Burkholder was so gung-ho he extended his tour for an additional six months. He was given 30 days leave and upon his return to Nam he served in A Company as company commander as a Captain.

Six months later in the fall of 1967 he became the battalion intelligence officer. His job was to collect and process intelligence on enemy movements and strengths. "This was information gleaned from interrogating prisoners of war, area over-flights and some reports from informers," Burkholder said of the duty.

In December 1967, he was finished in Vietnam and sent home. Burkholder was then assigned to Fort Ord where he served on the general staff for a year. He was then sent to the Defense Language Institute in Monterey, Calif., to study the Arabic language in preparation of an assignment in Saudi Arabia as an airborne advisor to the Saudi army.

After a year of language classes, he went to Saudi Arabia and was an advisor to the Saudi Arabian Parachute

resources unit for one year. Although not shunned, the Saudis made it clear they did not want the Americans in their country. Some looked upon the U.S. personnel as spies.

Following this tour Burkholder returned to Fort Benning and attended the Infantry Officer Advanced Course for one year. Then he worked at getting his college degree and graduated from San Diego State in 1972. Burkholder was promoted to major and worked on the staff of the infantry school.

After three years he was selected as a public affairs officer as a secondary specialty and was sent to Indiana to Defense Information School. Next, he worked in public affairs in Heidelberg, Germany, for three years.

Next, he was ordered to Fort Sam Houston and put with the Fifth Army staff and, for a time, was Post Public Affairs Officer. Burkholder served in that capacity for three years and then retired after 20 years of military service. By this time, he had also earned a master's degree in educational administration.

Looking back at his 20 years in the military Burkholder said he enjoyed the tour in Germany the most. It was an opportunity for him to travel, which he did, visiting Scandinavia, the Canary Islands, Greece and much more.

Burkholder also used the GI Bill to attend law school. He practiced law in San Antonio, Texas, for several years and retired in 1999. In 2000 he moved to the Village from Marble Falls, Texas.

The interview concluded with a discussion on what lessons were learned from our involvement in Vietnam. "I've thought about this for years, number one, to seriously consider the ramifications of getting involved in conflict, particularly when the issues of self-interests of the country are arguable. And secondly to commit ourselves whenever we do get involved to do it completely with full support," said Burkholder. He concluded by saying there were too many self-imposed restrictions during the Vietnam War. "That is the way I felt about it then and it hasn't changed since."

War Stories

Curt Carlson served as a Navy corpsman attached to the USMC in Vietnam

Statistics vary, but whatever source one uses there is little doubt the cost in terms of U.S. casualties was high during the fighting of the Vietnam War. An estimated 58,148 were killed as the war seemed to drag on forever. Taking care of the many battle casualties were doctors, nurses, Army medics and Navy/Marine corpsmen. Curt Carlson was one of those corpsmen who experienced the Vietnam War and many difficult situations in which he was called upon to do his duty.

After high school graduation he briefly attended Kansas University. Then in 1963 he decided to enlist in the Navy. "I always thought I wanted to be a doctor, so I told them I'd like to go to Hospital Corps School," Carlson said. He began his training in San Diego for basic and later was sent to nearby Balboa Naval Hospital for Corps School training. The 16-week course taught basic first aid, anatomy, and physiology. On what was known as a 'dream sheet,' he requested duty at Olathe, Kan., Pensacola, Fla., or Miramar, Calif. Instead, he was sent to Guam.

At Guam, he was assigned work in the orthopedic-neurosurgery ward at the hospital there. Later he was sent to an outpatient clinic on the island. A year later, Carlson was put with Fleet Marine Force, went back to the U.S. and trained as a field medic with the U.S. Marine Corps.

Next, he went to El Toro where he got his orders for duty in Vietnam. "We loaded on an LST, the USS Sumner County, and went to Japan," said Carlson. At his assigned base he ran the Marine dispensary. While there he learned

Jeffrey L. Meek

he didn't have enough time left on his enlistment period to go to Vietnam. "I asked them what I could do to get over there and they said I could reenlist for three years. So that's what I did," Carlson said.

He was flown to Vietnam and volunteered for helicopter duty aboard the UH-34D Sikorsky chopper. He was now a Navy corpsman attached to the Marines. He began his tour at a base in Chu Lai, was then sent to Ky Ha and put with Marine Air Group 36. As a corpsman he carried what was called a 'unit one,' the basic medical bag – such things as bandages, hemostats, compresses and morphine.

There were several corpsmen at Ky Ha, so Carlson would not have to pull duty every day. He and a friend did their duty plus volunteered for as many other missions as they could. "We had a competition going, which when you think back on it was kind of stupid," Carlson said of his voluntary missions. Asked why he did it, he answered, "I don't know. It was kind of exciting and you felt like you were really doing something (important)."

Heading out on the flights Carlson said he never knew whether or not the mission would be to a hot landing zone (LZ) until they arrived. However, the night missions, several of which Carlson volunteered for, were usually into the teeth of the enemy.

On one of his first missions, they flew into a hot, chaotic LZ where several men had been killed and wounded. Under enemy fire the chopper dropped down and Carlson and the others did their duty, then took off as fast as possible. When they returned to base, they counted 17 bullet holes in the helicopter.

War Stories

That's when the realization of being a combat corpsman in Vietnam really sunk in. This was a dangerous place and a dangerous, ugly job. Despite the danger, he kept volunteering for missions as needed.

On one night mission Carlson had a man with a sucking chest wound. The man begged Carlson not to let him die. In the dark, Carlson worked to locate the wound and do what he could to save his life. "I was doing it (the examination) by feel. I finally found an opening in his back, just a little tiny hole. I could feel the air coming out of it. I put a cigarette wrapper on it to seal it, bandaged it and last I know he was alive," Carlson said of the experience.

There were many times, back on the base, when he would sleep on a stretcher under a chopper, so he'd be ready at a moment's notice. "Sometimes they'd wake me by firing up the engines," Carlson recalled.

There was also a mission when he was hit in his armored vest by an enemy round. "We were coming into a hot LZ and I caught a round right smack in the chest. It knocked me across (the helicopter), didn't kill me, but it hurt like hell," Carlson said. Carlson was also hit by shrapnel once when his base came under attack but was not seriously hurt.

Without question his toughest mission involved a friend. It wasn't easy for Carlson to tell this highly emotional story, but he pressed on and told of the day he learned a friend from back home was at a nearby base. Carlson flew to the base and found out his friend David was not there. David was out on a mission. David was two years younger than Carlson and because Carlson was a corpsman, David wanted to be a corpsman.

Jeffrey L. Meek

Later Carlson was called out on a mission that pulled out several wounded and dead men – including his friend David. At first, he didn't know it was him, until he rolled him over "and it was him," Carlson painfully said.

Years later, in the 1990s, Carlson was preparing to run in the Twin Cities marathon in Minnesota. He had read an article about a runner named Tom who was running his 15th marathon in honor of all medics and corpsmen from all wars. Carlson also learned from the article that Tom had been in on a same operation as Carlson back in Vietnam. The story told how a corpsman came to the aid of Tom's friend. That corpsman was Carlson's friend David.

Carlson, now working for the Veterans Administration as a nurse, talked with Tom, ran together with him for a while in the marathon and have become good friends ever since.

The following July, David's mother, Carlson, and Tom all met at Great Lakes Naval Station in Chicago to honor their friend and loved one, David. "Tom ran all the way from St. Paul, Minn., to Chicago, 20 miles a day, five days a week and arrived on July 4th," said Carlson of the experience he will never forget.

Tom presented a flag to David's mother in appreciation of her son's service. "It was a very emotional day, but I'm glad I got to do it," Carlson said. Also attending the ceremony was friend Charles Lindberg, the one remaining member of the group that raised the first, original flag at Iwo Jima in February 1945.

Carlson left Vietnam in August 1967 and was stationed at Long Beach Naval Hospital for one year,

War Stories

working in the orthopedic ward and was later made Senior Corpsman of the ER before his September 1968 discharge.

As a civilian he went to work in the insurance business for 23 years, then changed careers at age 48 to become a nurse for the VA. It was a way to give back to those serving in the military.

Twelve years later, in 2007, he retired, and with wife Diane, moved to Hot Springs Village. He has two children, Shane, and Mandy and three stepchildren, Teri, Tim and Tom.

The Vietnam War had a big impact on him and his hometown of Lindsborg, Kan., population 2,200. Seven men from Lindsborg were killed in the war. Carlson knew six of them; friends, teammates and church members that grew up together, became young men and went off to war in the service of their country. Carlson's is one of many that show the unbelievable courage shown by those in unform. That courage, that devotion to duty deserves our respect at all times.

Jeffrey L. Meek

"Bub" Cooksey served with Fourth Infantry in Vietnam

The U.S. Army's Fourth Infantry Division was first formed in 1917 for the fight in France during World War I. On June 6, 1944, as part of the D-Day Normandy invasion the Fourth stormed Utah Beach as the first assault forces came ashore. In September 1966, elements of the division landed in Vietnam. Joining them a year later was 'Bub' Cooksey.

Shortly after finishing high school in 1967 Cooksey received his draft notice and reported to Fort Campbell, Ky., for basic training and then went to "Tigerland" – Fort Polk, La. There he learned about weaponry as well as continuing his physical training preparing him for a likely tour in the jungles of Vietnam. The conditions at the snake infested camp were hot, sticky and the drill instructors tough on their newest trainees.

After a 30-day leave, Cooksey was sent to Fort Lewis, Wash., for the trip to Cam Ranh Bay, a natural harbor in the Khanh Hoa Province south of Nha Trang. "It was kind of like Phoenix, 114 degrees when we got off (the plane)," said Cooksey of his arrival in country.

Soon the men were put in different units, Cooksey initially with the First of the 14th of the Fourth Infantry Division at Bong Son. Then, the next day, he was made a member of the First of the 35th Infantry at Pleiku which sat atop a plateau, 225 miles NE of Saigon and the home of the Fourth Infantry Division's Camps Holloway, Schmidt, and Enari. Cooksey was issued an M-16 and put with a weapons platoon and sent out on a hill for observation purposes.

War Stories

He was soon moved to DaNang taking daily sniper fire as the men moved about one thousand meters per day. Near DaNang, his outfit moved from landing zone to landing zone. At times he'd also do mine sweeping work with U.S. Marines in the area.

Then in January 1968 during the Tet Offensive, Cooksey was sent north of Pleiku to Kontum where they had numerous firefights including one, he'll never forget at nearby 'Mile High Hill.'

When the men were first assigned to the densely forested area, scouts had to be dropped to clear timber so choppers could off-load the infantry units. Three companies were set up which were to patrol the area. One day part of Cooksey's unit moved out toward the bottom of the hill. Cooksey was up top with his mortar platoon. As the men moved on down the hill they came upon a large dug-in North Vietnamese Army (NVA) unit. "That was the heaviest fighting our company got into," said Cooksey of the memorable day of battle.

The U.S. troopers were in big trouble and called for mortars to be dropped right down on their positions. As gunner, it was Cooksey who had to fire 81 mm mortars rounds down near or on his own men. On that day he would fire 1,620 mortar rounds to drive back the enemy. "We burnt two tubes, melted them. They get hot and just collapsed," Cooksey said of the seven-hour battle. Later he received the Army Commendation Medal for his work that day.

And there was a time when, once again, he found himself in a similar dire condition when F-14s fired their guns on top of his unit to get the enemy to retreat. His outfit had moved toward a Village when rocket propelled grenades (RPGs) rained down on them. During a second attempt to take the Village the NVA charged and that's when the F-14s strafed the enemy to drive them back. Unfortunately, three Americans were killed in the fight.

The war could get very up close for those like Cooksey humping along the countryside. One day he was walking along when suddenly a man behind him shot an NVA sniper that had popped up out of a hole Cooksey had just walked past.

Cooksey said they also had some good times too. Like when they'd find a water-filled bomb crater where they could take a swim or bathe. On one occasion Cooksey, out of water, drank from a rice patty. Doing so resulted in a two week stay in the hospital as he fought a 105-degree temperature.

Finally, his year-long tour was up and in September 1968 he left Vietnam. Aboard a Braniff jet, and still in his combat fatigues, he landed in Seattle. He had survived and was finally back home.

Soon he had a fine meal and received a new dress green uniform. Next, he flew to Chicago where he received a rude welcome home at the airport.

"I got some really bad name-calling there," said Cooksey of his homecoming. He talked about walking through the airport when 10 to 12 people walked along side of the returning men calling them baby killers and the like. Cooksey said nothing and kept walking.

After a 30-day leave, he was ordered to Fort Benning, Ga., and put with a service company raking yards, cleaning gutters, pulling KP and guard duty. At no time did

War Stories

he get an opportunity to share his training and experience with new troops, which was troubling to him.

After discharge Cooksey went to work for Eli Lilly for 33.5 years working as a process technician and process operator. He retired in 2001, and with wife Mary Evelyn, he moved to the Village from Lafayette, Ind., that same year. Staying busy, Cooksey later ran a window cleaning service for several years before retiring again. He and Mary Evelyn have three children: Troy, Benjamin, and Andrea.

Reflecting on his military service Cooksey said the experience was something he'd never trade but would never do it again.

Jeffrey L. Meek

Hugh Doyle served on the USS Kirk during Saigon's evacuation

Operation Frequent Wind was the final act of the Vietnam War when nearly 7,000 at-risk Vietnamese and U.S. civilians were evacuated from Saigon, South Vietnam. During the final days of April 1975, planes, helicopters, and ships were used to remove civilians, as enemy troops moved into the city. One of the vessels participating in evacuation efforts was the USS Kirk, a destroyer escort. On that ship was Hugh Doyle, brother of Hot Springs Village resident Ed Doyle. While in town for a visit, Hugh sat with me to share his amazing experience which was also chronicled in the PBS documentary. "The Last Day in Vietnam."

Doyle grew up in the Philadelphia area, attended Villanova University and entered the school's ROTC program. He decided to follow brother Ed into the Navy, was commissioned, and began his training in aviation, but voluntarily dropped out. He had decided to 'go to sea,' as he put it, and was assigned to the USS Montrose, an old WWII attack transport, as a gunnery officer. Soon they left for a nine-month deployment in the western Pacific, in and out of Vietnamese ports.

In 1969, the Montrose was decommissioned, so Doyle was ordered to the USS Inchon, which was brand new. He thought he'd be headed to the Mediterranean, but in 1972 the assignment was Vietnam as a psychological operations advisor to the Second Coastal Zone in Nha Trang. The job was to attempt to win the hearts and minds of the people as the war neared its end.

War Stories

A year later, after attending destroyer schools, he was assigned to the USS Kirk as a chief engineer in charge of the propulsion, electrical and other plants/departments. In 1973 the Kirk deployed to the Indian Ocean with the USS Kitty Hawk battle group where they did patrols. Seven months later they returned to the U.S., then months later deployed again in 1975, back to the western Pacific.

On the way to Pearl Harbor, they learned the Kirk would be escorting the USS Hancock to Vietnam. At Pearl, the Hancock's planes were removed. Why no planes on a carrier? So there would be room for many heavy lift helicopters for the evacuation of Saigon.

At high speed the ships sped to Guam, the Philippines and then later to Vietnam. Operation Eagle Pull came first, which was the evacuation of Embassy personnel in Cambodia. The Kirk and other ships then went to Singapore for what was to be a break and to await orders. But the very next day the ship received orders to sprint to the coast of Vietnam, "where we waited for something to happen," Doyle said.

On April 28, 1975, the USS Kirk and 50 other ships got involved in Saigon evacuation efforts. Helicopters flew into the city and took off with evacuees from Saigon and Tan Son Nhut Air Base. The Kirk was providing protection support for the carriers when suddenly a Vietnamese Huey approached for a landing on the destroyer escort. Down came the chopper with 20 on board, included a Vietnamese two-star general. The chopper didn't have enough fuel to return to Saigon, so it was pushed off to the side of the ship's small deck. But then another helicopter approached, landed, and damaged the first chopper.

Jeffrey L. Meek

This second chopper was pushed overboard and the first repositioned.

Still more helicopters approached the Kirk, and after off-loading their people, were also pushed over the side because there was no place to put them. Eventually, Doyle said they pushed 14 helicopters overboard and others crash-landed alongside the ship as the chaos continued.

In all, 157 refugees were taken on board and a tent city was created on deck. A day later those people were transferred to another ship so the Kirk could resume their patrols.

Then a call came in for the Kirk to come alongside the USS Blue Ridge, a command ship, and a man named Richard Armitage was transferred to the Kirk. He was a former Navy officer and an agent for the U.S. Department of Defense. Armitage said the Kirk was to sail to Con Son Island off the coast of Vietnam where Vietnamese ships were amassing. These ships not only had their crews aboard, but family members as well. Upon arrival, Doyle said there were approximately 50 vessels of all shapes and sizes. "Our job was to escort them from Con Son to the Philippines," Doyle said.

A decision was made to select 32 ships that were seaworthy enough to make the 1,000-mile journey, form them into two columns and set sail. "You could only go as fast as the slowest ship, so it was four to five knots across the sea for 1,000 miles. It took us, I think, five, almost six days to do it," Doyle said.

It wasn't long until the armada ran out of medical necessities and simple medications but were soon re-supplied by C-130 drops from Clark Air Base in the

War Stories

Philippines. Then food ran short, and a supply of rice was delivered, which had bugs in it, but still eatable according to a Vietnamese man on board.

Along the way, word was received that the Philippine government had formally recognized the new Vietnamese communist government, which meant that all 32 ships were flying a Vietnamese flag for a country that no longer existed. The Philippine government said the ships could not enter port flying that flag, so U.S. flags were found and flown on all 32 vessels, which was legal seeing as the ships had been previously owned by the USA. And the ships had to be disarmed, so crews took time to throw guns and ammunition overboard before entering Subic Bay.

While in port, Doyle supervised the cleaning of the ship's boilers which took about 10 days. They then sailed to Guam, where they encountered some of the refugees that Kirk had hauled to the Philippines and had now been transferred to Guam. Following this stop the USS Kirk continued their patrols and later returned to the U.S.

Doyle left the ship and became material officer for Destroyer Squadron 5 for the next two years, then went to New Zealand as part of an exchange program where he was the Nuclear, Biological, Chemical Defense and Damage Control officer for the New Zealand Navy.

Two years later he returned to Newport for an officer course. In 1981, he was put on the USS Fanning as Executive Officer. While on the Fanning, Doyle once again aided in picking up refugees from Vietnam which were referred to as 'boat people,' people escaping Vietnam in small boats and any other way they could.

Jeffrey L. Meek

In total, Fanning rescued approximately 140 Vietnamese. One of those boats had lost power and been adrift for approximately 80 days. When found by the Fanning it wasn't a pretty sight. The boat left Vietnam with 80 people. When found, 29 were still alive. One woman was holding a dead baby in her arms. "All the rest had starved to death and were pushed over the side. It was really grim. Most of the rest of them were catatonic," said Doyle. The living were taken aboard, treated and quickly taken to Subic Bay.

The Fanning then completed her patrols and returned home. Doyle then attended the Naval War College for a year, then became Commissioning Officer of the USS Taylor. Around this time his family situation changed and so did his job. Doyle became a Curriculum Standards Officer until he retired in 1987.

As a civilian he worked in management consulting until retiring in 1993. Doyle has three children: Kathleen, Stephen, and Paul. For more on the USS Kirk and the evacuation visit www.kirk1087.org.

War Stories

Ed Doyle served on four Navy ships as an officer

Ed Doyle grew up in the Philadelphia area, attended Villanova University and participated in the school's ROTC program. He graduated with a Bachelor of Civil Engineering degree in May 1966 and was commissioned as an Ensign.

In June, Doyle attended Damage Control School at the Philadelphia Naval Base. There he took several courses on such topics as firefighting and nuclear, biological, chemical defense. "We studied how to keep a ship alive in a battle environment," said Doyle.

I asked him what was involved in repairing a damaged hull. "Obviously below the water line is a lot more of a problem than above the waterline, but what you have to do when a ship goes to general quarters is, you set 'condition zero,' which is when all water-tight doors are shut and not to be opened. You then have to go to the hull, get pumps going and somehow plug the hole with whatever you can," he answered. Beams, boards, metal pieces and whatever other nearby materials are used to plug a hole. Doyle said two-by-fours and four-by-eights are used to brace the materials, which could even include a mattress and a sheet of plywood.

They also had a simulator to learn to fight fires, sometimes in smoke so thick they couldn't see their hand in front of their face. When battling a blaze, the men worn oxygen breathing equipment and a rubber-like suit and boots.

Doyle finished school in September and reported to the USS Monrovia in Norfolk, Va., as the Main Propulsion Officer. The ship was an old World War II attack transport.

Jeffrey L. Meek

As propulsion officer he was in charge of two divisions – machinery and boilers. Propulsion of the old ship involved a single prop and two boilers. The boilers produced steam that was fed into turbines which turned the prop.

In November, the ship went to Todd Shipyard in Brooklyn, N.Y., for overhaul, which took four months. After completion in April 1967 the ship went on a refresher-training cruise to Guantanamo Bay, Cuba. For six weeks the crew trained, doing whatever the ship was assigned. Those assignments included landing men on the beach. A U.S. Marine battalion was also on the Monrovia and the crew would practice loading them up and sending them in.

As for living conditions, Doyle said they were good. "As officers we had it pretty nice," he noted.

In January 1968, the ship did a Mediterranean cruise with the Amphibious Forces of the Sixth Fleet. They conducted several full-scale landings of troops at places like Crete for example.

In July, Doyle transferred to the destroyer USS Forest Sherman as Damage Control Officer. In August the ship did the refresher cruise to Guantanamo and drilled day and night preparing for future assignments. He then reported to Naval Destroyer School in Newport, R.I., in November. At the school the men learned to become one of three things – an Engineer or Weapons or Operations Officer.

In May 1969, Doyle was sent to the USS Waldron as Engineer Officer on the old WWII vessel. As such he was in charge of the engineer department which oversaw everything mechanical as well as all auxiliary equipment, even the small items, like an ice machine. Doyle said the

War Stories

only thing not under his watch were electrical matters, like radar. On this cruise they operated with other destroyers as an anti-submarine screening unit for Sixth Fleet.

In May 1970, Doyle reported to the USS Sumter while under construction in Philadelphia. Doyle's job was to get equipment installed on the ship and to see that it was working properly. In August the Sumter was commissioned and made its way through the Panama Canal to its home port in Long Beach, Calif.

In April 1971, the Sumter went to Vietnam. Their mission was to evacuate USMC motorized equipment from DaNang. Along the way they towed two patrol boats all the way to Vietnam. Much of that Marine equipment "was pretty well used," said Doyle. Once loaded they went back to the U.S. and, in June, Doyle was interviewed about staying in the Navy. He declined the offer and was discharged in Long Beach on June 23, 1971, as a Lieutenant.

As a civilian, Doyle spent 30 years with Kaiser Aluminum, then nine years with the Aluminum Foil Container Manufacturers Association, retiring in January 2002. In May of that year, he and wife Paula moved to the Village from Palos Park, Ill. They have two children: Tom and Jill.

Reflecting on his Navy service, Doyle said it was a terrific experience. "I wouldn't trade it for anything. It gives you confidence," said Doyle of his military experience. Completing tasks, setting goals, teamwork, they were all a part of what he learned as a member of the United States Navy.

Jeffrey L. Meek

Jim Faurot served with an aviation group in Vietnam

The U.S. Army 12th Combat Aviation Group (CAG) was in charge of all helicopter operations and support missions for the III Corps area in South Vietnam. Based out of Bien Hoa, III Corps was responsible for the approaches to and defense of Saigon. With the 12th CAG was Jim Faurot.

Faurot grew up in Oklahoma, attended East Central State University in Ada, Okla., graduating in 1966. After two years of teaching, he was drafted by the Army in July 1968.

He then took several tests and was assigned to Fort Polk, La., for basic training. "For eight weeks we did nothing but run. We ran everywhere, hardly ever walked. I lost 45 pounds in eight weeks and ate everything I could. When you only have about four minutes to eat there's not a whole lot you can eat," Faurot said of boot camp.

Basic training also included learning the M-14 machine gun at the hot, sticky Fort Polk. Faurot's first assignment following boot camp was to 6th Army Headquarters at the Presidio in San Francisco where he worked as a basic clerk.

The Presidio was built by the Spanish in 1776 and later given over to the United States by Mexico in 1848. In October 1994, the base was transferred to the National Park Service after 219 years of military use. Faurot said the Presidio was a beautiful place with a nice golf course he got to play a few times, a fine hospital and a great view of San Francisco Bay and the Golden Gate Bridge.

The day of his arrival was memorable not only because it was the beginning of his service there, but also

War Stories

because of the demonstration taking place at the front gate. Faurot said it was the day of 'The Presidio 11,' when 11 uniformed military personnel protested the war. "They arrested all of them, had a major trial and sentenced them to Fort Leavenworth. Some of the 11 had less than a month left in the military," Faurot said of the protesters.

Faurot checked in and was told to report to the personnel office. Once there he was asked if he'd like to work in the personnel department and said yes. He was immediately given a desk and became the Personnel Management Specialist for the 6th Army area from Arizona to Montana, handling all U.S. Army Reserve and ROTC enlisted personnel. "I handled their promotions, their movements, discharges and things like that," Faurot said of the job. At first, he had to repeatedly hand type rosters, but later helped get records on to data processing cards which greatly sped up the process. Ten months later he got new orders. He was headed for Vietnam.

Off to Fort Lewis, Wash., Faurot went, and from there flew to Japan and then Cam Ranh Bay, South Vietnam, in June 1969 where the heat was immediately noticeable as the thermometer rose to as high as 120 degrees. Shortly after his arrival he was put on KP duty.

Now an E-4, Faurot was then flown aboard a C-130 to Bien Hoa and then to Long Bin where he was assigned to the 12th CAG Headquarters at what was called 'The Plantation.' The compound was once a French rubber plantation, first occupied by the U.S. back in 1966.

Once again Faurot worked with personnel records for the 12th which covered promotions, assigning men back to the states and other matters. Each day Faurot dealt with the paperwork, worked out and sometimes would catch a movie in the evening. "There were two types of assignments in Vietnam, good and bad and I was in what I consider one of the good assignments," Faurot said of his duties. The compound was surrounded by fencing with bunkers here and there for protection. Faurot and the others had their flak vest, helmet, and weapon just in case an attack occurred.

During the January 1968 Tet Offensive the area had been temporarily overrun. And the area would still be occasionally shelled once or twice a month, usually in the morning according to Faurot. So, the area was considered pretty safe, but not without concern.

During one mortar attack a round hit just 40 yards from Faurot, but usually the attacks targeted the parked helicopters on the base. And there was a time when a Vietnamese man inside the compound was caught stepping off distances. "They arrested him and we never saw him again. He never came back," said Faurot.

During his one-year tour of duty in South Vietnam he got to take two R & R trips, one to Japan and one to Hawaii. In Japan at Camp Zama, he ran into a hometown friend and in Hawaii, while visiting his wife he again saw a buddy.

Much of Faurot's personnel work involved the paperwork necessary to return men to the U.S. "So I was a popular guy. Everybody wanted to know where they were going and we tried to help people out," he said of trying to send the returning troopers where they wanted to go or to extend their time in Vietnam so they could later get out of the service sooner once back in the U.S.

During his one-year tour he estimated 6,000 cases came across his desk for reassignment. One case was rather

War Stories

odd. Most men greatly looked forward to the day they could leave Vietnam, but one man was quite the exception. Faurot said there was one guy who was three times scheduled for transport back to the states but didn't show up. Finally, the man was found, put on the plane and handcuffed. "He didn't want to go. He had a girlfriend," said Faurot of the matter.

Faurot himself returned on June 30, 1970. Back in the U.S. the United Airlines plane landed in San Francisco. He said he did not experience much of the rude behavior from U.S. civilians upon his return. "There were a couple of people that said thanks to me in San Francisco and a couple of people down the (airport) corridor said something, but I didn't pay any attention to them," Faurot said of his homecoming. Upon his return he was discharged within hours and on his way home.

When he arrived at his house, he learned his wife wanted a divorce. "She gave me 24 hours before she hit me with the news," said Faurot.

As a civilian he went back into education in Oklahoma City at U.S. Grant High School teaching American history. Then in 1979 he moved to Westmore High in Moore, Okla., where he stayed until retiring in 1995. In January 2000, he and wife Pat moved to the Village from Moore.

Reflecting back on his service he said he was grateful for the experience. "It changed my whole outlook on life. It changed my appreciation for the United States, how lucky we are here and what a wonderful place we live in. It's not perfect, but it sure beats what I saw in Vietnam."

Jeffrey L. Meek

Mike Fisher served with Navy crash crew in Spain

U.S. Navy crash crew teams provide a vital service when dangerous situations arise. Their responsibilities include rescuing occupants from crashed or burning aircraft, putting out wheel fires from overheated brakes and other fires that may arise. Working in such a role 'back in the day,' was Mike Fisher who served from 1958 to 1961.

While living in Idaho, after his junior year in high school, Fisher decided to join the Navy. "It was a tradition in our town," he said, so he and a good buddy signed up in June 1958. Processing included a physical in Spokane, Wash., and his swearing in at Seattle. He then flew to San Diego for boot camp.

"It was certainly different. I'd never been away from home. I remember marching a lot, the physical exercises, after about a week I could hardly move. And I thought I was in pretty good shape," Fisher said with a smile. His good friend accidentally broke his leg in the shower, so Fisher moved on with his training, "and I've never seen him since," he added.

He graduated in September, volunteered for submarine duty and was sent to a radar technician school in Virginia. He did not enjoy the schooling and book work, and decided to make a change, so he put in for sea duty. He dropped out of the school and received orders to report to Naval Air Station Rota in Spain. Many of his mates were sent to Guantanamo Bay, Cuba.

Fisher flew to Rota via New Jersey, the Azores, and on to Madrid where he first stayed in a hotel for about a

War Stories

week with five other guys. It was exciting to Fisher, just 17 years old and far away from home.

Finally, the men flew in a DC-3 through a terrible storm to Rota as lightening and turbulence bounced the plane through the sky. "It threw us all over the place," said Fisher of the flight.

Upon arrival they were put in a barracks. Two days later he began working with others to secure a barge that had broken loose in the storm, then later put on a tugboat for four- or five-days doing harbor-related work. Two weeks later he joined the crash crew.

With that crew he started out as a 'lineman' on a truck, learning how to use hoses and put out various fires. Next, he would learn the turret position that sprayed chemical on fires. The training was almost constant. "When we weren't on watch we were training," said Fisher of the routine.

The training was done where an old airplane was situated, surrounded by hundreds of gallons of burning aviation fuel and two sawdust dummies inside the plane. "It would create a good-sized fire. It was frightening and you never got used to it," Fisher said of running into the flames.

The men wore rubber boots up to their hips and bulky coats and helmets covered with asbestos. Going into a fire was dangerous work and many times the men were slightly burned or have the hair on their arms burned off. "It was terrifying," said Fisher of the job. The hoses sprayed a syrupy foam to coat an object and thus extinguish the flames.

Another aspect of the work was going through the fire and into the plane to rescue those dummies. When wet, the dummies weighed more than Fisher. The crash crew

Jeffrey L. Meek

carried a special tool with them to cut straps to free the dummies and get them out as quickly as possible.

Fisher said the work included using different chemicals for different situations, like wheel fires, of which there were many, due to overheated brakes upon landing.

The crews would also do visual inspections of the aircraft to see if any problems could be spotted.

Another crew function was to make sure an incoming plane had its wheels down. They used large red paddles and a flare gun to communicate with pilots. Fisher said the crews were tested many times by planes coming in that had intentionally left their landing gear up.

During his time in Rota there were many fires to deal with. One involved an A4-D that wasn't sure his gear was down properly. After a few flyovers the crash crew wasn't sure either, so they foamed a runway with an 18-inch blanket of chemical and in came the aircraft.

Turns out the front landing gear was not locked in place and as the plane continued down the runway it was all over the place. As the plane came to rest the crash crew was already spraying more foam in case of a bad fire. "We got the pilot out and he was pretty excited," said Fisher.

Then there was a time when an A3-D twin engine bomber came in and missed an arresting wire that had been put in place. "He just kept going and off the runway he went through the cactus," said Fisher. The plane did not catch fire, and everyone came through the incident okay.

The worst incident Fisher experienced was at an air show when two F-8U Crusaders from the VF-84 Squadron began a maneuver. The maneuver began with one F-8U flying very low, upside down, and the other right side up,

War Stories

just above it. As they changed position the lower of the two planes crashed in a huge ball of fire. Fisher said he will always remember the crowd began clapping. "They thought it was part of the show," said Fisher. Later his crew went out to clean up the area. "I found part of his (the pilot) helmet. It still had part of an ear in it," Fisher recalled.

Three years later he returned to the U.S. via North Africa and Newfoundland, finally reaching their destination in Virginia where he was discharged on Oct. 31, 1961. Fisher also served in the Reserves from 1961 to 1964.

As a civilian, Fisher got into the restaurant and bar business in Boise, Idaho, and also in Iowa. Later he became an investigator with a division of a substance abuse agency. He retired in 2002. With wife Phranc, they moved to the Village in 2011 from Winterset, Iowa. They have three children: Mark, Michael, and Lori.

Looking back on his service to our nation, Fisher said it gave him a lot of confidence and he really enjoyed the others he worked with.

Jeffrey L. Meek

Jim Grant served two tours in Vietnam as helicopter pilot

Organized in 1921, the First Cavalry Division brought together horse cavalry units fighting Indian wars. In World War II the units fought on foot in the Pacific. In the Korean War the division was the first into Pyongyang, the capital of North Korea. On Sept.11, 1965, they became the first Army division deployed to Vietnam. Later that year they participated in the Battle of Ia Drang, the fight that eventually was made into the 2002 movie, *We Were Soldiers*, starring Mel Gibson.

Jim Grant served as a helicopter pilot, beginning his service with the 3rd Brigade, 7th Cavalry of the First Cavalry in February 1967. By the end of his service, he would log 1,461 combat flight hours and receive numerous medals including the Distinguished Flying Cross, Bronze Star for Meritorious Service, and the Purple Heart. This is his story.

After spending one year at Auburn University, Grant decided to enlist rather than be subject to the draft. By doing so he could get in a rotary wing flight school and learn to fly helicopters. After basic training at Fort Polk, La., he was sent to Camp Walters, Texas for primary helicopter flight school in March 1966.

Next came Fort Rucker, Ala., for instrument and tactical flying. "Everybody knew we were going to Vietnam after graduation," said Grant. He graduated in January 1967 and in February went to Vietnam with the First Air Cavalry Division. Upon arrival, like many other Vietnam vets I have spoken with, Grant immediately noticed the heat, and the smell.

War Stories

At the 90th Replacement Depot he was told that all single pilots should step to the left. The married pilots stepped to the right. He then learned he would be a scout pilot and was told to pick up a Purple Heart application certificate. "All you have to do is put the date on it, don't worry about not getting it (the Purple Heart). You will earn it," Grant was told. "I thought things could go badly from here. That's not a good sign," Grant said. He was assigned to the Headquarters Troop, 3rd Battalion, 7th Cavalry of the First Air Cavalry.

Grant mostly flew the old H-13 chopper with a turbo charger. His job was to go out and see what the enemy was up to. They would fly in pairs with one chopper down low and another up high. Grant flew several missions in the H-13 and recalled for me one memorable occasion.

"I did crash an H-13 trying to avoid a mid-air collision," said Grant. He came over a rise and there was another helicopter coming straight at him. Grant sharply turned the H-13 and because of the degree of the turn, he lost lift, went down, and hit a rice paddy. The chopper hit a dike and flipped over. "My head was underwater, but my feet were dry," remembers Grant. He found a way out of the destroyed machine and was later picked up and taken back to base.

Later during his tour of duty Grant flew Huey missions as the command-and-control chopper. On one Huey mission the helicopter was hit in the oil cooler. The pilot got the craft down safely. Later another ship flew in and picked up Grant and the others. That night he learned the helicopter had gone down in a minefield full of

Jeffrey L. Meek

'Bouncing Bettys.' The next time Grant's chopper was hit he wasn't as lucky.

He was the command-and-control chopper circling an operation when a 51-caliber enemy round hit the Huey. His copilot's legs were shattered, and Grant was wounded in the right knee. "It (the enemy round) took off the front of my knee," Grant said. Another round came in and took out the dashboard of the helicopter.

Grant got his helicopter down and later he and his copilot were hauled out of the area. Grant was taken to Japan for treatment and recovery in October 1967. After recovering he was sent back to the U.S. and became an instructor pilot at Fort Rucker.

Eighteen months later, Grant was ordered back to Vietnam for a second tour. However, he volunteered for a commission in the armor branch and was sent to Fort Knox for classes. Following this, Grant volunteered for Cobra School to learn the Cobra gunship.

By September 1969, he was back in Vietnam with the Air Cavalry, 11th Armored Cavalry in Quan loi. "I flew Cobras for the first six months and then I took over the Slick Platoon, those were Hueys," Grant said. His task was to insert troops in landing zones and pick them up after completion of a mission. The Hueys had no armor. Grant's only protection was a 'chicken plate' – a seven-pound ceramic vest worn over his chest.

In October 1970, and now a captain, Grant left Vietnam for service in Fulda, Germany. His assignment was with Air Cavalry Troop, 14th Cavalry. After his second tour of duty concluded he went back home and once again attended Auburn University. He also enlisted in the Alabama National Guard.

War Stories

In June 1972, and now a civilian, Grant went to McMinnville, Ore., and flew for Evergreen Helicopters. Later he flew in Bolivia, Rio Madre de Dios, and Cohiba in Bell 206B and SA315 Llama single engine aircraft.

In 1976 he worked in Alaska and became an Airline Transport Pilot. In 1977 Grant went to Galveston, Texas as Chief Pilot for gulf coast operations for Evergreen. In October 1978 he joined the Tenneco Aviation Department in Houma, Louisiana and stayed for 25 years flying offshore in the Gulf of Mexico.

Grant retired in April 2003 and with wife Peggy moved to the Village in January 2004. They have two children: Jennifer and DeHart. We concluded our interview with a short discussion of the war in Vietnam.

I asked Grant about returning home from Vietnam and the treatment he received. "That was pretty poor. In fact, I left the United States and didn't come back to the States until 1976," Grant said.

I then asked Grant why Americans turn so hostile against the war. "I think it was the losses of their own countrymen; the young men getting killed, wounded and maimed, like we have now in Iraq and Afghanistan," Grant answered. Was doing this interview difficult? "A little bit, yeah. I didn't do anything different from anybody else," said a humble Grant. "I was just doing my job."

Jeffrey L. Meek

Max Greeson served two tours with aviation companies in Vietnam

Max Greeson first began his military service by enlisting in the National Guard in 1951. Little did he know it would be the beginning of military service that would last for more than 20 years.

After joining the Guard, he went on active duty with the U.S. Army in 1953 and was first ordered to El Paso, Texas, for anti-aircraft 90 mm gun training. After completing the training, he was headed for Korea, but contracted meningitis which cancelled his orders. Instead, he was assigned to an Air Defense unit in the New York City area.

"We had a lot of 90 mm gun batteries set up in New Jersey, Long Island, Staten Island and all over and around the New York City area," Greeson said. He was based on Staten Island as a controller where the headquarters was stationed. After a three-year hitch, he returned home. Then circumstances were such that he decided to re-enlist in 1956 and was assigned to Army Security.

At Fort Devons, Mass., he learned cryptology and radio reception skills which allowed him to analyze codes and read radio traffic. By 1957, he was ordered to Germany with the 11th Army Security Field Station for code analysis and the operation of code equipment. He was there when, on Oct. 4, 1957, Russia launched Sputnik, the first satellite to orbit earth. Greeson and others knew it was going to happen a few days before the launch.

He returned to the U.S. in 1960 and was assigned to Two Rock Ranch in California for more crypto work. He also

War Stories

trained in the repair of teletype machines. In 1963, he was sent to Turkey to maintain a communication center near Ankara.

Five months later Greeson was asked if he'd be interested in learning how to fly. He decided to give it a try, was accepted and was to begin helicopter training in Texas.

Leaving Turkey would provide a memorable experience. You see the Greesons accidentally packed their passports in their now officially sealed belongings. "We went down to the Embassy and told them we didn't have our passports," Greeson said. He had done some work for the Turkish Parliament and the country's president so he decided to contact the duty officer at the Parliament to see what if anything could be done. While awaiting a return call he and his family got quite a surprise.

"This big black limousine drives up and lo and behold it's the president of Turkey," he said. Greeson was then allowed to open one of the sealed crates of the family's belongings and there were the passports. The crate was then resealed and the Greesons were on their way home.

He completed his helicopter training and was then sent to Fort Rucker for fixed wing training which began with an O-1 Birddog that was used for observation purposes. Next came Fort Ord, Calif., and U-1 Otter training. From there he was ordered to Vietnam in 1966.

He arrived during the monsoon season. "It was raining like crazy, and the raincoats didn't do any good at all because it was so hot and sticky even if you covered yourself from the rain, you sweated and still got soaked," Greeson recalled.

Jeffrey L. Meek

He was soon taken by truck to the company headquarters at Ton Son Nhut Air Base on the outskirts of Saigon. He was then assigned to the 54th Aviation Company for missions involving resupplying Special Forces camps and outposts in the Mekong Delta area in the U-1 Otter. Six months later the 54th combined with the 18th Aviation Company.

Greeson had several close calls flying those supplies into the Special Forces units. On one mission as he was flying out of a camp when he was hit in the tail section. The plane behind him was shot down and the pilot killed.

On another mission near Nan Trang, he was flying a U-1 on a low-level mission up near the DMZ. The Special Forces commander said he wanted to come along on the mission to see how bad the situation was. "I told them they were crazy," said Greeson. In all, three Colonels were on board with Greeson.

As he brought the plane in, they came under fire. "We came over a rise and five black pajamas (enemy fighters) stood up and had us cold turkey. They started unloading on us," Greeson said. He took the plane down, right toward the enemy, made a hard right-hand turn between two trees and flew off to his destination.

They landed safely at the Special Forces camp and the supplies were unloaded. While that was going on it was noticed his plane had over 80 bullet holes in the wings and tail area. All the holes were patched with duct tape. "We called it 100 mile an hour tape," said Greeson.

In another close one Greeson was flying at 10,000 feet when he received a call to immediately return to base. He turned the plane around and called in to see what was

War Stories

up. He was told there may be a bomb aboard his aircraft. A captured Viet Cong soldier had told base intelligence a bomb had been put in the gas tank.

Greeson made it back to base and the plane was parked in an isolated area. "We left it there four days and it didn't blow up, so we started flying it again," laughed Greeson.

Having completed his tour in Vietnam he returned home and served as a T-41 flight instructor at Fort Stewart. Three years later, in 1969, he was back in Vietnam flying the U-8 Beach Baron on electronic surveillance missions searching for enemy movements. Again, there were some hairy times for Greeson in his cockpit.

There was a mission in which he was ordered to find a lost unit. After searching for hours, he switched over to auxiliary gas tanks. Not long thereafter the engines stopped running so he had to go back to the main tanks. "We figured we had about 15 to 20 minutes of fuel left (before they would need to head back to base)," Greeson remembers.

He called in to headquarters about their situation and was told they were expendable and to stay out and find that unit. Ten minutes later they located the men, transmitted coordinates, and headed for home.

About five miles from the base's outer marker, they ran out of fuel, but managed to continue on and land without incident.

Near the end of this second tour, he had another harrowing experience. They were doing surveillance on a Viet Cong regiment and had just pinpointed their location when an urgent call came in telling them to return to base.

Jeffrey L. Meek

Enemy MiG fighters were closing in on them. Greeson flew into some clouds, turned left, and headed for the base.

Suddenly bullets hit his left engine and a fire broke out. They also lost their electrical system. For the next 25 minutes Greeson flew the burning plane in a slip position to keep the flames away from the fuselage. They had no idea if the engine would explode before they could get home.

As they approached the runway, the copilot cranked the landing gear down. Fire trucks began following them down the runway as he brought the plane to a stop. He and the crew got out with no one being hurt. "It was quite a day," said Greeson.

In 1970, he returned home and spent the remainder of his career as a flight instructor and flight commander.

As a civilian, Greeson spent 20 years with Texas Instruments and later opened his own networking business. He retired in 2003 and with wife Betty moved to Hot Springs Village from Germantown, Tenn., that same year. The couple has two children: Richard and Timothy.

Looking back at his career he wondered how he made it through all those close calls. "There were a number of times I shouldn't have made it through," said Greeson.

War Stories

Jim Gruenewald was wounded serving in the Vietnam War

The storied First Marine Division, famous for its service at Guadalcanal and Okinawa in WW II and at Inchon during the Korean War, was sent to Vietnam in March 1966 where they established a headquarters at Chu Lai. The division consisted of four infantry regiments: the First, Fifth, Seventh and 27th Marines. Jim Gruenewald served in the Fifth Marine Regiment during his time of service in the Vietnam War.

He came from a family of Marines and rather than be drafted into a different branch, Gruenewald enlisted in the USMC on Feb. 12, 1968. He was sent to MCRD in San Diego, Calif., for training. The initial few weeks were really rough on him, but like the others, he managed to get through it. During his leave he got married, then reported back to California. After receiving infantry training at Camp Pendleton, he was ordered to Vietnam as a rifleman.

The trip went through Hawaii and Guam en route to Da Nang where he arrived at 3 a.m. on Aug. 1, 1968. His arrival was also during an enemy attack. Men quickly disembarked the plane and made it safely to a nearby bunker where they waited out the attack. Welcome to Vietnam.

The following day Gruenewald got his gear, was put with a platoon and, by truck, was taken off to the Ho Chi Minh trail. On the way they were attacked twice. One of the attacks was carried out by an eight-year-old boy. "He was a young kid waving to the Marines coming through town," said Gruenewald of what seemed like an innocent young

Jeffrey L. Meek

boy. "Next thing we know he was throwing satchel charges in our trucks. It's hard to defend yourself under those circumstances." Eight Marines were killed in the attack.

After reaching their destination, Gruenewald settled in with a regiment atop a ridgeline.

The four-to-five-day missions he then participated in were to seek out and destroy the enemy, pure and simple, find them and kill them. "We were out there to destroy whoever we could," Gruenewald said.

Then he described his first combat mission. "We were all lying in a river with water rushing over our shoulders. We were in the river two days and finally a patrol came by our location. We jumped out of the river and killed the entire patrol," Gruenewald said. He would participate in 29 of these voluntary seek and destroy missions. The average was approximately 15. Why volunteer for such a dangerous job? "I got to know the terrain really well and my senses were sharp," answered Gruenewald.

He then contracted Type-II malaria and was flown out to Da Nang where he was placed in a freezer-like room for seven days, with only a sheet covering him. Upon his recovery Gruenewald was put with a security platoon about 10 miles off the base.

The men were there to protect General William Westmoreland's headquarters. About 30 of them occupied a ridge approximately one-half mile from the General's HQ. Along the ridge they dug fighting holes in case an attack would come. Those holes were usually filled with water from the heavy monsoon-like rains.

On Feb. 23, 1969, Gruenewald and the platoon had the shock of their life. They received word the North

War Stories

Vietnamese Army (NVA) was about to attack their position. About 1 a.m. and without warning the NVA were on them. They had dug tunnels under the ridge and attacked from the rear.

Suddenly the enemy was on top of them. "We were overwhelmed," said Gruenewald. It was raining and the men never heard them coming. Hand-to-hand combat broke out. Gruenewald said he killed at least five NVA.

During the fighting he received a head wound. Despite the wound, Gruenewald, by himself, grabbed the .50 caliber machine gun, ammo, tripod, extra barrel, etc., and got to a nearby hillside where he fired on the enemy. When it was over, 11 of the 30 men were still alive after a five-hour battle.

Later, Gruenewald and the others went back to the ridge and put their fallen comrades into body bags. What they didn't know was the enemy was still there. Once again, the NVA opened up and killed three more men. Gruenewald was treated for his wound at Da Nang the next day and later received a Purple Heart.

In June 1969, he was on patrol and witnessed a napalm air strike on a village. He and others were then sent in to gather the bodies for the all-important 'body count.' You remember, the numbers the media would feed the public every night during their news broadcast.

Gruenewald also spoke of something I had not heard of before – 'rock apes' is what they called them. They were monkeys, about five feet tall, that would throw rocks at the men. "You could smell them a mile away," said Gruenewald of the jungle menace.

Jeffrey L. Meek

With only one day's notice, he learned he was being sent home. He left Vietnam in December 1970 with the clothes on his back and a sea bag full of dirty clothes. Gruenewald was flown to Tokyo, San Francisco, Los Angeles, Chicago and finally to his home in Milwaukee. As he passed through the airports, he could feel the tension. No one spoke to him. Many gave him dirty looks, but he wasn't sure why. His return to his wife at the time, and later his mother, did not go well either. "That was my homecoming," said Gruenewald.

He struggled putting the war behind him. He said it was 2006, 36 years later, before he could put it away. "It took a long time. Otherwise, I wouldn't be setting here for this interview," Gruenewald said. "I'm 100 percent disabled with PTSD because of that war, and I wouldn't wish that on anybody. But I'm glad I came home safe and sound and was able to have a son and daughter. That's one of the good things that came out of my life," Gruenewald said as the interview concluded. He tries to give back by volunteering at the VA hospital in Little Rock. It's his way of helping his fellow veterans.

As a civilian, Gruenewald worked for the City of Milwaukee as a police detective for 20 years. He retired in 2000 and with wife Janine moved to Hot Springs Village in 2002.

Gruenewald has two children: Deborah and James, Jr.

War Stories

Tom Harrison served as weapons mechanic during Vietnam War

The country of Thailand assisted United States and South Vietnam forces during the Vietnam War by allowing military bases to be set up in their country and later added troops to the effort. As the war grew in intensity so did the number of units in Thailand.

This included several outfits in Korat like the 40th Military Police Battalion, the 388th Tactical Fighter Wing and the 553rd Reconnaissance Wing. Tom Harrison was there in Korat as a weapons mechanic with the 388th Tactical Fighter Squadron.

After being born in Berlin, Wisc., the family soon moved to Ohio where Harrison grew up. He briefly attended Ohio State University but decided to leave and in early 1966 enlisted in the United States Air Force (USAF) and signed on as a weapons mechanic. He was sent to Amarillo, Texas for basic and then was ordered to Colorado for the special weapons mechanic training. There he learned about weapons, missiles, and even nuclear weapons.

His next stop was McConnell AFB in Wichita, Kan., where he trained exclusively on the F-105 Thunderchief and to prepare for assignment in Korat. The F-105 carried 750-pound bombs and a 20 mm cannon that would fire 6,000 rounds a minute.

Harrison made his way to Korat in September 1967 and began his duties as a bomb loader, quite hazardous work. Later during his tour, he was put in the gun shop where he worked on that M-61 20 mm cannon. Before making that change Harrison had a few harrowing experiences. One was when he and the rest of the loading crew were attaching 750 pounders.

These bombs had a delayed fuse which would cause the bomb to explode up to two weeks later. They also had a booby trap mechanism that would cause an explosion if the enemy tried to defuse the bomb.

Early one morning they were loading the bombs when one of the loaders accidentally mishandled the fuse. "The next thing I realize he is crouched behind the pylon (which holds the bomb) shaking like a leaf with that fuse in his hand. I knew exactly what he had done," said Harrison who then calming talked to the loader. Harrison told everyone to leave the flight line, took hold of the fuse which was not armed and walked to the end of the flight line and successfully disarmed it.

The weapons mechanics worked hard, seven days a week and up to 16 hours per day. A typically busy day of loading bombs included attaching them to the pylons using a bomb lift. Lugs would then lock the bomb in place, usually that is. There were a few accidents when the lugs didn't hold and, after the bomb lift was taken away, a bomb would fall and hit the runway.

Not every happening Harrison experienced was dangerous. There were a few funny moments as well. Like the time an old, experienced pilot landed after his 100th mission, which meant he'd be rotated home. The jet landed and cruised down to the end of the flight line when the pilot threw off his flight suit and other clothing. He then taxied in and climbed out of the jet completely naked except for his garrison cap. "He turns around and snaps a salute to his

War Stories

wing commander and a woman standing there and internally I was just laughing," said Harrison of the event.

He also did a month of temporary duty in DaNang, Vietnam, where he worked on the A-1 prop plane used for close infantry support. A month later he was back in Korat for more duty loading the F-105s.

Harrison also spoke about a time when President Lyndon Johnson visited his base in Korat. He and the others were told to assemble on the flight line to hear Johnson speak. He had just finished a long grueling day and didn't feel much like listening to anyone, even the president, but he reported as ordered.

"I'll never forget it. Much to my amazement Lyndon Johnson was booed off the base. He tried to give us a 'we love you' speech and we didn't want to hear it. We were sick of the politics of the thing (the war, the bombing halts, etc.). Military guys are willing to serve but give us a chance to win, to finish the job and we weren't given that chance. Contrary to what people think we did not lose that war. We left the field," said Harrison.

About the bombing halts Harrison said he believes the enemy would agree to them just long enough to resupply their SAM sites and other installations because after the jet fighters would knock out a site later, after a halt, they would be shot down flying over the same area that previously had been hit by USAF attacks.

In September 1968, Harrison came home and served at Myrtle Beach AFB with a firefighting unit. His duties included firefighting on and off the base. Harrison finished his military service there and was discharged in February

Jeffrey L. Meek

1970. He returned to Columbus, Ohio and attended Ohio State University on the GI Bill, graduating on the Dean's List.

Harrison then spent 30 years with DuPont as an auditor and senior business analyst. He retired in February 2003 and with wife Ramona moved to the Village that same year.

The Harrisons have two children: Matthew and Marjorie.

Looking back on his service Harrison had a point he wanted to make. He said when they returned from the service the men didn't want to be known as a Vietnam War veteran, so they shrunk into the woodwork, didn't join a VFW or American Legion. This changed for him 29 years later when a friend took him to a VFW meeting and a woman welcomed him and thanked him for his service.

"I looked at her and I said what do you mean, I don't understand. She said, 'no one properly welcomed you back and thanked you for your service so I'm doing that right now.' It hit me like a ton of bricks. I'd never really thought about it, but it was true. You were just looking to survive, get home and get on with your life. Now I see how people are treating Iraq and Afghanistan troops and I'm very happy about that, thrilled about it."

War Stories

Philip Heinrich served in Vietnam, narrowly escaped injury

Philip M. Heinrich was born in Elgin, Ill., grew up in West Dundee, Ill., where he attended school through his high school years while he worked at several jobs because he wanted a car. After graduation he worked at a factory for a time, but even though the Vietnam War was raging, he decided to join the U.S. Army. "My Dad was in World War II and my grandfather in World War I with the German Army. He was in the trenches. The German trenches. So, the Army runs in our family," Heinrich explained.

Heinrich enlisted on Jan. 1, 1969, and was sent to Fort Bragg, N.C., for basic training. Next, he was off to Ft. Eutis, Va., for helicopter training. Here he learned the basics of helicopter maintenance. "We were also taken up in the Hueys to know what it was like in flight with an M-60 machine gun onboard."

After a 30-day leave, he received orders to report to Vietnam where, after a 16-hour flight, he landed in Long Binh, near Saigon, on July 19, 1969. Heinrich was assigned to 'D' Troop, First Squadron, 10th Cavalry, which was attached to the Army's Fourth Infantry Division. On a C-130 he was flown to their base at Pleiku in the Central Highlands. "We did reconnaissance for the Fourth Infantry Division," he said of the assignment. I asked him what his first impressions were upon arriving in Vietnam. "It was like, Oh geez, what's that smell? It was the smell you had to get used to over there. It was like a fog; the smell of human waste being burned."

Jeffrey L. Meek

Heinrich started out as a door gunner/crew chief on a Huey UH-IH. Their job was to take out scout troops, aerial infantry platoons, that would be inserted into landing zones when intelligence had provided information needed to be checked out. His chopper would then land somewhere nearby and wait for further instructions. Sometimes they'd be heading back into a 'hot LZ,' hot landing zone, now under enemy fire. "They'd let us know if the LZ was hot so we could provide suppressing fire on the way in."

After a few months on the job, he was encouraged to transfer into the scout platoon, which he did. "The aerial scouts were assigned missions usually entailing long-range aerial reconnaissance of areas assigned by the division. Our recon involved two observation helicopters reconnoitering the area hovering at treetop level. Each helicopter, a Hughes OH-6, had a pilot and a scout-gunner who was armed with an M-60 machine gun and various grenades. The scout ships were covered by two Cobra gunships circling above them." Heinrich said the pilots would take time to teach him how to fly the OH-6 in case the pilot became incapacitated. "They taught us how to fly it back to base and land it. I never had that happen, but I knew other guys that did. They'd say if you can hover it, you can fly it."

"Upon receiving fire, the scout-gunners returned fire with their M-60s and while existing the area, they'd mark it with smoke grenades. Those gunships covered our exit with their munition which included rockets, mini-gun fire and grenade launchers. Once the area was 'prepped' by those gunships the aerial rifle platoon would be inserted to make contact with the enemy units."

War Stories

And then there was a mission that he'll never forget. "We started to receive heavy enemy fire. I was half out of the helicopter on the skid and as we were existing the area, I felt something hit the back of my helmet. The impact pushed the helmet over my eyes. I first thought that something from the helicopter flew off and hit me because it would get hit with a lot of enemy rounds."

"Once we exited, the pilot told me to check my head for any wounds, seeing as it looked like I was shot through the helmet. When we landed at our forward LZ I looked at my helmet along with most of the guys on the mission and sure enough, there was a hole through the top of my helmet. Looking at the inside of the helmet you could see the bullet path through the Styrofoam padding."

When asked why the OH-6 could take such a beating and stay in the air, Heinrich said, "That ship was really tough. It could stay up because there was an armor plate around the engine, and it had very little hydraulics that could be shot out. Because of that it would still fly even when hit by a lot of enemy rounds." Heinrich was apparently unmoved by the near-death experience because he upped for a second tour and kept doing the same dangerous missions.

He left Vietnam on Jan. 1, 1971, and was assigned to the 18th Airborne Corps at Ft. Bragg. He was discharged on Nov. 18, 1971, as an E-5, Specialist Five, Sergeant.

As a civilian he served in law enforcement, starting in 1974. From 1978 to 2004 Heinrich was at the Crystal Lake, Ill., P.D., retiring as the Patrol and S.W.A.T. Commander. During that time, he also served on the executive board of the Illinois Tactical Officer's Association, a statewide

Jeffrey L. Meek

organization of tactical/ S.W.A.T. officers that provided training and assistance for S.W.A.T. teams in the state of Illinois. After leaving Crystal Lake P.D., he worked for the McHenry County Sheriff's Department as the Commander of Court Security, retiring again in 2017. He and wife Cheri moved to the Village in 2017. They have three children: Brian, Robert, and Sarah.

As I usually do at the end of a 'Veteran Vault' interview, I asked Heinrich to do some reflecting. How did your time in service affect you for the rest of your life? "I was always proud of what I did. I never regretted it. I never had any remorse. I was taken aback on how the public back home saw the war." He added that during the times he came home on leave for example, he'd arrive at an airport around 4 a.m. and the protestors were not there so he personally did not witness and experience the public anti-war protestor sentiment.

War Stories

Ron Jansen served as driver in Vietnam, receives Purple Heart

Ron Jansen grew up in Kansas and Missouri. After high school graduation he attended Central Missouri State University, but only for three months. He quit school and was about to be drafted, but instead enlisted for three years. After reception at Ft. Leonard Wood he went to Ft. Hood, Texas, for basic training with the Second Armored Division.

Jansen said he remembers being on the bus to Ft. Hood, arriving at night, getting off the bus and immediately getting yelled at by a Sergeant. "Your life completely changed right there. It was culture shock," said Jansen of his military arrival.

Basic training included the usual, including marches. He recalls a march when the men were running with their rifles out in front of them and in full packs. Jansen said some men fell out, collapsed face first, but he was able to keep going. "I'll never forget that day," he said.

Believe it or not Jansen actually gained 20 pounds during his time in basic training. "The mess hall made the best pancakes you ever ate. I had cold chocolate milk with pancakes every morning," said Jansen.

After a leave, he began his advanced training. For him that was all about trucks – changing tires, batteries, driving and more. As a driver he needed to know all about the vehicles and how to maintain them.

In November 1967 he received orders for Vietnam. He arrived on Dec. 15, 1967, just days before the Tet Offensive. At Long Binh, Jansen was told he was going to

Jeffrey L. Meek

Pleiku. There he was placed with the 563rd Transportation unit.

Jansen remembers when Tet kicked off, the unit was kept in their compound and later there was talk of evacuation by helicopter, but it never came to that. "That was a scary moment in my life," he told me. Jansen said at the time he had no idea of the enormity of the enemy attacks.

As a driver of heavy trucks, he drove in long convoys, sometimes 15 miles in length. "So there were times they'd hit a convoy that you really wouldn't know about, wouldn't be a part of," said Jansen. Usually he drove a five-ton tractor-trailer, hauling supplies inland to Dak To, a large base near the Ho Chi Minh trail.

From An Khe to Pleiku, one had to go through the Mang Yang Pass. "You'd get hit a lot of times on that pass," said Jansen of the small arms fire the convoys would receive. On one trip a rocket went over his head and on another he and his truck struck a land mine that blew off an axle of his truck.

"That day I was hauling a big load of lumber to Dak To, and I was the fourth truck in the convoy," he said. The blast also ripped open the gas tank and it threw gas up on the truck's canvas top which caught fire. "I tried to open the door to get out but it was jammed so I had to crawl out the door headfirst. I got out of the truck and I ran away from it and hid in a brush pile (in case he might be fired upon) until the gun trucks came up. At first, I thought a rocket had hit the load," Jansen said. His hair was singed and his arm burnt. "And the noise punctured my ear drum," he added.

War Stories

Once he came to his senses he was picked up by a helicopter and taken to a hospital in Pleiku for treatment. He was off the job for about a month because a lot of noise hurt his ear drum. During that month he took care of the enlisted men's club where the guys would go for a drink or two. Eventually, in Oui Nhon, a two-star General by the name of Richards pinned a Purple Heart on his chest. Once recovered, Jansen rejoined his unit, hauling a lot of napalm to the Air Force in Pleiku.

Life at the motor pool included maintaining trucks. There were three things Jansen always checked closely — that his M-16 was clean and, in his truck, and that air and fuel filters were clean. Dirty filters could halt a truck and make for a good target.

The convoy trips were along 60+ miles of roads filled with ruts and holes. The drivers would travel approximately 40 to 50 miles an hour as they bounced their way to their destinations. Jansen recalls a time he picked up an infantryman seeking a ride to Pleiku. By the time they arrived the man's side was really hurting from all the bouncing around in the truck. Near the end of his time in country he drove a refrigerated truck filled with food for the Fourth Infantry Division.

When his Vietnam service ended, he went to Ft. Lewis, Wash., and was put with another transportation outfit as an assistant platoon Sergeant. "I also played baseball, centerfield," he said with a smile.

I asked Jansen if he experienced any negative treatment upon his return stateside. "Not personally. I knew there were people against the war but no, not personally," he said. As a civilian Jansen spent 30 years

Jeffrey L. Meek

selling cars and retired in 2006. He moved to Hot Springs Village in 2015 from Edinburg, Texas.

Reflecting on his time in uniform he said, "It helped me for sure. It was a disciplined operation, but over in Vietnam after the Tet Offensive, you know, I can remember driving through Pleiku and seeing all those dead bodies piled on each other. I'll never forget that. And after an ambush you'd drive, and you'd see the dead Viet Cong lying along the road. That part, that wasn't good," Jansen softly said.

War Stories

David Jaspers served as Air Force aerial recon navigator

David Jaspers grew up in South Dakota. In high school he was an all-state clarinetist and helped start a bowling league. After graduating from Northern State University in 1966 he got a teaching job at the University of Arizona in Tucson. Six weeks later Jaspers lost his deferment and learned he was about to be drafted. Instead, he enlisted in the U.S. Air Force. His first stop was Officers Candidate School, then went to Mather AFB, Calif., for nine months of navigator training.

Following the completion of the training in 1968 he learned he was going to be put in the back seat of F-4 jets for reconnaissance duty. The F-4 was the first jet to have terrain avoidance radar which was a real necessity as they would be flying very low, sometimes because of the weather and very fast, up to 600 miles per hour.

Next this new airman attended several survival schools including how to land with a parachute, what to eat and not to eat, escape and avoidance, sea survival and interrogation school which was pretty tough on Jaspers. Once his 'interrogator' literally picked him up and put him against a wall, then later left him in a cage to see what it might be like if he was captured in enemy territory.

Then Jaspers went in jungle survival school in the Philippines in late 1968 before heading for duty in Udorn, Thailand, where he was assigned to the 14th Tactical Recon Squadron for one year's worth of flights, regardless of how many that turned out to be. His first flights were over Laos and the Ho Chi Minh trail.

Jeffrey L. Meek

A 'typical' mission format involved marking targets and taking photographs, usually at 500 feet above the ground. Missions usually lasted about an hour and 45 minutes. Fighter aircraft would perch above the recon planes and wait for enemy movement or fire as the recon planes almost dared the enemy to fire at them as they flew over taking photos. "If we saw a flash on the ground, it would be pretty easy to say where they are," Jaspers said of the flights.

The jet had the capability of knowing what was being fired at them, which helped with avoidance maneuvers. "You had techniques to increase your chance of avoiding it. If you could see it come off the ground then you could influence the guy on the ground's direction (of fire)," said Jaspers who ended up flying an incredible 193 missions during his one-year tour of duty. And then there were the night missions which Jaspers said were scarier that the daytime flights.

With no fighters with them, screaming through valleys in the dark, the missions were very dangerous. The jets did have an infrared system with flash capabilities for taking photos, but the flashes would also give away their position thus making them a target. "They were so bright it would silhouette the airplane," Jaspers said.

For the period July through September 1969, his plane earned outstanding crew honors for their night flights. "We achieved 100 percent target acquisition, but more to our credit no matter how much they shot at us we did not once sustain battle damage," Jaspers said.

During his tour he did get some R and R and was once able to go to a place he really wanted to see – Sydney, Australia.

War Stories

The unit had a 100th mission tradition in which the flyers would be dunked in a barrel of ugly green water, then party with others in the unit.

In November 1969, Jaspers returned to the U.S. and was placed with the 12th Tactical Recon Squadron at Bergstrom AFB, Texas, doing the same job. He also served temporary duty (TDY) in Alaska. On one flight they finished their mission and then took a slow ride over the Yukon River. Suddenly a distress call came in that a Boy Scout troop had a member in trouble. Using the jet's radio, they contacted Fairbanks for a helicopter which flew in and got a boy out who had a ruptured appendix. Jaspers also got a jet ride straight up Mt. McKinley which was quite a thrill.

Jaspers ended his military career in April 1972. Of his service he said he grew up a lot, then spoke of his experiences after returning to civilian life. He said he was never spit on but felt he was just ignored. He told of being in night school: "The girls would just basically turn their head away. They could tell by the haircut you were Air Force, and they didn't want anything to do with you."

Jaspers also shared another time when he was back home with his parents. His father asked if they could take a ride after church to visit family in the area. "I guess I was just rude. I told him no. I thought if I could come halfway around the world after what I'd been through, if they wanted to see me, they could come here. So, there was a little bit of resentment or aloofness. But you get over it," Jaspers explained. He added that he never sat and talked about his experiences with his parents, and they didn't ask much.

Jeffrey L. Meek

As the interview neared its end Jaspers said only a few people knew anything about his military service. Asked if his family would learn something about him by watching the interview Jaspers said, "Yeah, I think they'll learn some. They won't get the perspective of how scared I was and how often I was (scared). I think part of that's because we never got hit."

"Just because you don't get hit doesn't mean you don't experience the fear and the trauma. I'm thankful I don't have PTSD or any of those kinds of things." Jaspers said he's never been asked to join a military organization, nor has he ever applied. He's just moved on.

As a civilian he worked 29 years with Texas Instruments in accounting and finance. After obtaining his CPA he was transferred to one of TI's subsidiaries – Geophysical Service – to become controller for two international assignments in the seismic exploration for oil: in 1978 in Dhahran, Saudi Arabia, and in 1980 in Rio de Janeiro, Brazil.

He returned to the U.S. in 1982 working in many different roles for the company. Jaspers retired in April 2001 and later moved to Hot Springs Village in 2004 from Garland, Texas. He and wife Rose Mary have a son Phil.

War Stories

Dean Johansen served in Thailand during the Vietnam War

Dean Johansen grew up in LeMars, Iowa and also attended college there. After graduating he went to work in the retail store business in Iowa, but was later transferred to Brainerd, Minn. After moving he received an Army draft notice on April 1, 1968. "I said it had to be an April Fools letter, but it wasn't," said Johansen of that day. Not having any children at the time, he was considered 1-A.

He began his service with basic training at Fort Lewis, Wash. Following this he was off to Arizona to attend a clerk-typist school. After completing the coursework, he was ordered to Ft. Jackson, S.C., to begin his regular duties.

At Fort Jackson he started as a mail clerk, but soon became the morning reports clerk at the company headquarters. "The morning report clerk is responsible for preparing a report, every day, for the commanding officer on the strength figures for that company. It's the general numbers on where everybody is," said Johansen of the work. While doing his job he once received a citation from his commanding officer informing him, he had been chosen as the soldier of the month for the entire base.

Approximately seven months later he was told he'd be going to Thailand. This surprised him somewhat because he had only 10 months left of his two-year stent of duty.

In March 1969, Johansen left the U.S. for overseas. By plane he flew to Hawaii, Guam and then to Bangkok, Thailand. From Bangkok he was taken by military bus to Korat where, at a processing center, he was unexpectedly chosen as a replacement for a job there at that base.

Jeffrey L. Meek

Johansen learned he was going to be assigned to the 256th Personnel Services Company and be based at what was called Camp Friendship. "It was a small Army establishment, mostly personnel soldiers that worked with the 256th. There were other aspects of it, but I didn't see much of the camp other than the building I worked in," said Johansen. His job was to requisition replacements for the senior enlisted grades from sergeant and above.

He was also given a secret clearance because he would be working off of data showing troop strengths of various units. The data contained a soldier's name, his job, how long he'd been in service and also their rank. When their ETS – end term of service – came up, Johansen had to identify who was going home and, within 60 days, find someone to fill their position. On occasion he would be issued weapons when the camp's perimeter was being threatened by enemy or unknown forces.

The weather was humid and hot with temperatures reaching 120 degrees. On the base would be Thai natives who worked in the barracks as a house boy or girl doing such jobs as cleaning the barracks and shining shoes for a little extra money. The countryside around the base was quite interesting. Wild creatures like Bengal tigers, large bears and cobras roamed around at will.

One night Johansen decided to take a shower. "I turned on the light and there was a cobra in that shower. It was on the floor standing up looking at me," Johansen recalled. He shut the door, found an MP, and told him of the unwanted visitor in the shower. The MP went into the shower and opened up with his M-16 machine gun. "There

War Stories

were splinters all over, but they got the snake and drug it off," smiled Johansen.

While at Camp Friendship he got a chance to see a Bob Hope Troupe Show. Before the show began, he received a notice telling him he would be interviewed by Hope during the show. Johansen arrived at the designated location but learned Hope's troupe was delayed and the interviews had to be cancelled. It wasn't a total loss because he got to watch the show from one of the wings of the stage. It was during this time that he got to shake hands with Neil Armstrong who had recently returned from his walk on the moon. After the show, Hope had a photo taken with Johansen and others, but he has never been able to find a copy of the picture.

In March 1970 he began his journey back to the U.S. He and the others returning home had learned of the protesting and dissension back home. "That was a little disheartening," said Johansen of his homecoming. "It seemed to be targeted at the individual soldier," he added.

Arriving in Oakland, Calif., one of the first things the men were told was to consider switching from military uniform to civilian clothes. "It was disheartening that you couldn't feel the pride of serving your country," said Johansen of the experience. He added that even in civilian clothes it was pretty obvious who was in the military because of their short haircuts. He was discharged on March 27, 1970.

As a civilian, Johansen worked in the retail business for 10 years, then worked for Wal-Mart for 11 years and then decided to open his own retail stores in Houston, Texas. In 1996 he retired and with wife Sandra moved to

Jeffrey L. Meek

Hot Springs Village in 2001. The couple has a daughter Jocelyn.

Reflecting on his time in service, Johansen said it was a great experience. "It was a tremendous asset. I got to see a lot of places I probably will never see again, like Thailand, and I learned an awful lot of things. I think it was a valuable service for me," Johansen concluded.

War Stories

Tom Johnson served with Army intelligence in Vietnam, Pentagon

For Tom Johnson it all began at the University of Alaska when he enrolled in an Army ROTC program. Little did he know it would be the beginning of a distinguished 28-year military career.

His first stop was at Fort Benning, Ga., where he took the Infantry Officer basic course and attended Ranger School in 1965. Later that year he was put with the First Battalion, 36th Infantry, 3rd Armored Division and sent to Friedberg, Germany, as a Second Lieutenant, and platoon leader (later he would become the Company XO). The mission there in Germany was to be prepared to defend the Fulda Gap should any advance be made by Soviet forces.

Then in 1967 Johnson moved to Heidelberg and was assigned to U.S. Army Headquarters Intelligence. "I got to sign for a million dollars' worth of vehicles to make sure they were maintained and ready to go to war," Johnson said.

Following this he was sent to Counterintelligence School at Fort Holabird, Md., which made him a Special Agent in the Department of the Army. "We learned how to investigate security challenges, problems and to do background checks on people for security clearances," he recalled.

In 1968, Johnson went to Saigon, South Vietnam, as part of the Special Operations Group (SOG) –Studies and Observations Group, where he became a targeting officer for covert and clandestine operations in Cambodia, Laos and North Vietnam. The work involved selecting targets

Jeffrey L. Meek

along the Ho Chi Minh trail for B-52 strikes, capturing of prisoners, and watching roads for enemy movements by use of acoustic sensors along the trail.

Johnson also made 13 training-related jumps in Vietnam teaching captured NVA to jump, after they had been 'turned' and prepped to return to North Vietnam for intelligence gathering, most of which garnered no useable intelligence.

In 1969, he returned to the U.S. and worked as the South Vietnam desk officer and 'black book' briefer at the Pentagon. In that role Johnson briefed the secretary of the Army every Saturday morning.

Two years later he attended Defense Intelligence School in Washington, D.C., taking the Strategic Intelligence Officer course. Upon completion of the course he became J-2 of the Alaska Joint Command at Elmendorf Air Force Base at the Indications and Warning Center which was well below ground. "We watched Soviet aircraft off the coast of Alaska," said Johnson of his work.

Just across the street from his quarters was a VIP building for colonels and above. In 1972, Johnson saw President Richard Nixon and Japan's Emperor Hirohito during a visit. "I got to welcome them at the hanger when they arrived," Johnson said. That night secret service agents with machine guns ringed the building and Johnson was told to close his blinds and turn out the lights.

The next morning Johnson went outside and offered the agent some coffee and was invited, along with his family, to see the president and Hirohito. At 4:30 a.m. the following morning Johnson, his wife and two young children were escorted across the street where they watched the

War Stories

two leaders enter a limo. "That was exciting. And I also got to brief Henry Kissinger," Johnson added as almost an afterthought. He read the black book information to Kissinger but got no response.

In 1974, Johnson attended Army Command and General Staff College at Fort Leavenworth, Kan. His neighbor while there was Wesley Clark who would later become a General. "He was the leader of our class," said Johnson.

After a promotion to Major, Johnson left for Seoul, South Korea, in 1975 for a stint as Operations Officer with the 502nd Military Intelligence Battalion. A year later he returned home for duty in the Albuquerque Field Office, 901st Military Intelligence Detachment as Commander of counterintelligence and operation security in support of the nuclear testing program.

In 1979, he moved to the 470th Military Intelligence Group at Fort Clayton, Panama, and became a Lieutenant Colonel. While there, his wife died. Also working in Panama was a talented linguist named Karen who also was the translator for the U.S. and Manuel Noriega, military governor of Panama until being removed from office during a U.S. invasion in December 1989. Karen would later become his wife.

In 1982, Johnson joined the I Corps at Fort Lewis, Wash., as an intelligence staff officer. Two years later he transitioned into the Combat Developments Experimentation Center and worked as a researcher testing new Army equipment.

Three years later the Johnson's moved cross-country to Fort Meade, Md., where he worked in the Army's

Jeffrey L. Meek

Investigative Records Repository as the manager. The facility contained hard copy files on everyone who had ever been issued an Army security clearance.

By 1987, he became commander of the Special Access Programs Security Detachment handling 'black programs,' like the Stealth Bomber program for example. Everyone that worked there was polygraphed once a year.

Three years later Johnson attended Defense Intelligence College in D.C. where he designed and managed a course concerning Strategic Arms Limitation treaties and inspections in support of those treaties. The course taught scientists, inspectors, CIA personnel and others the art of inspecting Soviet missile sites.

Johnson also traveled to the USSR in diplomatic status to observe inspections. Asked if he ever felt the Russians were hiding anything Johnson said, "No, I felt they were totally open," and added that he and the other inspectors were treated very well as they were escorted around by a KGB colonel.

In 1993, Johnson retired, ending a fascinating 28-year career. Wife Karen retired the same day after 20 years in service. The couple moved to the Village from Washington, D.C., that same year. Johnson has two children: Linda and Carl.

War Stories

Karen Johnson served with CIA, Army intelligence

It's not often we get a story from someone that has 'rubbed shoulders' with a name just about everyone will know when they hear it. That's the case with Karen Johnson as you'll soon see.

After graduating from the University of Missouri at Columbia with a degree in Spanish, Johnson contacted several agencies in her attempts to get a job. "The Central Intelligence Agency answered first so I flew to Washington, D.C., and took an intensive language course because they were sending me to Brazil, so I had to learn Portuguese," Johnson said. Following the completion of the course, in 1968, she went to San Paulo, population nine million, where she would begin her career as a case officer for sources.

"It was a time of unrest in Brazil. You had a man by the name of Carlos Marighella and he wrote the book on guerilla warfare. He had a unique capability of organizing the far left and the far right into his terrorist organization," she said of the times.

The city had three-fourths of the country's banks so there were almost daily bank robberies by Marigehlla's organization to secure funds for their operations. "Marighella was responsible for kidnapping the U.S. Ambassador. (It was) the first time a U.S. Ambassador had been kidnapped by terrorists for the release of 'political prisoners'," Johnson said.

The Ambassador was taken in September 1969, interrogated for days and revealed the name of the CIA station chief, all the chiefs of base and all the CIA case officers. But the CIA didn't know this until six months after the kidnapping, thus they all had to leave the country and Johnson became case officer for students and a surveillance team. Marighella was later killed in San Paulo by police in an ambush on November 4. Johnson was also in country when an Army attaché was machine gunned to death in front of his family.

She returned to the U.S. in 1970 and was told she was going to be sent to Paris. Johnson said no, she wanted to stay in the United States "so you didn't have to worry about being in the wrong place at the wrong time," she said. The CIA said she had to stay onboard for six months before she could resign. During that time, she worked in counterinsurgency also known as 'dirty ops.'

She returned home to Missouri, worked a few jobs and in 1973 decided to join the U.S. Army. She talked to a Women's Army Corps (WAC) recruiter and at 11:30 p.m. in her parent's living room was given a direct commission based on her college degree.

Johnson attended WAC basic at Fort McClellan and from there went to military intelligence school in Fort Huachuca, Ariz., for a basic course. Next, she applied and was chosen as a command briefer for the onsite commanding General and was the first woman to hold the job of Military Area Intelligence, aka human intelligence. Johnson stayed for four years as an instructor and instructor trainer.

In 1978, she was told she'd be going to Germany, but instead was sent to Panama and was placed with the 470th Military Intelligence Group at Fort Amador. At this time Colonel Manuel Noriega was the Chief of Intelligence in Panama.

War Stories

Johnson met Noriega at a social function and became his personal translator during headquarters functions. On one occasion Noriega asked her if it were true that Americans entertained in their homes. Yes, said Johnson. Noriega asked if that was how you socialize with others? Yes, said Johnson. "Then he said, 'why haven't I ever been invited into any American homes?' I said I don't know, but you're certainly welcome in mine and he said 'when'," remembers Johnson.

She found Noriega very interesting, and they conversed freely. She doesn't see him as portrayed by the U.S. as an idiot. "He was an intelligent man and loved his family," said Johnson who would get bubblegum for his daughters. Johnson said she feels Noriega got railroaded at his trial following Dec. 20, 1989's Operation Just Cause when U.S. troops ousted the General who surrendered on Jan. 3, 1990, and was given over to the Drug Enforcement Agency.

Also during her tour in Panama was the revolution by the Sandanistas in Nicaragua. Noriega came to her with information. "I passed on that the Sandanistas were looking for money to pay their solders because they hadn't been paid in six months. And he said, 'you will win their hearts if you will just give them the money.' And the U.S. said no, we're not going to interfere. Well, now we have a leftist government in Nicaragua," said Johnson of the turbulent times.

At the time Johnson worked as assistant operations officer, 18 hours a day, seven days a week. In 1982, she left Panama for duty in Arlington, Virginia to work with the

Jeffrey L. Meek

Inspector General of the Intelligence and Security Command.

Later she was part of a group that went to Panama in 1983 to do an inspection of the 470th. While there, Noriega assumed command of the Guardia Nacional as General. As a courtesy, Johnson contacted Noriega's secretary to let them know they were coming. "When I got there Noriega had sent invitations for the whole team to attend his assumption of command. We were in the box seats and at that time Noriega presented me with the Guardia Nacional's Honor of Merit certificate and ribbon for the work I had done in Panama," said Johnson. "It was totally unexpected," she added. That was the last time she ever saw or heard from the General.

For the next three years she worked as an Inspector General and traveled the globe to Japan, Korea, Turkey, Germany, and Austria for intelligence compliance. During those years she also took a four-month systems automation course in Indiana.

In September 1985, Johnson was put with the 902nd Military Intelligence Group at Fort Meade, Md., commanding auto data processing at the Systems Security Detachment. In that role she was with counterintelligence, inspecting U.S. Army facilities worldwide that had computer facilities. In November 1987, she was made the S1 (Personnel) for the 902nd and then S3 (Operations) in June 1988.

In 1989, Johnson completed studies from the Army Command and General Staff College. In July, she was assigned to 8th Army in Yongsan, Korea as Chief of the

War Stories

Counter-Intelligence Branch for U.S. Forces – Korea and G2 (Intelligence/Security) for 8th Army.

In September 1990, she returned to Maryland with the Special Operations detachment as Deputy Director for Support. Their mission was to find people betraying their country. During this time she was involved with the arrest and conviction of a retired Army Master Sergeant in Germany that had been selling secrets for 15 years and later helped nab an Army Warrant Officer in the U.S.

In April 1993, Johnson retired and was awarded the Legion of Merit. That same year she moved to Hot Springs Village where her parents were living. Johnson has two children: Carl and Linda.

Of her time in uniform she simply said, "It was an honor to serve my country."

Jeffrey L. Meek

Tom Laginja survived USS Forrestal disaster

The USS Forrestal was America's first super carrier. The ship was enormous and had a crew of 5,400. While serving during the Vietnam War, it suffered one of the worst disasters in U.S. Naval history. On July 29, 1967, a missile misfired on the deck of the carrier. That missile hit a jet and started a chain of events that killed 134 and injured 64 of its crew. Several bombs and missiles ignited and blew up, causing $72 million damage. In all, 21 planes were destroyed and 35 damaged. Holes were blown in the ship that went down seven decks.

On board the Forrestal was a young pilot named John McCain. When his plane was hit, he jumped out and rolled through fire to safety. A few months later he would be shot down and spend many years as a prisoner of the North Vietnamese.

Also on board was Tom Laginja. He served as a fire control radar technician. He was working with American Airlines in Chicago when he received a draft notice. He had scored well on tests so had an option to enlist if he chose. Laginja decided to enlist in the Navy and was sent to San Diego for basic training.

His next stop was at a base in Kingsville, Texas, awaiting electronics school. He eventually received that training in Memphis, Tenn. Laginja learned to be a fire control radar tech. His job was to man radar which guided weapons to their targets. He worked mostly with Phantom F-4 fighter jets and Sparrow missiles. He was assigned to Squadron 74 on the USS Forrestal and shortly thereafter was on his way to Vietnam.

War Stories

Laginja was awed by the size of the carrier. The flight deck measured four acres, had 17 decks, and seemed enormous. "It even had a dentist, snack shop and a hospital," said Laginja. His personal quarters were situated under the flight deck. He worked 12 hours on, 12 hours off schedule.

The night before the disaster the ship was about 10 miles off the coast of Vietnam. He could see the flashes and hear the explosions of the fighting on shore and thought about his relative safety out there on the ship, yet so close to a fierce war.

On occasion, Laginja would get a chance to talk to pilots about their missions. One of the pilots was McCain. McCain was in a different squadron, so Laginja didn't know him, but he had heard about him from others. "His reputation was that he was a very good pilot, a good officer, good leader and didn't sweat the small stuff," remembers Laginja.

July 29, 1967, is a day Laginja will never forget. He had worked the night before and was down in his bed when he heard an announcement of a fire on the flight deck. He could hear something above him that sounded different but was not sure of what it was.

"I could hear footsteps that were different. There was urgency to them I'd never heard before and I thought something was different up there," said Laginja. A few minutes later the call to general quarters was made. "That was the most serious situation you could have aboard ship," he said.

He rolled out of his bed and was about to put clothes on when he noticed smoke coming in his compartment.

Jeffrey L. Meek

Next, Laginja heard a bomb go off. He later learned that was the bomb that blew up near McCain's jet. This caused Laginja to rush out of his compartment and on through the deck. Suddenly, he saw a big flash and heard a huge pop. "The next thing I knew, I was on the deck (floor) and there was debris all around me," he said.

Now, there was fire behind him and up ahead. He went over into a corner. "I thought well this it is. I just hoped it wouldn't be a slow death," Laginja said. Then, behind him, he saw movement and decided to search for a way out in that direction. The smoke was thick, but he made his way out of the compartment. He and others went down some ladders to a lower deck where the hospital was located.

Laginja came upon some others who gasped when they saw him. He didn't know it, but he was bleeding all over from the shrapnel that had hit him from the blast. They took him to sick bay, and he sat down next to a man whose skin was burned off. He was then moved to another area where a sailor was repeatedly saying, "Please don't let me die."

A corpsman removed shrapnel from his face and legs, and he was kept overnight for observation. The next day dawned sunny with a calm sea. Laginja said it was then he learned that nine bombs had exploded on the flight deck.

In footage of the event, you see men pushing jet planes overboard to get rid of the explosives and ammo on board. It was the quickest way to get the live ordinance away from fire. Had that not been done, it is likely more explosions would have occurred.

The ship sailed to Subic Bay in the Philippines for repair. On the way, men were given a chance to go to their

War Stories

quarters to see if any personal effects were still there. Laginja went to his compartment which was still covered with about 18 inches of water. As he was walking in his area, his foot bumped into something. Thinking it may be something of his, he reached down in the water and picked it up. It was a severed hand.

In the Philippines, Laginja got new clothes and new glasses. About a week later the ship left for a slow trip back to the U.S. "You could still smell the smoke," said Laginja. A month later the ship docked in Norfolk, Va. After many repairs and updates, the Forrestal was assigned duty in the Mediterranean.

The ship and their planes patrolled the area for nine months. Upon returning, his enlistment period was nearly over so he was discharged in August 1969.

Looking back on his experiences on the Forrestal, Laginja said, "I think back to those guys, and I'm still amazed the Navy could take a bunch of young men, 18 or 19 years old, and put them on a ship like a carrier doing technical, sophisticated, important work and they do the job. Everybody does their job because they know somebody else is depending on them."

Jeffrey L. Meek

Bill Long served several tours in Vietnam during 23-year naval career

Bill Long served 23 years in the U.S. Navy, earned two degrees, served on five ships, and received numerous decorations for his time spent in Vietnam. It all began in 1962 during the Cuban Missile Crisis. "We were mad as hell and wanted to do something about it," said Long.

He joined the naval reserves so he could finish his current college semester and then reported to boot camp in San Diego. Long loved it. "I found it fascinating and loved hearing about ships," Long said.

He then joined the regular Navy and was sent to Charleston, S.C., where he became a radioman, finishing third in his class of 75 people.

Next, Long chose duty aboard a Landing Ship Tank (LST) and in 1964 was assigned to the USS Middlesex County for duty in Panama. In Panama his job was to help train Marines in a jungle survival school.

Long was next assigned to the USS Meeker County and joined the ship in Boston before sailing on to Guam. After a few days there, Long was on his way to Vietnam.

LSTs were one of the real workhorses for the Navy in Vietnam, hauling ammunition, supplies, vehicles, and personnel as needed. Long became part of Landing Ship Squadron Three and arrived in the harbor at Vung Tau in early 1967.

On their first mission upriver, Long was stationed on the bridge listening to radio traffic, and the sound of gunfire. "There was a heck of a firefight going on up the river," said Long. It turned out that an LST, under South

War Stories

Vietnamese control, had been attacked and badly damaged in the fight. Long said it was on that morning that he realized there were a lot of people out there that wanted to kill him and that throughout Vietnam many would die that day. His ship eventually made many trips upriver to deliver supplies to Saigon.

On another mission the ship came under mortar fire while on a beach. "It was another one of those moments when you thought, this might be it," Long said.

Another time as the LST was attempting a landing at Cua Viet, Long recalled seeing a female body floating in the water. He was told to back away and not touch the body. As suspected, it was later determined the body was booby-trapped.

In 1968, Long had another close call that led to him receiving a Combat Action Ribbon. They were hauling ammo to Marines fighting the North Vietnamese near the demilitarized zone (DMZ). After off-loading the ammo, they came under heavy fire. The ship backed off quickly as rounds fell all around them. A nearby destroyer relieved the situation by pouring fire into the area.

Long's LST later went back in with another load and once again they were attacked. This time a battleship poured rounds into the area. "You could see the mountain disappearing," Long said of the shelling.

Long told me how the enemy would also float things down the rivers, like a Coke can, that were booby-trapped. Because of this tactic, men on the ship were assigned as lookouts and would shoot the items as they came into range. On one occasion Long's ship was near another ship that was struck by one of these devices and six sailors were killed.

He also remembers pulling into a beach one day and seeing 42 body bags lying there. "That's a vivid thing in my memory," said Long.

His tour in Vietnam finally came to an end and Long entered the Navy Enlisted Scientific Education Program (NESEP). The program led to him earning a degree in Electrical Engineering at the University of Texas in 1972.

Later that year he was back in Vietnam aboard the LST USS Fresno for duty off the coast in an Amphibious Ready Group (ARG) with Marines and SEAL teams also aboard. The Group was to be ready at all times to make a landing if needed. Long remembers dropping off SEAL teams for missions and later picking them up. Never would the SEALS talk about what they did.

Long did three different six-month tours from 1972 to 1975 with the ARG and recalled for me one mission at the end of the war. They had sailed into Saigon picking up supplies and Long recalled seeing the South Vietnamese people frantically trying to get aboard any plane or ship that could take them to safety before the enemy entered the city.

While anchored out in the river that night the crew, with fire hoses, fought off civilians trying to get onto the ship. It was a sad sight and a sad ending to America's involvement in the war.

Long also saw the 'boat people' trying to make their way to the Philippines. He saw times when a 30-foot boat would hold up to 100 people. The U.S. Navy provided them

War Stories

with supplies and on some occasions when the people would deliberately sink their vessel, take them on board.

After the war, Long earned a master's degree at the Naval Postgraduate School in Monterey, Calif., in 1977. His final three years of service, 1982 to 1985, Long worked as an assistant professor and deputy department head for the Department of Electrical Engineering at the U.S. Air Force Academy in Colorado.

In civilian life Long spent 14 years working for defense contractors. In 2000 he moved to Hot Springs Village. Long has a daughter, Tammy, who is an engineer with NASA.

Our interview concluded with a talk about some of the nagging questions that surround the Vietnam War. I asked him what lessons we learned from our participation there. "I wish I could say that we learned something," said Long. "We lost 58,000 men in a losing situation."

He went on to say that during his first tour of duty he felt like the U.S. was there to win. Four years later and back in Vietnam he wondered why we weren't winning. I asked why, in his opinion, did the American home front turn so violently against the war. "There's another one I don't understand because I missed it. I missed that transformation because I was over there. I was astonished when I came back and found all that stuff going on in the United States," Long said.

Finally, I asked about visiting the Vietnam War Memorial Wall in Washington, D.C. Long said it was difficult to visit the Wall. "I have close friends on that Wall," said the 23-year Navy veteran.

Jeffrey L. Meek

Frank MacCallen served with the 497th Engineer Company in Vietnam

In Vietnam, Army engineers and Navy Seabees built and upgraded roads, extended highways, constructed ports and buildings, and installed pipelines and railroads. With an Army engineer unit during the war was Hot Springs Village resident Frank MacCallen.

While working in California, he became a married draftee in September 1966, and went to Ft. Lewis, Wash., for boot camp where he got in shape, received weapons training, and went on night marches, much of the time in wet, rainy weather.

After a leave, he was sent to Ft. Leonard Wood, Mo., in Jan. 1967 for attendance in a heavy equipment operator school. With the 4th Engineer Specialist Training Brigade, he was immediately approached about being a platoon leader. Next came leadership school and then a trip to Ft. Hood, Texas where he was put with the 16th Engineer Battalion, First Armored Division. There he started by doing guard duty.

MacCallen said he operated a loader and did "a lot of busy work." In August 1967 he got a 30-day leave, then left for Cam Rahn Bay in Vietnam as a single replacement. After several stops, he arrived at the air base there and clearly remembers his arrival. "I'll never forget hitting that door to go out (of the plane) and getting a whiff of Vietnam. I can still smell it today. The humidity and the musty, moldy smell, it was something you don't forget," said MacCallen.

He was ordered to the 35th Engineer Group, 497th Engineer Company, 87th Engineer Battalion for port construction work. "It was a small company. We had divers,

War Stories

we had pile driving barges, some heavy equipment, and operators," MacCallen said, then added that he felt fortunate to be in the 497th with such a good bunch of guys. "The guys taught us a lot. They really helped out. We learned really quick we had to cover each other's back."

Their first big project was making a petroleum off-loading jetty. Bulldozers ran 24/7 to get a pipeline in place. One night on the job, MacCallen accidentally punctured a JP-4 (jet petroleum) line. "I met a lot of people that night," chuckled MacCallen. "I was given some bad information," he added.

From there, he and others did projects in the Cam Rahn Bay area for the next several months, day and night. This included repairing roads due to damage done by a monsoon.

Later he and another man were told to get their dozers on an LST, which they did, and off they went cruising the bay. As they approached a beach, mortar fire came in. The LST pulled back, waited, then came back in. Troops showed up to unload the LST. "They were Koreans," said MacCallen, known as the White Horse Division (9th Korean Infantry Division, 30th Regiment). The men made their way to a compound and were told they were to clear the jungle peninsula from one end to the other. So, he and his buddy began bulldozing the area. "It took us just short of a month. It was like a big parking lot when we were done," MacCallen said. When finished, the two men returned to their base, but in doing so, his good buddy accidentally lost a finger during the transitioning.

Near Cam Rahn Bay the outfit worked on Hwy 1 repairing bridges and included work on the 87th's compound south of the base, supposedly to push heavy

Jeffrey L. Meek

rocks, but the D-7 dozers couldn't do it. The work just tore them up.

At night the compound would get hit by enemy fire. MacCallen and others would sit in a bunker waiting out the attack. During the Tet Offensive, things got hairy for his unit, which in tough times became a reactionary force as needed.

At the base during a night attack, the engineers became infantrymen told to guard a bridge. It was a tricky assignment because on one side was the base, on the other those Koreans, so where would the firing be aimed?

Enemy mortars came in and blew up fuel bladders at the base. "Basically, we just hunkered down and waited it out," said MacCallen. Luckily for them, the bridge was not attacked.

Now promoted to E-5 he continued to work along Hwy 1 as necessary. With about 45 days left in country he was asked to accompany a group of dump trucks headed for the Cambodian border. He had already turned over his dozer to another man, so he was available, so he said he'd do it. "Biggest mistake of my life," said MacCallen.

The trucks left Cam Rahn Bay loaded with gravel and eventually were out on a dirt road with a drop off on one side and a high cliff on the other, perfect ambush area. "I thought, this isn't a good situation, but we made it all the way and spent the night," MacCallen recalled.

That night, sitting in their trucks, enemy fire came in, but he was not hurt. He safely made it back to base and was asked to go again. Sgt. MacCallen answered, "You can take this stuff (sergeant stripes) off my arm. I'm too short (referring to time in country). I'm not going back there."

In September 1968, he returned stateside and was soon discharged out of Ft. Lewis. In dress uniform he

War Stories

headed home through San Francisco. MacCallen called it "the greeting committee," protestors at the airport. He didn't want to say much about the experience other than to say it was not a good situation.

Now at home, he went to a shopping mall with his wife at that time. Some youngsters set off some firecrackers inside the mall and, "I almost knocked my wife down getting to the ground. It was just a reaction," he said.

"Living in California you never told people you served in Vietnam. Until I moved to Arkansas, I never wore a Vietnam hat because people here will thank you. There, people, once they were aware, you felt like they were looking down on you," he said.

As a civilian, MacCallen worked for a tractor company as a sales representative, then general manager for a farm equipment dealership and then got into the lawn and garden industry. He retired in 2013 and with wife Saundra moved to the Village from Carmichael, Calif., that same year. MacCallen has a daughter, Lisa.

Reflecting on his Vietnam experience was difficult for MacCallen. After a long pause he said, "I didn't realize how much it changed my life. Back then the VA wasn't aware of all the problems the guys were having coming back. I remember going to the VA with a bad back," he said. After waiting four or five hours, and still not being called in for his appointment, he walked out, had a couple of drinks, and drove home. "It's hard to explain. It changes you," MacCallen said.

Obviously very emotional, he spoke about those he served with. "This interview is for them. There's a lot of

Jeffrey L. Meek

them that don't have this opportunity. I want to say thank you to the men I served with in the 497th for their dedication to duty and country."

War Stories

Bob MacDevitt served in U.S. Army supply capacity

Bob MacDevitt grew up in New York. After attending Long Island University, he was drafted into the U.S. Army in 1966. "I got my greetings notice in the mail," MacDevitt said with a grin. He reported to Fort Hamilton, a processing center, which was under the Brooklyn Bridge. "They had us count off by threes and congratulated all the number ones and said congratulations, you're now a member of the United States Marine Corps. The remainder of us they put on a plane for basic training and flew us all the way to Fort Ord, Calif.," said MacDevitt.

Turns out there was a spinal meningitis scare at Fort Ord, so the men were quarantined for three weeks, then flown back to Fort Dix, N.J., for basic training. He began that training during the cold months of 1966 – 1967. Advanced infantry training also took place at Dix.

With a big smile on his face, MacDevitt talked about his 'wonderful' drill sergeant. "He had a scar that went from his eye down to his lip that he had gotten in a bayonet fight in Korea. And he had two gold front teeth, so he was a formidable figure; 6-foot, 2-inches and there wasn't an ounce of fat on the guy," MacDevitt said.

He added that in his training he learned that it was unbelievable to him what the human spirit can do when you feel you are mentally or physically exhausted. "You can still do things and that was a lesson that went with me throughout my life." MacDevitt qualified on several weapons, including scoring #2 in the group with an M-14.

Jeffrey L. Meek

Back at Fort Ord, MacDevitt had been offered the opportunity to attend Officer Candidate School (OCS). He did so and was offered three choices for duty – infantry, artillery, or quartermaster. He chose the latter and reported to Fort Lee, Va., for OCS training in March 1967. The 23 weeks of training started with 164 trainees, of which 91 graduated. MacDevitt said OCS was tough, running 2.5 miles several times a day, but also tough was the constant testing and drilling, all in an attempt to identify leaders. Ranking of each man took place every few weeks and those who were at or near the bottom were weeded out.

Leadership development, map reading, calling in artillery, simulations (including becoming a POW) were part of the OCS training. "It was to prepare us for what we might face," said MacDevitt.

In Sept. 1967, he was sent to Fort Carson, Colo., to be with a mechanized infantry unit. Although a supply officer he worked in a maintenance division. A typical day for MacDevitt included reviewing what the company needed, things like repair parts for example. He would meet with his Commander every day for a briefing about parts, vehicles, and readiness. "Readiness was always the key. How long would it take you to be 100 percent efficient," MacDevitt explained.

While there in Colorado he volunteered for placement in Thailand. In July 1968, he reported there after a few stops in Vietnam. From Tan Son Nkut Air Base to Bangkok, then on to Korat, Thailand, for duty with the 247th Maintenance Support Group. MacDevitt said the base at Korat was so built up it was like being in the U.S., tennis courts, movie theaters, maid service and more. Six months

War Stories

into his tour he was sent to Sakon Nakhon. "Everything was a dirt road. They'd come around at night with these defoggers and the guys would be wearing these huge tanks on their backs because the mosquitoes were so bad. With the defoggers they'd shoot (spray) the place where you lived."

The work was hard, but MacDevitt said he enjoyed it as, daily, he'd check in with his computer guys to look at inventory.

MacDevitt told a story about a guy who had ordered 100 tires, but somehow the order was accidentally changed. As a result, the base received 10,000 tires. MacDevitt was asked if he could use some, so to help out, he took a few, but had no room for thousands of them. "It was one of those glitches. What they did was to send a ship and take the tires to Vietnam and that's how they got redistributed," said MacDevitt.

And there was a time when he received a big container of size 42 blue denims for the Navy. The Navy? Why Navy items at an Army base in Thailand? Good question. MacDevitt said he gave them out to all the men to take to a tailor to make blue jean suits.

The work was constant, 10 hours a day, six-plus days a week. The political thinking there at the time was to help build roads that farmers could use to get produce to the southern part of the country where the most population was located in an effort to better their economy.

In Aug. 1968, MacDevitt was promoted to First Lieutenant, then in July of 1969 he returned home on a crowded Continental Airlines flight, eventually landing at Travis AFB in California. Late at night he boarded an air-conditioned bus. MacDevitt recalled, "I thought I was going to freeze to death because I hadn't been exposed to air conditioning in a year. It was a bus ride from hell for me. It seemed like it would never end. My teeth were chattering." Thailand was so hot he once saw a man fry an egg on a truck hood, so the AC on the bus was a real shock to his system.

From Los Angeles he flew home to New York where his father picked him up. At his house the family had put up a big sheet with 'Welcome Home' on it. After discharge, MacDevitt was put with a Military Police unit in the Reserves, working the Fort Dix stockade.

As a civilian he worked for Pan American World Airways as a service representative evaluating flights and new crew members. He was soon promoted to being a supervisor for flight service personnel. Later he took a job as assistant Director of Personnel at a Salvation Army-owned hospital, retiring in 2003. He and wife Sue have four children: Aaron, Melissa, Jason, and Kelly.

When asked to reflect on his Army service, MacDevitt said it made him grow up as a man and that he later never felt he couldn't get something done, that it removed his self-doubt. "It hardened me a little bit, but I think I needed some of that," he concluded.

War Stories

Tom McCamey served with the First and Third Infantry Divisions

The U.S. Army's First Infantry Division has a storied past, serving at Cantigny and elsewhere in World War I, in North Africa, Sicily and Normandy, France on D-Day, June 6, 1944. The First, known as 'The Big Red One' also fought in Vietnam, arriving in October 1965 for duty in III Corps. As a division they were awarded many medals, including 11 Medals of Honor, 67 Distinguished Service Crosses, 905 Silver Stars for bravery in action and the Vietnamese Cross of Gallantry with Palm. With the First Infantry Division in 1969 was Tom McCamey who served as a rifle platoon leader and was the recipient of the Purple Heart Medal and Combat Infantry Badge to name just a few of his distinguished awards.

McCamey grew up in Texas and after graduation from Abilene Christian University he received a draft notice in November 1966. This led him to enlisting so he could stay out of the infantry, but as you will see that isn't how things progressed for him.

He first went to Ft. Bliss, Texas for basic training, then to Fort Wachuca, Ariz., to await Officer Candidate School (OCS). A few weeks later he went to Ft. Sill, Oklahoma for OCS prep for eight weeks of artillery training. "That was unusual because I was an infantry candidate," McCamey said.

Then, in July 1967, he received orders to report to Ft. Benning, Ga., for six months of OCS. McCamey told me he loved the schooling and that the leadership and training was outstanding. "I found out I could do things I didn't know

Jeffrey L. Meek

I could do," he added. Most of the schooling was on leadership matters and skills.

In December 1967, as a Second Lieutenant, he reported to Ft. Knox, Ky., where he became a motor pool officer for two months. Then came his overseas assignment. McCamey was headed to Wildflecken, Germany, with the Third Infantry Division, 2nd Battalion, 15th Infantry Regiment. The unit was a mechanized infantry outfit whose job was to meet any enemy that may cross the Czech border. McCamey said the Wildflecken area saw lots of winter weather, adding that summer lasted about two days. There his job was supervising that motor pool.

In March 1969, he was ordered to Vietnam. Upon arrival it was an 'oh my' moment as he watched others leaving in their worn-out boots and uniforms. "It's rather solemn," he said of the sight. He joined the First Infantry Division as a rifle platoon leader assigned to 'D' company. McCamey praised his platoon sergeant. "He kept me alive," he said.

His first three weeks in the jungle were a real eye-opener. "I was afraid I was going to die, and it was getting to me," said McCamey of the pressures of combat and the many nightly ambushes in the area of the Michelin Rubber Plantation, 30 days at a time on duty. McCamey was told he was replacing their leader who had got out of a helicopter and was shot dead before he touched the ground. Not exactly a comforting thought.

The men did not wear socks inside their boots to keep out moisture. McCamey did not take his boots off for three weeks. "We were constantly moving, constantly ambushing, doing something and I didn't want to take my

War Stories

boots off because if you get caught in an ambush or firefight, you're barefooted and got to move. That was unacceptable so my feet turned into rubber and pulp. I'm a spiritual man and I had to come to grips with the reality that, Thomas, you can't keep doing this, you have to make peace with dying and responsibility. After that I did really well," McCamey said of overcoming his fear and becoming the necessary leader he needed to be for his men.

On the early morning of Aug. 11, 1969, his platoon was pulling out of an area when suddenly out of nowhere two enemy soldiers walked right into their position. Startled, both sides began firing and McCamey was hit in the leg. "I didn't even fire a shot, but I did see them run off," he remembers.

And then there was the time when one of the men with him had a seizure during a firefight but made it out okay.

In the battalion he was in, McCamey later joined S-3 (Operations) to work on air strike coordination and mission support at a tactical ops center. McCamey would be in on the radio coordination of ground and air actions.

One day an Australian pilot asked to be in on the ground war instead of in the air. "I told him 'Good luck'," laughed McCamey who added that the pilot returned weeks later unharmed. "He was brave and foolish," said McCamey.

His battalion was known as 'The Black Scarfs' which they wore around their necks. Their call sign was 'Dracula.' Later he found out the enemy was aware of the unit and had a great deal of respect for them.

Jeffrey L. Meek

In November 1969, he headed home and was discharged on December 1. As a civilian he went into human resources as an executive in the health care industry. On July 1, 1998, he retired. Oh, and he was also a scuba instructor for three years as well. He and wife Maureen moved to Hot Springs Village in November 2001 from the Florida Keys. He has two children: Kendall and Keelan.

Reflecting on his days in uniform, McCamey said he was glad he served and found out a lot about himself. "It's been very, very helpful to me," he concluded.

War Stories

Bill Mulcahy served three tours in Vietnam

Between 1966 and 1972, Bill Mulcahy served three tours of duty in Vietnam with the U.S. Navy. This Chicago native earned 52 Air Medals during his flying career as well as other numerous awards as he logged a total of 11,200 hours in the air. It all began in July 1948 when he joined Naval Submarine Reserve Unit 9-225 at the Naval Armory in Chicago. He was only 17 so his father had to accompany him for sign-up.

His initial training was on the USS Silversides, an old World War II sub. Other training involved sub school and attending the Naval Reserve Officer Candidate School (ROCS).

In 1951, while still in the reserves, he attended ROCS at Treasure Island, Calif. This training and completion of college would make him an officer.

During his third year in college, he got a draft notice from the U.S. Army. "I called them and said you guys made a big mistake. I'm in the Naval Reserve," said Mulcahy. He was told no; you are now 21 so you're no longer in the reserve. Mulcahy got things straightened out, re-joined an active reserve unit, and completed college. In September 1953, he was commissioned as an Ensign and sent to Combat Information Center School in Glenview, Ill. Other training stops included basic flight school, multi-engine advanced flight training, helicopter training, and fleet airborne electronics school.

In January 1961, he joined Helicopter Anti-Submarine Squadron 10 in San Diego as an instructor. In July 1966, Mulcahy was sent to Vietnam with the J-2 Military

Jeffrey L. Meek

Assistance Command. His job involved writing command objectives. "It really wasn't what I wanted to do," he recalled.

There was a new squadron forming up and Mulcahy wanted in. It was called the Helicopter Attack Light – Squadron Three (HAL-3). It was the Navy's only gunship squadron in Vietnam at that time. He was told he could not get in the unit but did find a way to log some hours in the air, despite the setback. On his days off he flew combat missions as a copilot with the Army, spending a total of 300 hours in the air flying a UH-1 helicopter.

In August 1967, Mulcahy was sent home and reported to the Naval War College and also, at night, attended classes at George Washington University where he earned a master's degree in international affairs. In June 1968, he was back in San Diego as commanding officer of Helicopter Combat Support Squadron Three.

A year later Mulcahy was sent to Vietnam for duty aboard the USS Iwo Jima for operations along the coast. While on the ship he participated in the recovery operations of Apollo 13 as operations officer. "I saw the chute open. It was a very thrilling thing," Mulcahy said. That evening he dined with two of the astronauts.

His third tour in Vietnam came in July 1971. This time he was able to get into the HAL-3 unit as commanding officer. "It was like a dream come true. I was able to fly helicopter gunships," said Mulcahy. He was stationed at Binh Thui. The squadron consisted of 150 pilots, door gunners and maintenance men: a total of 650 men in nine detachments with 47 helicopters.

War Stories

It was at this time that America's involvement began to lessen in Vietnam. This unit closed down in March 1972. Mulcahy was asked to take over another squadron running out of Saigon. He joined the Naval Helicopter Logistics Unit as Officer-in-Charge. The flying was thrilling according to Mulcahy. Every month he got 100 or more hours in the air. "My last three months I was flying 160 hours each month," he said.

Mulcahy then related a mission he won't forget. The mission was in support of a Navy Seal operation. They were going to insert the Seals on an enemy-held island in the Mekong River. Mulcahy led the flight in and encountered surprisingly tall trees in the landing area chosen to drop the Seals. A vertical descent was required.

With a heavy load of men and equipment on board, Mulcahy began to lose rotor speed. A red warning light came on and a loud warning horn sounded. The Seal team leader heard the horn go off and, while still 25 feet in the air, ordered his men to jump. "These guys were tough," Mulcahy added.

Now with a lighter load, Mulcahy was able to cushion his landing and not crash. His assent was without incident. About 30 minutes later he was called back in to pick up the Seals. They were in trouble. "I could hear all the firing in the background," Mulcahy remembered. Again, he led the helicopters in, landed and extracted the men as the Viet Cong closed in. "I was shooting an M-16 at them, and my .45 (pistol)," he said. "It was like the Fourth of July. As I pulled up I heard the rotor blades hitting the trees. I still relive that incident," Mulcahy continued.

Jeffrey L. Meek

In January 1973, he returned to the U.S. and worked at the Pentagon as Program Coordinator for the Light Airborne Multi-Purpose System. He retired from the Navy in July 1975. In civilian life Mulcahy continued to fly helicopters. He got a job with Petroleum Helicopters, Inc. During the next 18 years he flew in the Gulf of Mexico, Saudi Arabia, South America, and Central America.

He retired in 1993 and relocated to Cebu, Philippines, where he worked as a part-time FM radio newscaster. In 1996 he and wife Barbara moved to Hot Springs Village. They have four children: Richard, Michael, Cathy, and Claudia.

War Stories

Mike Murphy served with U.S. Marines in Vietnam

Mike Murphy grew up in Michigan, played basketball and football in high school and attended Central Michigan University. In 1966, as a junior, he had two big events occur in his life. He met his future bride Vicki, and he joined a United States Marine Corps (USMC) Platoon Leaders Class (PLC) which he said is similar to Army ROTC. Typically, just 50 percent of PLC attendees end up with a commission.

He graduated college on Feb. 1, 1968, with a degree in business administration, got married two days later and two days after that started a financial planning job. Because of an injury in the final phase of his USMC training at Quantico, Va., he was set back one year as his injury healed.

In August 1968 he finished the PLC requirements and was commissioned a Second Lieutenant. Murphy stayed at Quantico and attended a six-month basic school of which Murphy said everyone took very seriously knowing they were headed for leadership roles in Vietnam. He also stayed another two months thereafter for special training in communications.

While there, some of his fellow Marines had already been killed in action and returned home. "We often ended up on burial detail at Arlington National Cemetery," said Murphy who then added that one of the men had been killed the same day as his daughter was born. Murphy said the experiences he had up to this point matured him quickly.

In May 1969 he was sent to Vietnam, joining the Third Marine Division, Third Tank Battalion as

Jeffrey L. Meek

communications officer and as reaction platoon commander. The RPC's job was to take approximately 100 Marines out on the line to stop any attack on their base, sometimes needing tank and artillery support.

Did the training he received adequately train him for his responsibilities I asked? Murphy said at first he was extremely nervous about his job, but had good NCOs for help and felt the training did in fact prepare him for the job ahead.

Murphy said their assigned area was very mountainous which channeled tank movements along predictable routes. One day two tanks were ambushed, and three other tanks rolled in to help, including the tank commander of the outfit in his own tank. Unfortunately, that commander was killed, just one day before he was to rotate back home. Murphy said Oliver North was also involved in this attack and has written about it in his book.

While Murphy was in Vietnam, U.S. troops were beginning to be pulled out. His Third Marine Division was relocating to Okinawa, to be replaced by an Army unit. But Murphy received orders to remain and join Special Forces with a recon unit, but the orders were rescinded and off he went to Okinawa with his fellow 'Devil Dogs.' Murphy said the nine-day trip was great and the Navy treated them well, "like returning heroes," Murphy said.

At Okinawa they settled in and started a basketball league. Because he had played the sport in high school, he was designated the coach of their team. The team had several former college players and won all their games against other units and advanced to the division championship game, which they lost. But there was a silver

War Stories

lining in that loss for Murphy. Instead of moving on to Japan for the next level of competition, Murphy came back home, right on schedule.

In May 1970, he was sent to Philadelphia as officer-in-charge of unsatisfactory equipment reporting (UER). The unit would get defective equipment, usually from Vietnam, consult manuals and usually fix or re-design the equipment to make it functional. Also, at this time Murphy was given a top secret clearance and made crypto officer. He told me he couldn't talk much about that work other than to say it involved how communications could be sent without the enemy understanding transmissions.

Approximately a year later, Murphy said it was decision time. Should he remain in the Corps or move on. He was offered a regular commission which meant several more years in uniform and was also strongly recruited by his former civilian firm to return to the job. Murphy chose to leave the Corps and moved back to Lansing, Mich.

There, Vicki became a teacher and Murphy went back to his former job. "But something was missing, the Corps," said this Devil Dog. So, he decided to join the USMC Reserves and got with the local unit in the 24th Marines. He spent the first two years as an infantry platoon commander, then a few years as executive officer of the company.

During his first drill he was made casualty officer – the guy who goes to the home of those who have had their Marine killed while on duty. Murphy said his first call was to the family of a fighter pilot. That dead pilot was a former roommate and friend of his. "That was a tough one, but they're all tough ones," Murphy said of the sad, emotional work.

Jeffrey L. Meek

In 1975, Murphy was reassigned as commanding officer of the Marine infantry company in Grand Rapids – the 24th Marines, First Battalion, 'A' Company. He said everyone took the job seriously, wanting to be sure their troops would be ready if called. The training even took troops to the Arctic, Alaska, California's mountains, and the jungles of Panama. They also did amphibious landings on both U.S. coasts.

After three years as commander and now a Major, Murphy was assigned as battalion intelligence officer. Two years later he chose to become company commander, then later made the decision to go with staff work at Reserve Command and Staff College at Quantico. He stayed in that role for three summers, then in 1989 decided to retire, at which time he was a Lt. Colonel.

Murphy continued to work in the financial planning field and retired from it in 2011. That same year they moved to the Village from Dyer, Ind.

Murphy was concerned about the disconnect of the public from those in uniform. "You have a tendency to forget," he said of the sacrifices made. He wants to see veterans thanked, churches praying for them and people providing services for them, things like visiting VA hospitals. "All those things really take a relatively minor amount of time and effort, especially when one remembers that the troops are working 24/7 putting their lives on the line for us so we can enjoy our freedoms," he told me.

Looking back on his USMC service he summed it up simply. "Looking back, I don't think I'd change a thing," Murphy concluded.

War Stories

Gene Rasure served in U.S. Army in Korea and Vietnam

The U.S. Army's 25th Infantry Division has a storied past – Guadalcanal and Luzon in World War II, the defense of Pusan during the Korean War and beginning in 1966, deployment to Vietnam. During the Vietnam War the 25th operated in the Central Highlands and participated in major battles in regions between Vietnam and Cambodia, including Operation Junction City and the Tet Offensive. Overall, this division suffered 34,484 soldiers killed or wounded in action. Gene Rasure was with the 25th Infantry Division in 1970.

He grew up in the Dallas area, graduated high school in 1966, then enrolled at a junior college. He dropped out, got a draft notice, but decided to enlist. Soon he was off to Fort Polk, La., for boot camp in October 1967 during a short cycle of seven weeks training then moving on. Rasure qualified for the Green Berets but did not enter the unit. After finishing boot camp and a two week leave, he got orders to report to Fort Lee in Virginia for small arms repair and supply organization schooling. The small arms training taught him how to disassemble everything from a .45 pistol to 106 recoilless rifles, back then, mounted on the back of jeeps. The M-16, M-79 grenade launcher, machine guns, you name it, Rasure could repair them all.

After another leave, he reported to Fort Lewis in Washington for assignment to Korea with the 45th Transportation Company, arriving in April 1968. "It was a helicopter maintenance unit. I thought I was going to be their small arms man, but they already had a Sergeant in

Jeffrey L. Meek

there that out-ranked me. So, they put me into the technical part of supplying parts and requisitioning parts for helicopter," said Rasure.

He also did two weeks of duty guarding bunkers. Rasure said he was never told what was in them, but they were constantly guarded.

In May 1969, he returned to the States after 13 months in Korea. After a leave, he reported to Fort Bragg, N.C., to train others that were in their basic training period and became an assistant drill instructor. As such, he walked with the troops and filled in for other drill instructors on marches and at rifle training sessions. Rasure also handed out rifles and worked as training NCO keeping records.

Eighteen months later he was ordered to Fort Ord in California followed by a trip to Long Bin in Vietnam, where he based out of Chuchi for small arms repair work there and at other fire bases as needed, sometimes as much as three times a week, getting there by chopper.

One of those brief stops at a base is still remembered vividly by Rasure. "That was the scariest part I ever had in my life," he said of the time at a base where there was just a berm between the enemy and those inside the fire base. Attack by enemy forces was a real possibility there and all he had to defend himself was a .45 pistol, so it was a long sleepless night for him.

Six months later his unit was ordered back to the U.S., but not Rasure. He was assigned. During the waiting period, he got some R & R in Thailand, then put with a different unit where he was made part of a supply outfit handling all sorts of parts for numerous things.

War Stories

In jeeps and other vehicles, he and others would drive to other supply depots for the necessary parts. One day, almost at his destination along Hwy 1, he came upon a Vietnamese bus that made a sudden U-turn. Rasure had two choices – slam into the bus or head for the ditch. He chose the ditch, rolled the jeep, and was injured. "I got nerve damage to my left leg. They eventually medevacked me and took me to Japan. I spent two weeks in a neurology ward in Japan," Rasure remembers. He also had a separated right shoulder.

Doctors there thought the nerve problem was in his back, but that turned out not to be the case. In total, he spent two weeks in a hospital in Vietnam and two weeks in hospital in Japan and was then taken back to the States, ending up at Fort Hood, Texas.

After several tests, it was determined the nerve damage was in his leg, which was still very swollen. After diagnosis, in 1971, he was told the swelling would eventually go down, which it did, "but the nerve damage has remained," said Rasure. He was sent home to Dallas and put on a temporary disabled list. Seven months later he had one more test which determined the damage to be permanent. On July 25, 1972, he was honorably discharged. The leg still bothers him today.

As a civilian, Rasure got into the auto parts industry, then spent 30 years as a food broker, checking on everything the company represented, which was over 400 items. That work also involved new item placement and securing the best positions on store shelves. He retired in 2012. He and Beverly have a daughter Carmen.

Jeffrey L. Meek

Reflecting on his time in service, Rasure said it helped him "understand that there's more ways to do things than just my way. The Army instilled in me a pride of my country I hadn't thought about. It also helped me calm down. It took a while," he said with a laugh, "but it did calm me down. I credit military service for that."

Rasure said when he came home from Vietnam, he didn't wear his uniform, "but I've never been prouder than how things are going now for the service, and I've never felt more welcomed than here in Arkansas. "I truly mean that," he said, and explained that many times he's been thanked for his service.

War Stories

Steve Rittenmeyer served in Vietnam with USMC

The Third Marine Division has a proud history dating back to World War II invasions at places like Guam and Iwo Jima. Later, in March 1965, the division was chosen to land the first combat troops in Vietnam where they were assigned the job of protecting the Da Nang airfield. Steve Rittenmeyer later served with the Third Division in 1966-1967.

Shortly after graduating from high school in Iowa, Rittenmeyer was drafted into the Marine Corps in January 1966. Training at MCRD and Camp Pendleton included learning tactics, strategies and how to handle numerous weapons. Following this he was assigned the job of Armor Crewman which meant he would be put with tanks, amtracs or ontos.

After a 30-day leave, he reported in and was asked one question. Can you swim? The answer was 'yes' so he was put in an amtrac unit. The resulting training took place in the summer of 1966 in Del Mar, Calif. The vehicle was a 36-ton armored amphibious craft designed for ship to shore movement and could also continue on as an infantry support vehicle.

Next, Rittenmeyer was prepped for jungle warfare in Vietnam. In August he flew to Okinawa, then on to Da Nang. "When I walked off the plane the first thing that hit me was the smell. It wasn't particularly pleasing. Smell and fear. I thought I might get shot at any moment," said Rittenmeyer. After checking in, he was put on a truck and taken to a nameless base camp for tanks and amtracs.

Jeffrey L. Meek

Rittenmeyer was now with the First Platoon, 'B' Company, First Amtrac Battalion, Third Marine Division.

Upon arriving he noticed the camp was practically empty. The units stationed there were out on a mission. "I spent my first week basically alone," said Rittenmeyer, who ate, slept, and moved about as he pleased. He met another Marine named Martinez who was there for a court marshal for shooting another Marine. "He was my only friend and he befriended me," Rittenmeyer said of their relationship which grew closer when their camp was hit and overrun.

Both were watching an old Elvis Presley movie when enemy sniper rounds smashed through the movie screen. The men went to their tents and Rittenmeyer fell asleep. Soon he was awakened by Martinez and the sounds of explosions and gunfire. The two ran through the darkness and jumped into a drainage ditch. With chaos all around them Martinez told him to stay put, then left. "I spent the rest of that night sitting in that ditch because I had no orders, didn't know where anything was or where to go," recalls Rittenmeyer.

The next morning, he crawled out and wandered about the camp amongst dead enemy bodies dressed only in a loin cloth. Later he found out Martinez had hooked up with a patrol that went outside the wire to rescue a pinned down Marine patrol. His actions helped him later at his court martial where he received a shorter sentence.

During his 13 months in Nam, Rittenmeyer's unit did long range security patrols for Da Nang air base and provided infantry support and ran supplies. During this time Rittenmeyer had one mission he's not likely to forget.

War Stories

He was driving an amtrac with infantrymen on top along with a second amtrac as they made their way back from a Village where they had picked up some enemy prisoners. As they rumbled down the road toward their camp, Rittenmeyer drove over a mine which exploded and blew the other amtrac crew member out of the vehicle. Rittenmeyer received minor injuries but was okay. "It was a remotely detonated box mine made of materials that were undetectable," he said of the experience. Their amtrac had their track laid out and some armor peeled back but was able to limp the thing back to camp.

Months later, PFC Rittenmeyer and his unit moved to another base where he soon learned they were putting together a battalion landing team – BLT 1/9 (First Battalion/9th Marine Regiment). At Okinawa they prepared, sailed to the Philippines for practice landings, then, in January 1967, made an amphibious landing in the Mekong Delta as part of Operation Deck House Five. "We were told it was the largest amphibious landing since Chosin Reservoir," said Rittenmeyer.

After days of shore bombardment, Rittenmeyer drove his amtrac off the LST at 4 a.m. and headed for the beach with 35 infantrymen on board. They had been told there was the possibility of concertina wire up ahead near the beach. If so, it could foul the tracks of the craft and stop them dead in the water.

Rittenmeyer managed to get across the beach and move inland about 200 yards before the infantrymen were deployed from the vehicle. After this the job was to move supplies where they were needed.

Jeffrey L. Meek

Next the outfit moved north of Fu Bi where they provided security for a fuel dump, then it was off to Cua Viet where Rittenmeyer's job changed. Besides driving an amtrac he would also be called upon as a regular infantryman on an as needed basis doing mechanized infantry patrols on a main line of defense.

The patrols did not encounter many small unit contacts but did come under heavy artillery and mortar fire at times. Many of the unit's vehicles were destroyed.

One big gun in particular was causing a lot of damage and was proving to be difficult to locate. Even a B-52 air strike could not knock the troublesome gun out of commission. Eventually the gun was spotted and taken out by a recon unit.

Rittenmeyer finished his Vietnam service there near Cua Viet and rotated home in October 1967. Because he had signed on for three years of duty back in boot camp, Rittenmeyer's service continued on for another 18 months. First, he was put with an artillery unit for fire direction control training, then in February 1968 ordered back to amtracs until his discharge in February 1969.

In civilian life he became a police officer in Iowa City, then earned degrees in political science and sociology, and then attended law school in Seattle. After graduation he became an assistant professor at Western Illinois University and at the same time opened a law practice until retirement in 2006. He and wife Mary Ann moved to the Village in 2005 and have a son Tyson.

Reflecting on his Marine Corps service Rittenmeyer said our military didn't learn much from their involvement in Vietnam except for not letting the press have such

War Stories

complete access to the battlefield. "The American press brought the reality of (the Vietnam) war to America and put it on television while everybody's having supper. Americans saw war was for what it is, not the John Wayne variety where people get shot and got a little hole and they sort of fold up and issue some profound statement before their eyes close and people shed a few tears. This is war where people get blown apart and horrendous, unspeakable things go on that go on in every war and America didn't like it," said Rittenmeyer.

He concluded by saying the Marine Corps was, at that point in his life, the best thing that could have happened to him. He learned about himself, to be confident and it gave him the courage to go forward in life.

Jeffrey L. Meek

Don Russell served two tours in Vietnam during 20-year Army career

An important aspect of any army is their intelligence branch. In 1885, during President Grover Cleveland's administration, a Military Information Division was formed which, later became Army Intelligence. During World War I the intelligence units took on a more significant role which grew in importance as America fought in other wars. Don Russell worked for U.S. Army Intelligence serving two tours in Vietnam during a distinguished 20-year career.

Russell grew up in the Arlington, Va., area and attended college at what is now Virginia Tech. At the college he was in the ROTC program as well as a program called the Cooperative Engineering Program. Russell hoped it would lead to an engineering degree. After graduation in 1958 he attended ROTC summer camp and later went to work for North American Aviation.

Next, he moved to Aberdeen Proving Ground to attend the Basic Officers Course for the Ordinance Corps. At the same time Russell also worked with rockets and nuclear reactor control rods. After completing the courses Russell got a surprise. The Army chose not to use his expertise, but instead wanted to make him a Motor Maintenance Officer.

Russell said the job didn't appeal to him and asked what his options were. He was told he had only one option – to become a Bomb Disposal Officer. Russell took the job and was sent to Explosive Ordinance Disposal School in Maryland.

Next, he was assigned to a Bomb Disposal Detachment at Raritan Arsenal in New Jersey, later

War Stories

becoming the Commanding Officer of the detachment. The work involved removing igniters stuck in missiles, picking up leftover munitions and their disposal and occasionally responding to a bomb scare in the area and policing the firing range at West Point.

In 1962, his unit was put on alert for service in Germany. In April they deployed because of tensions in Berlin. "We were primarily at Bremerhaven to be in position to assist if nuclear weapons were shipped to Germany," Russell said of the assignment. Most of the duty turned out to be training with dealing with nuclear weapons as well as storing and maintaining the weapons. On a few occasions the unit was required to recover old World War II ordinance in the Bremerhaven area.

Many of Russell's friends in Germany were in the field of intelligence. That interested him so he applied for military intelligence in 1964 and was accepted. In July 1965, Russell was sent home and attended the Army Intelligence School at Fort Holibird, Md. At the school he learned aerial surveillance/photo interpretation and, because of his engineering background, stayed on as an instructor of math classes. During this time things were heating up in Vietnam and the pace of instruction was accelerated. At times, Russell would teach 12 hours per day.

In August 1966, Russell was ordered to Vietnam as an Army Intelligence Officer with photo interpretation. He was assigned to the 525th Intelligence Group, Combined Intelligence Center-Vietnam in Saigon. At the center he worked with the South Vietnamese to develop the intelligence. "We spent a lot of time looking for trails because the biggest concern was infiltration of the North

Jeffrey L. Meek

Vietnamese and the logistical support to the local guerrillas that came down those trails from North Vietnam," Russell said of his duties. A year later he returned to Fort Holibird and rejoined his family there.

Russell then took the Army's counterintelligence course and the career course. In December 1968, he finished the courses and was assigned to the 502nd Intelligence Group, Special Operations Section in the Washington, D.C., area where he remained for 18 months. Russell was not at liberty to discuss the work he did during this time.

In June 1970, he went back to Vietnam, again with the 525th, and became a desk officer. "I was privileged to be selected as one of six desk officers in the all-source intelligence center at MACV (Military Assistance Command-Vietnam) headquarters. We briefed the MACV staff daily and we briefed General (Creighton) Abrams and his staff weekly. I had the Cambodia desk. My responsibility was for what was going on in Cambodia," Russell said.

The desk watched for enemy troop movements in Cambodia and into the third military region and also for logistical movement in support of enemy actions. During this assignment Russell would also be occasionally flown to Phnom Penh to brief the then-U.S. Ambassador.

Russell spoke about dealing with General Abrams who had taken over the MACV command from General William Westmoreland in July 1968: "He was a great guy, very business-like of course, but personable and interested in you. I admired him greatly."

After Russell's tour was completed, he was sent back to the U.S. and then immediately sent to Germany

War Stories

again as Special Security Officer for the VII Corps Headquarters in Stuttgart where he handled highly classified intelligence. Only 10 to 12 people were privy to the materials he handled. Much of it was Russian-related.

Three years later he returned home and was assigned to a program that tested new concepts. Russell's special unit was located at Fort Hood, Texas. Describing the work Russell said their job was "to test new utilization of strategic assets to support tactical forces."

He left that job in September 1979 and became a part of the staff element of the Army Intelligence Staff at the Pentagon that ran the program at Fort Hood. By June 1980, he'd had enough of the Pentagon assignment and decided to retire as a Lieutenant Colonel.

As a civilian he was offered several consulting positions and chose a job as a systems engineer for a consulting firm, where he stayed for 18 years.

Retiring again in 1998, he and his wife Pat moved to Hot Springs Village that same year from Fairfax, Va. The couple has three children: John, Cindy, and Pam.

Looking back at his military career Russell said it was very challenging work that was, at the same time, quite exciting.

Jeffrey L. Meek

John Schrage served in U. S. Air Force, flew tankers

John Schrage attended Robert E. Lee High School in Texas, played football and baseball. He joined the U.S. Air Force ROTC program in 1966 and later earned an economics degree. After graduation he was commissioned and sent for initial pilot training in 1970. A year later he went to Castle AFB, Calif., for KC-135 training. The Boeing KC-135 Stratotanker jet was an aerial refueling aircraft that could cruise at speeds over 500 miles per hour, carry as much as 200,000 pounds of fuel and was powered by four turbofan engines.

At Castle, he learned the plane's systems, practiced refueling and then went to Dyess AFB, Texas, in 1971. At Dyess, Schrage was assigned a crew and the entire squadron was then sent to Kadena AB in Okinawa with the 917th Air Refueling Squadron. The mission? To support U.S. efforts in Vietnam and provide aerial refueling to bombers and fighters.

Practically every other day Schrage flew missions to refuel B-52 bombers in various areas including South Vietnam. Most of the missions were 4.5-hour flights. He also did 12-hour radio relay missions in the Tonkin Gulf. These flights monitored North Vietnamese radio transmissions. The information gleaned from them was then relayed to other units. At 25,000 feet they were just above surface-to-air missile (SAM) range, fairly safe, except for encountering a possible MiG fighter which was a rare thing Schrage said.

War Stories

There was one mission Schrage isn't likely to forget. He was flying into Ton Son Nhut, a major air base and commercial airport on the outskirts of Saigon. There had been some close attacks recently, so caution was at a premium.

The runway was pretty short for the big fuel-heavy KC-135s and this time Schrage had to come in at night with his lights off. On approach he was escorted in with a C-119 gunship on one wing and a C-130 with lights on near the other wing. "I felt like a sitting duck. They were lighting me up," said Schrage of the other planes guiding him in which could possibly draw enemy fire directed at his tanker. The missions to Ton Son Nhut usually carried film from SR-71 Blackbirds meant for analysis before heading to Washington, D.C.

Schrage said the flights were with a four-man crew which included a boom operator lying down 'flying' the boom out the back of the tanker with a 'stick.' Aircraft approached the Stratotanker from behind and hook up as the boom was extended out. Several hook ups were rough, but never caused any damage. 'Breakaways' also took place when he would determine things weren't going well and the two planes would quickly separate.

In 1972, Schrage was part of Operation Linebacker and was the lead tanker of a huge flight of 72 tankers divided into three cells to meet up with 72 B-52s for what was later called 'The Christmas Bombing,' an attempt to get the enemy back to the negotiation table. The hook ups were made at night which made the missions even more dangerous. Keep in mind the pilots did not have GPS, just celestial navigation.

Jeffrey L. Meek

In 1973, Schrage returned to Dyess but was sent back in 1974 and 1975 flying out of Thailand and Okinawa. Even though the war had ended, recon missions and fighter operations still took place and those planes needed fuel.

Schrage said he was also flying, temporarily, out of U-Tapao Air Base during the 1975 'Mayaguez Incident' when the Khmer Rouge fired on and boarded the container ship USS Mayaguez which was to then sail to Poulo Wai.

Informed of the seizure, President Gerald Ford had recon aircraft locate the ship and contacted the Chinese to help communicate with the Khmer Rouge for the ship and crew's release. Eventually, on May 15, a rescue operation began with the task of reclaiming the ship and crew. Schrage's missions, at 15,000 feet, would refuel the attack planes as they carried out their flights. Also, during this time period, he spent two months in Spain on training missions.

In 1975, he was sent to the U.S. as a squadron instructor pilot at Dyess, training others in the KC-135.

In 1976, Schrage was ordered to the 24th Strategic Recon Wing at Eilson AFB, Alaska, to fly RC-135-S aircraft, mostly out of Shemya AFB not far from Russian territory. He was there when Russia was launching ICBMs targeted for Kamchatka Peninsula off the Russian coast to refine their target capabilities.

The U.S. would orbit the target area to take pictures, collect signals and monitor the exercise.

In Alaska, Schrage's job was flying the RCs and working as a receiver instructor pilot and squadron instructor pilot in charge of all training. In November 1978, while in Alaska, Schrage separated from the Air Force.

War Stories

As a civilian, he stayed with flying, first, in Jan. 1979, in Clear Lake City, Texas, with Metro Airlines flying the DHC-6 Twin Otter, Beech 99 and Shorts 330 aircraft. Later in 1997 he became a federal mediator based in D.C.

In 2002, he went with Express Jet Airlines handling labor relations from which he retired in 2012.

In 2008, he and wife Dee moved to Hot Springs Village and have five children: Bill, Teresa, Amy, Jennifer, and Leann.

Looking back on his USAF career Schrage recalled a memory of his time at Shemya. "I have to say each landing at Shemya was a real adventure. It's a relatively short runway for an aircraft (RC-135) like that," he began. "And the weather is horrible. It's in the middle of the Bering Sea. If you've ever watched 'Deadliest Catch' you know what the weather is like. It's not uncommon to have 50 to 75 mile per hour winds with a 35 to 50 knot crosswind component. Then you have snow and ice to go with it all."

Once it took three tries for him to get his plane on the ground. The successful attempt included descending to just eight feet off the runway to even see the runway.

Schrage holds dear the time spent with crew members and is proud and feels privileged to have served his country in the United States Air Force.

Jeffrey L. Meek

Tony Shields received bronze star for actions in Vietnam

The U.S. Army First Cavalry Division was the first Army division deployed to Vietnam on Sept. 11, 1965. At that time the division consisted of nine battalions of air mobile infantry. Other combat elements included air reconnaissance, artillery, and the 11th Aviation Group. Tony Shields served in the First Cavalry as an infantry medic in 1970-1971.

In 1969, at age 17, Shields enlisted in the U.S. Army and reported to Fort Polk, La., for basic training. He next reported to Fort Sam Houston for medic training and truck driver training. "They taught us everything from giving shots to starting IVs and bandaging people. I would call it advanced first aid," Shields said. The trainees were also shown gory films and told this is what they could expect in Vietnam.

Shields then attended jump school at Fort Benning, Ga. During his second week of training, he caught pneumonia and was put in the hospital. This meant he had to begin his jump training all over from the beginning.

While waiting in a holding unit he was ordered to Vietnam, but soon thereafter the orders were changed, and Shields was off to Panama where he became part of the 601st Medical unit. While there he was a medic for the Jungle Expert and Recon schools. Six months later he volunteered for Vietnam and by December 1970 was 'in country.'

He was immediately impressed with the extreme heat, and the smell. Shields was eventually put in the First

War Stories

Cavalry Division. After a one-day class, filling out a will, and being given a Bible, he was taken to a Headquarters in Bien Hoa as a medic.

He was put with 'A' Company, 1st of the 12th Cavalry and flown to a fire base. That same day he was flown out to the jungle to join a platoon and replace a medic who was rotating back. Every night the patrol would set up what Shields called "an automatic ambush." Claymore mines, a fragmentation grenade and white phosphorous would be placed along the back end of their trail.

"We mostly killed animals in them, everything from chicken to a small bobcat and monkeys. And a few gooks," said Shields. He would go out with the man setting up the ambush in case he was injured.

After a few weeks in the bush, Shields was sent back to the base for a break. Later, after eight months of patrols, he was able to go to Hawaii to meet up with his pregnant wife for some rest and relaxation.

Shields then told me about a few of the patrols he accompanied through the jungle of Vietnam. He began by giving me some information about being out in the jungle. Shields said the men didn't shave because they could cut themselves and risk getting an infection. He also said many of the guys didn't wear underwear or socks. When supplies would be brought to them, there would be other clothing items but never socks or underwear, so he asked why. Shields was told they didn't wear them because they just rotted off.

The water the men had to drink tasted terrible, but Shields was able to get around that because his mother sent him lots of Kool-Aid mix.

Jeffrey L. Meek

Along some of the trails the patrol would find venomous snakes tied to tree branches. For this and other reasons, the men didn't use the trails very often. In some areas the leeches were so thick the men would use shoestrings from their boots to tie around their pant legs so the leeches couldn't craw up their legs.

During one patrol the men walked into an L-shaped ambush. "All hell broke loose," said Shields. "Bullets were hitting the bamboo right beside me." RPGs, rockets, and other gunfire poured down on the men, but Shields managed to survive.

Their machine gunner panicked and left his weapon, and the situation was tense. Gunships were called in to support the men fighting on the ground. After three days of sporadic combat, the fighting stopped. It was then they learned they had stumbled on to a battalion-sized enemy complex.

On another patrol the troops were out looking for a downed helicopter. Eventually they located the burned-out chopper, half under water with the other half on dry land. The chopper still had the crew in it. They were all dead. One had been decapitated.

On another occasion Shields was flown in on a combat assault mission. They landed in a field which they soon learned was full of mines and bobby traps. As they were setting up camp for the night there was a huge nearby explosion. One of their squads was attacked and Shields ran off through the area to treat the wounded.

Another mission found Shields with a patrol that came across an enemy hospital complex. Shields said they didn't take prisoners and some men cut off ears and made necklaces with them.

War Stories

One other patrol he experienced came upon an enemy unit bathing in a creek. "I'm not proud of it but we opened up on them," said Shields.

After a total of 10 months in the jungle Shields was replaced and sent back to the fire base. That same day he had to go out and replace a medic who had been killed in action with a different company.

While with this company he contracted malaria and was again taken back to the base. After recovering he was ordered to the battalion aid station where he had sick call duty, gave shots, and did other medic-related work as needed. While there he received the Bronze Star for his actions in the field of battle. Shields remained there until he was sent home in late 1971.

Shields returned to Oakland, Calif., and was then flown to Dallas, Texas, and later Fort Sill, Okla. He was put in charge of the base's emergency room and crash team.

He stayed in the Army until 1978 and later got a nursing license. Shields also worked for seven years as a paramedic and later as a nurse until he retired in 2008.

Looking back on his year in Vietnam, Shields told me he wonders how he ever lived through it all. During his time in Vietnam, he was wounded twice but never had the time to fill out the paperwork because he was always filling out the paperwork on other soldiers' injuries. He also told me he experienced nightmares for some time and that certain smells, like burnt meat, would bother him for some time. Shields said he was put in for a Silver Star but never got it. He said that doesn't bother him, he's just glad he lived through it. Shields was deemed 100 percent disabled, a victim of Agent Orange. He has five children: Sara, Tom, Christina, John, and Marshall.

Jeffrey L. Meek

George Sisterhen served in both the U.S. Army and Navy, becomes aviator

George Sisterhen was born in Hawaii, grew up in Savannah, Ga., and elsewhere. In 1967, he enlisted in the U.S. Army "on a whim," he said. "It seemed like a big adventure." He first reported to Columbus, Ga., for boot camp, then on to Ft. Dix, N.J., for advanced infantry training.

While there, he took several tests and was offered West Point Prep School or Officer Candidate School (OCS). He chose OCS and reported to Fort Benning, Ga. For him, Sisterhen said, the experience was a lot of fun. "We got to shoot every weapon in the Army inventory, drive tanks, had airplane and helicopter rides which would lead me to the next step. It was exciting," he explained.

One day during an extraction, choppers flew in and the men hopped aboard. The winds, the smells, all of it struck him. He called it an awakening. It dawned on him that flying would be really cool, so later he approached his Commander and told him he'd like to take flight training. He applied and was accepted, then send to Fort Gordon, then Fort Stewart, Ga., for training in fixed wing aircraft.

Four months later he took advanced training at Fort Rucker. After receiving his wings, he assumed he'd be sent to Vietnam, but that was not the case for Sisterhen. Instead, in March 1970, he got orders to report to Ouijongbu, Korea, for service with 8th Army flying U6 DeHavilland Beaver aircraft. Usually this meant flying bigshots and other personnel all over the area, sometimes including near the DMZ, where he had to be very careful on his course.

War Stories

After one year in Korea and some upgrade training in a U-21 at Rucker, he was ordered to Vietnam. He was assigned to Command Aircraft Company in Long Thon near Saigon. "We flew all over southeast Asia. I learned a lot that year," said Sisterhen. In March 1972, due to reduction in force (RIF), he was discharged as a Captain.

Sisterhen attended Louisiana Tech University on the GI Bill for a degree in aviation. At the school Colonel Miller took him under his wing. Soon he had a job flying and met his wife while there.

One day in the student union he saw a Navy recruiter and learned that the Navy needed pilots. "So I went back in the military, this time with the Navy and started all over again (in November 1974)," said Sisterhen.

With his wife he went to Pensacola, Fla., for flight training. "I had more (flight) hours than a lot of the trainers," said Sisterhen with a smile. After another trip through OCS, he flew T-41s to begin with, then went to Texas to fly T-2s and A-4s. Later he was assigned to S-3s, a twin engine anti-submarine warfare plane, flying mostly out of Jacksonville, Fla. He also flew off carriers like the USS Forrestal and Independence during cruises in the Mediterranean. In all, Sisterhen did over 750 carrier landings during his career, over 250 of them at night. About carrier landings he said they were fun during the day. Night landings were a different story. "Nighttime, nobody volunteers. You do it to maintain your qualifications but it's a lot more stressful. Things get tense, but it's doable," he said.

Describing a night landing, Sisterhen said you pay close attention to the 'meatball,' which tells you about elevation. "It will take you to touchdown around third wire.

Jeffrey L. Meek

As soon as you touchdown you firewall it, full throttle (in case the pilot misses the wires they can get back up in the air)," Sisterhen said. He added that everyone has had that happen, the missing of the wires which he said is called 'Bulter.' "I'm not sure where that came from," he said of the word Bulter. Hooking the wire slows the plane from about 130 knots to zero in 40 feet, he told me. "It's over pretty quick."

On July 31, 1990, Sisterhen retired as a Commander with 20 years of active duty Navy service. His last deployment was with a troubled squadron where he became Executive Officer. Rather than put in another three-year tour, he decided to leave the military.

As a civilian, Sisterhen flew for Continental Airlines and Federal Express, flying Boeing 727s, DC-10s and A-300s. He retired in December 2010, and in October 2013, moved to Hot Springs Village from Collierville, Tenn. He and wife Patricia have two children, Laura, and Lesley.

Looking back at his many years in uniform he said being in the military affected everything in his life going forward. "It gave me everything; being able to send my children to school, to provide for my family. It changed the course of my life."

War Stories

Bruce Stair served on carrier during Vietnam War

The USS Oriskany (CVA-34) was named after the August 1777 Revolutionary War battle in New York. The 30,800-ton ship was 911 feet long, carried a crew of 2,600 and earned five battle stars for her service during the Vietnam War. One of those on board during that time was Bruce Stair who served with Air Wing 19, Attack Squadron 215.

Stair grew up in Alaska, graduated high school and knew he'd soon be drafted, so he decided to join the U.S. Navy. He did so with nine other guys from Anchorage, then returned home for a few months awaiting the call to duty.

On Dec. 28, 1967, he reported to boot camp in San Diego where he also took several tests. Stair wanted into aviation. "I did not want to be on a ship," he recalls. In Florida he attended an 'A School' to become an aviation electrician, taking classes five days a week.

Next, he was sent to Lemoore Naval Air Station in California, known as 'Corsair College' and put with the VA-122 Squadron, a new A-7 Corsair jet bomber location. By this time Stair had attended other schools learning about things like navigation and fuel. For the next two years he worked there and trained others in aviation maintenance skills.

One morning when coming off duty he was told to check out a machine that gets hooked up to a jet to get it started. Stair said no, he wouldn't do it. "I was leaving, and I told him I wouldn't check it out because I would be responsible, but then a day crew would have it. So, I walked

Jeffrey L. Meek

off my shift, went to my barracks and came back that night. When I showed up my chief said 'you no longer work here. You got transferred down to the 'crud crew." This crew cleaned airplanes.

So, Stair reported to the 'crud crew' station and was told no, he wasn't on the roster. Stair went back to his chief and was told he was to now report to a prop crew. "Sure enough, that's where I had been assigned," said Stair. These men took care of 10 T-28 trainer and C1A aircraft. "We were called the Corsair Dropouts and we even had our own patch," he said with a smile. As an electrician he took care of batteries and a simple navigation system.

Sometimes he would get to fly the backseat in the aircraft as pilots did practice bombing flights. In the back he would see what damage was done and tell the pilot.

In November 1970, Stair got new orders. He was headed for sea duty with VA-215, the 'Barn Owls' Squadron which did maintenance on A-7s at Lemoore. Then he was ordered to the USS Oriskany and put with a line crew on the dangerous and busy flight deck during flight operations. "That was scary," said Stair of the almost chaotic flight deck.

The ship made a stop in Hawaii where it picked up its nuclear weapons. Stair, after some training, was part of the loading team.

Next, the ship sailed on to Subic Bay in the Philippines, picked up supplies and went on to the Gulf of Tonkin for duty. Stair was put on the night shift working 7 p.m. to 7 a.m. each day doing maintenance work on 14 planes, six to eight of which would usually need attention.

Stair said at night the flight deck was quiet and most planes were chained down. Also, at night the ship would blow its smokestacks to clean out the soot which made for

War Stories

some pretty dirty air to breathe at times. If all their work was done the men got to go below deck to see a movie.

The Oriskany patrolled for eight months, but every 35 days went offline for liberty in either Japan or the Philippines. In Japan, he and two others found themselves in the middle of a riot. They ducked into a theater, watched a movie, then came out to find the area calm, so they safely went on their way. Stair also got liberty in Hong Kong which he enjoyed and later officially became a 'Shellback' after the ship crossed the equator.

In 1971, Stair began his last tour of line duty. During his time on the ship they did lose some pilots that were shot down. One of them was John McCain who was downed on Oct. 26, 1967.

Stair also remembers a time when a plane was catapulted off the ship, turned on its side, went down and the pilot killed. The second time it happened the catapult was shut down for many days. The problem turned out to be bad struts on the aircraft.

Coming home for Petty Officer Third Class Stair took almost three weeks. "When I walked off the ship I was out of the Navy," said Stair who was discharged there in Alameda, Calif. He was asked to stay in the Navy, declined, and served two years in the Reserves

As a civilian he first worked for the City of Hanford, Calif., in a program that hired veterans. Then later he got into the swimming pool business. He retired in 2003 and moved with wife Sandy to the Village in 2004 from Visalia, Calif. They have one child, Deanne.

Reflecting on his military service, Stair said today the country seems so proud of the military, "which is fantastic,

Jeffrey L. Meek

but when I was in the military in the Vietnam War we were looked down upon, never honored in any way, of any kind. I was not proud of being in the Navy because everybody looked down at you. I'm glad that attitude has changed."

War Stories

Tom Vaughn served in Vietnam, is wounded twice

The U.S. Army's Americal Division was formed during World War II. The name comes from a phrase in New Caledonia, an island in the Pacific theater of war.

Reactivated in September 1967, the Americal Division, officially a part of the 23rd Infantry Division, suffered 17,565 casualties during the Vietnam War and received the Cross of Gallantry with Palm from the South Vietnamese government in recognition of their combat service.

In 1970, Tom Vaughn served with the Americal Division in Vietnam as a rifleman with the 11th Light Infantry Brigade. Twice during his service, Vaughn was wounded, first in the hand and later in the leg. As he told me his story in graphic detail, I was actually sweating near the end of the interview. It's a story I'll never forget.

Vaughn remembers the Dec. 1, 1969, lottery drawing at Selective Service Headquarters in Washington, D.C. He didn't have to wait long for his birth date to be called. His lottery number was 72. Shortly thereafter he received his draft notice, reported, and was sworn into the United States Marine Corps – briefly. At the last minute, he and four other men were taken away and sworn into the Army instead. After finishing basic and advanced infantry training, Vaughn took a Leadership Preparation Course (LPC) on how to lead others. After a 30-day leave, he was off to Vietnam and landed in Long Binh, a logistical complex on the outskirts of Bien Hoa.

He shared what happened after the landing. "The door (of the airplane) opens, and a sergeant jumps on the

Jeffrey L. Meek

plane and said, 'Welcome to the Republic of Vietnam. In case of rocket attack deplane immediately and run to the shelter to the right'," said Vaughn. Vaughn also remembers the extreme heat and a terrible odor.

A few days later Vaughn was assigned to the Americal Division, Bravo Company. His first day of combat was as a part of a patrol through an area the men called 'sniper alley.' The unit had been there before and each time they went, someone got shot.

As Vaughn continued along the trail, AK-47 rounds started coming in. Because everything alongside the trail was booby-trapped, the men had to stay on the trail.

Vaughn was totally exposed near the front of the firefight. He fired his M-16 and grenades from the attached grenade launcher. Doing so drew enemy fire even closer to his position. "I knew I was in big trouble," said Vaughn.

As he got up to move an enemy bullet struck his weapon and ricocheted into his left hand. "There was jacketing sticking out of my knuckles," he remembered. The squad leader pulled the unit back and Vaughn noticed he was bleeding profusely.

Vaughn was then flown to the rear and treated. "It was great. I got to sleep on a cot with a blanket, listen to rock and roll and watch a movie," said Vaughn. That movie was 'Easy Rider.' The next day he was sent back to the line.

Vaughn recalled another time when U.S. forces had shelled a bunker area near 'sniper alley' that also contained an underground aid station and hospital. The area had been pulverized by U.S. artillery.

Vaughn and two others were told to crawl down into the facility and drag out any bodies that may be inside. "It

War Stories

was like the inside of a slaughterhouse. It had the smell of copper and feces," said Vaughn. There were many dismembered bodies. Vaughn and the others had to tie ropes to the dead so others could drag them out. The work took 90 minutes.

Sometime later Vaughn's unit was located in a compound of their own. Intelligence had been received that said the area was going to be hit by a large enemy force that evening.

Near sunset, while preparing for the attack, he was setting up an M-60 machine gun on top of a bunker when suddenly there was a huge explosion. "When I came too, I couldn't move and I couldn't hear," said Vaughn. He then realized he was now lying out in front of the bunker amid concertina wire.

Soon a company medic and others untangled Vaughn and carried him inside the bunker. Vaughn knew he was badly injured. His left wrist, legs and stomach had been burned. His boots had been blown off his feet and he was in great pain. He was given morphine and flown to the rear where for three days doctors worked to stabilize his condition. After a couple of other stops, Vaughn was flown to a burn hospital in Japan. The treatment there would center on the debridement of his wounds.

Doing so meant that on a daily basis he would be put into a stainless-steel tub filled with warm water and disinfectant. Then a nurse would come in and with a razor, begin to shave every open wound on his body. She would then scrub the wounds with a small towel to remove the dead and dying tissue. "I thought being burned was bad. Being healed was far worse," said Vaughn.

Jeffrey L. Meek

Screams of pain throughout the ward filled the air each day as Vaughn and many others fought for their lives. "I saw more men die in that burn unit than I did as a rifleman," Vaughn said.

Eventually Vaughn was sent back to the U.S. and spent a month recovering at Ford Ord, Calif. Later he worked in a printing office before discharge.

I asked this Purple Heart warrior if talking about all this was difficult. Vaughn said, "It's not easy, but I know this is important. Young people today have no idea what that war was like."

How about lessons learned from America's involvement in Vietnam? "We learned a great deal about warfare, but not about guerilla warfare. We learned that defending a corrupt government is simply not worth it. We did not learn that if you enter into something you have to enter it large scale. You can't piecemeal your armies. We should have been more aggressive with North Vietnam."

Vaughn then made another observation: "We learned the way to be defeated is to have the public made to believe the war is wrong," concluded Vaughn.

He went on to a career in corrections, becoming warden at Chuckawalla Valley State Prison in California where he retired in 1994. Before that he had been at an institution for women where Charles Manson follower Leslie Van Houten served as his personal clerk.

He and wife Cynthia moved to Hot Springs Village in 1995 and have four children: Nicole, Allison, Cindy and Amy.

War Stories

Ron Wilging served in the U.S. Army for 17 years

Ron Wilging grew up in Milwaukee, Wisc., graduated from Washington High School, then took some classes at Milwaukee Area Technical College. On March 27, 1970, he was drafted by the U.S. Army. "I got a letter that said greetings," said Wilging. He was working nights at Faulk Corporation at the time.

For training he first went to Fort Campbell, Ky. A school there had piqued his interest. The schooling was on computers, NRC500s. He saw an opportunity and grabbed it, is how Wilging put it to me. Doing so made him extend his military commitment another full year.

Wilging was sent to Fort Lee, Va., where he learned about accounting, supply and stock control. Then into mechanized aspects of those three areas. Once completed, Wilging was chosen as an Honor Graduate and later a Distinguished Graduate. "That qualified me to go to Atlanta Army Depot (in Forest Park, Ga.) for additional 90 to 120 days (of training) where I learned depot operations," Wilging said. In August 1970, he was put with the Director of Maintenance in the 'high priority repair' parts division. There at the depot he handled priority parts and orders for items such as helicopters and motor vehicles.

Months later Wilging was told to report to Oakland for transfer to Vietnam. He arrived in January 1971 and was assigned to the 228th Supply and Service Company in Tay Nink. But a 45-day delay came about during which time he was with the 25th Infantry Division, but eventually he joined the 228th in Binh Thuy. It was there one night that he would be wounded, and his life would change.

Jeffrey L. Meek

At Binh Thuy, he was assigned to the Two, Four and Seven yard, "which was major end items (like vehicles for example)." Wiling's job was to check quantity and be sure the requests for equipment were authorized. Then he would forward that information to the depot for processing.

At the base, Wilging said, there were many night attacks, but nothing all that dangerous. But one night in April 1972 an attack hit the base's ammunition dump. Wilging was part of a reaction force near the ammo dump.

The men moved into a defensive position in case of an attack. When the dump continued to explode a fellow soldier was severely hit in the leg by flying shrapnel. Wilging crawled over to him and dragged him over to a building for better cover, then elevated his leg and crawled on top of him to keep him warm.

As help was on the way, Wilging was also hit. It shattered his ankle and cut into the upper part of his leg.

His buddy was hauled off by a forklift of all things, then Wilging was taken out. He was given morphine and taken by helicopter for treatment at Can Tho Army Hospital where he came to and awaited surgery, as was his buddy.

After surgery a doctor told him he was lucky and might be able to rejoin his unit at some point. After six weeks of recovery, he was in fact sent back to his unit, now there in Can Tho. In April 1972, Wilging received the Purple Heart and Bronze Star for Valor. "They pinned it on my pillow," said Wilging of receiving the Purple Heart.

He was in Vietnam a total of 16 months, then returned home and assigned to Fort Leavenworth, Kan., in June 1972. "My Dad asked me 'are you in or at

War Stories

Leavenworth'," Wilging said with a smile. Soon he was assigned to Munson Army Hospital, placed with a medical equipment detachment. In the unit he ordered supplies and equipment for the depot, selected the typewriters for them, then wrote the specifications for what was wanted.

In March 1973, Wilging ended his term of service, went home, and was assigned to a Reserve unit, the 5091st U.S. Army Reception Station in Milwaukee. There he was made an E-5 and Company Supply Sergeant. He quickly rose to E-6 and E-7 and in December 1977 was selected 84th Training Division Soldier of the Year. Each year each command would submit a candidate who was tested on operations. "They didn't think I could win because I wasn't a Drill Instructor. They called me a bean counter. I was very surprised," Wilging said of the honor bestowed on him.

At about this point he got involved with mobilization planning for the Army, especially in terms of what would be required. In 1980, he participated in an exercise at Fort Hood, Texas. "We learned a lot about identifying problems. It was very interesting," Wilging said of the operation. He remained on this assignment until September 1983, but later that same month returned to active duty, assigned to the Third Battalion, 351st Regiment, 84th Division in Milwaukee. "They made me an offer I couldn't refuse," said Wilging.

In this job he was a logistical advisor and worked with other supply Sergeants, working on inventory control. He stayed there until January 1987. His exit from the Army was unlike any other I can remember during the past 15 years of doing veteran interviews.

Jeffrey L. Meek

In early 1984 he had gotten really sick, was in ICU and comatose. Wilging said, "The Army took a dim view of that." He was sent to Fort Sheridan, then ordered to take a physical, and meet with a medical board in 1985. Some on the board decided he was unfit for duty, others disagreed. Wilging appealed his case and was later told in a letter from a high-ranking officer that he was unfit for duty. But Wilging pushed back.

In 1986, he received a letter from the Surgeon General of the Army, basically saying he had grown tired of the whole matter. Wilging told me the Surgeon General said he could come to work for him in St. Louis, but as a civilian and that he'd be proud to have him. He was also told he could retire at 40 percent of his base pay for life and that his family would be taken care of.

Wilging added that he was told if he did not want to do that, he would be ordered to Fort Sheridan for another physical and found 10 percent disabled and out of the Army. So Wilging agreed to leave. "I would not have gone under my own volition. I'd have stayed there," he said.

As a civilian, Wilging worked at the VA and retired in 2004. He moved to Hot Springs Village that same year from Milwaukee. He and his wife Marie have two children: Michelle and Chad.

Reflecting on his nearly two decades in uniform, Wilging said the real story for him started at the VA where he could help others, teach others, and explain to veterans what they themselves could do. "A lot of these guys just needed training and understanding the skills they possessed," Wilging said. During this time Wilging also hired several others to do the job. "We helped soldiers get their reward," he noted.

War Stories

Chapter IV: Cold War Veterans

Ed Brick served on the submarine USS Razorback

The submarine USS Razorback first put to sea on Jan. 27, 1944. She went to Pearl Harbor and became a part of the U.S. war effort in the Pacific. She saw duty near Luzon in the Philippines, Midway Island and many other sites. She was also in Tokyo Harbor when the Japanese signed the surrender documents ending World War II. In 1970, the sub was transferred to the Turkish Navy, but later made her way home where she currently sits as a floating museum in the Arkansas River. Ed Brick served aboard the submarine during his U.S. Navy tour of 1954 to 1958.

Realizing he wasn't likely to go to college, Brick enlisted in the U.S. Navy shortly after graduating from high school. Making it official on Aug. 1, 1954, Brick was sent to Great Lakes Naval Station near Chicago. After basic training, Brick was ordered to San Diego, Calif., to attend electrician school. Here he learned all about AC and DC current, control panels and other electricity-related skills.

Upon completion of the training, Brick requested submarine school. His request was granted, and he was sent to New London, Conn., to learn his chosen craft. He talked about becoming a submariner. "You couldn't wear glasses and if you were claustrophobic you'd never be put on a submarine," Brick said. He also said the showers were so small a man dares not drop anything because he couldn't bend over far enough to pick it up.

The air quality was another thing submarine veterans are not likely to forget. Smelly stale air was not

Jeffrey L. Meek

uncommon. "After you'd been there awhile you don't notice it," smiled Brick. He went on to say when men would leave the sub and later return, the foul air was very evident. "It stunk like fuel oil." One good thing about being in a sub was the food. Brick said they ate plenty of lobster, steak and even ice cream. He learned to handle torpedoes, how to make submarine dive and other skills. Each man had to know how to do the other's job in case of emergency situations. He was then sent back to San Diego and assigned to the USS Razorback as an electrician.

At that time the submarine was being used as a target boat. Later the sub was sent to Hunters Point and put in dry dock. During this time Brick completed his training and testing and became a qualified electrician.

Brick and the Razorback once made a trip to the Far East to be a part of war games with the 7th Fleet. "Every time you popped a periscope you'd see a destroyer on your butt," Brick said.

As needed, the Razorback would typically run 65 feet below the surface when charging their batteries. The Navy called it snorkeling. This usually took approximately six hours.

The sub would also dive to 'test depth,' 400 feet down. Brick said the sub would be crushed at 600 feet deep. The crew once spent 56 consecutive days under water. Following the games, they sailed to Japan where they stayed for four days. If one didn't have work to do, you could take liberty and explore the country.

Brick also experienced a hurricane during his service while the sub was snorkeling. The storm grew stronger, so the sub followed proper procedure and surfaced to ride things out. The sub dragged along a buoy that could be

War Stories

released if they sunk, but the storm was so violent it tore the buoy loose.

On another occasion Brick was in the forward torpedo room when water started coming in from above. This was not a good sign. He was told to get out of the room while others went to work on the problem.

Then, as fast as possible, the sub surfaced. Brick was now in the officer's mess room. As the sub quickly reached the surface Brick remembered all the dishes sliding off the table and crashing to the floor.

The men found the problem. The packing, or insulation, had come loose from what is called the 'pit sword.' The pit sword is a blade that extends into the water beneath the sub's hull. Its purpose is to measure the vessel's speed. The issue was soon corrected and to give the crew confidence in the sub's seaworthiness, the captain took the ship down to 400 feet to show that everything was okay.

Brick said the Razorback had 252 batteries to power the vessel. Once a week these batteries had to be checked to be sure the cells had the proper amount of water in them. That job fell to the electricians. "You'd be sweating and there would be sparks flying and it would give you a pretty good shock," Brick recalled. The resulting battery acid would ruin whatever pants he wore while doing the work.

After a stop in Hawaii, Brick returned to San Diego for Christmas 1957. Off the U.S. coast they would again be involved in maneuvers. Brick said they once sank an old LST during an exercise.

Jeffrey L. Meek

He continued his duties until his discharge in July 1958 and drove straight through from San Diego to his home in Minnesota.

In civilian life, Brick spent 31 years with Texaco Inc., mostly in sales. He retired in 1994 and moved to Hot Springs Village in 1996. He and his wife Phyllis have three children: John, Kelly, and Tom. And yes, they have toured Dad's sub, the USS Razorback.

War Stories

Charlie Brown served with United States Coast Guard

The U.S. Coast Guard serves as a maritime, military, and multi-service branch of our Armed Forces. It operates under the auspices of U.S. Homeland Security or can be transferred to the Department of the Navy during times of war. It was created by Congress in 1790 to collect custom duties at seaports and has remained a vital part of our nation's defense units. Serving in the USCG from 1986 to 1991 was Charlie Brown.

He was born in Ft. Smith, Ark., but moved around a lot, ending up in Eunice, N.M., because of his father's occupation. It was there he graduated high school, and it was then that he got involved with being in rodeo events both as a bull rider and a rodeo clown.

In late 1986, Brown was working at a petroleum plant in New Mexico and was not enjoying the associated smells of the place. It got him to give thought of what he really wanted to do with himself. He felt he had spent so much time in the desert, exploring ocean possibilities might be in order, so he enlisted in the Coast Guard that November.

His boot camp training was at Camp May, N.J. He found it shocking, regimented, but good for him as he learned protocol, seamanship, knot tying and other essentials. Eight weeks later he received an assignment in Kodiak, Alaska, to work at a communications station. His duties included maintenance, support and standing watch to monitor communications equipment for distress signals that came in.

Jeffrey L. Meek

Typically, Brown's day began at 5 a.m. after which he and the others would have breakfast, clean the barracks, and take a bus to a transmitter site about nine miles away, located near the Buskin River.

There he was lead seaman keeping an eye on all matters involving the men's duties. As he awaited further schooling, he continued working there monitoring all electronics. Sometimes that meant receiving distress signals which resulted in deploying a search and rescue helicopter or vessel to save those in trouble.

Eighteen months later, in July 1988, Brown went to Air Station Humboldt Bay, McKinleyville, Calif., to work in the support center and to prepare for aviation 'A' school. He had gotten some search and rescue mission experience back in Alaska and thus wanted to get more into the aviation aspect of the job. He enjoyed the experience of going out and helping others in need. As Brown said, as others flee from bad weather, a 'coastie' does the opposite, plunging headlong into the associated danger. Brown said the men learned to live their motto: "You have to go out, but you don't have to come back." He also remembers a sign that said, "So others may live," a reminder that their job was to serve others in need.

In January 1989, he received orders to report to aviation technical school in Elizabeth City, N.C., where he trained in aircraft engine maintenance, five days a week, from C-130s to Dauphine helicopters. Six months later he reported to Air Station New Orleans, Belle Chasse, La. There he worked on the HH65A Dauphine chopper and at the same time qualified as part of a flight crew for law enforcement and search and rescue missions.

War Stories

The training was intense and involved learning hoist operation, hand signals and pilot communication. Brown loved the job. "It was the best job I ever had. Every day was exciting," he said, and added that every day was an opportunity to go out and help others.

The USCG was and is instrumental in our nation's war on drugs. Brown said their missions seized many tons of illegal drugs headed for the U.S. He went on several of these missions and recalled one for me when he was on deployment to South Florida for patrol duty.

They came upon a vessel that was suspect. From the chopper they would direct Coast Guard vessels to the scene, then provide support from above. With intelligence in hand, they would confirm the vessel's registration numbers, call that information into the center, and watch as the surface vessel would board the suspected boat.

Brown served 18 months in New Orleans and was approached to re-enlist, but for family reasons he declined.

As we continued the interview Brown spoke about the Dauphine helicopter, with a crew of three, and said they had hauled aboard many a frightened people who had just survived a scary time at sea that may have taken place many miles offshore and in 25-foot seas.

Brown was the crewman who would lower the basket or a swimmer into the water to rescue panicked survivors. He said there were times when the people in distress would attach the chopper's cable to their vessel, "just so you don't go away," said Brown.

Just before discharge, on his final search and rescue mission, he had an experience he'll never forget. It was the only time he had a victim die. Two people were in a small

Jeffrey L. Meek

fishing boat on Lake Pontchartrain that had capsized and spilled the elderly gentlemen into the water. "When we arrived on scene, I put the swimmer down in the water because both seemed to be unconscious away from the boat that had broken up in six-or-seven-foot seas. The rescue swimmer began doing CPR on one of the victims in the water. At that time a Coast Guard patrol boat arrived and began to help one of the victims who was unconscious. The boat determined that gentleman was already deceased. The rescue swimmer readied the other victim, and I got him in the cabin and also administered breathes and compressions, and picked the swimmer back up, and we went enroute to a local hospital where we landed on top of the hospital to drop off the victim," said Brown. A short time later he learned the man had died. Watching Brown tell of the incident I could tell it was still quite real to him after all these years.

In July 1991, he was discharged. As a civilian he eventually went to work in the U.S. Justice Department, Federal Bureau of Prisons, retiring in July 2015. He and wife Michelle have four children: Wesley, Larissa, Mattie, and Megan.

Reflecting on his days with the USCG, Brown said being in the service affected him in two ways. First, the pride he felt from serving his country and secondly, it got him to realize what he wanted to do in the future. "It made me realize that a regular day to day job that didn't have to deal with a lot of intensity and stress probably wasn't going to be for me. I wanted to stay in something that was going to deal with emergency and stressful situations."

War Stories

Tom Dalgity served in Germany during Berlin Wall crisis

The 1962 Cuban Missile Crisis and the Soviet – U.S. faceoff in Berlin over the Berlin Wall in the summer of 1961 are the two most significant confrontations the United States and Russia have ever faced.

On the night of Aug. 12-13, 1961, barbed wire began to be put in place along the border of East and West Berlin to halt the flow of East Germans to the west. Some called it the 'brain drain' as many intellectuals were leaving the east for safety and freedom in the west.

Later. U.S. and Soviet tanks stood face-to-face awaiting each other's next move. Streets began to be torn up, fences erected, and markings placed on the streets all signifying a big change was taking place. In time, a concrete wall would be erected, guard towers manned and for 28 years this barrier would stand as a symbol of good versus evil in Berlin, Germany.

Finally, on Nov. 9, 1989, word came that the wall would be coming down. Tom Dalgity served in the U.S. Army from 1960 to 1966 and was there in Berlin when those tanks squared off.

Dalgity was born in Alabama, but grew up in Oakland, Calif. Times were tough for the family, so he thought it best to join the military and did so in May 1960. Soon he was in boot camp at Ford Ord where, in eight weeks' time, he was considered a rifleman.

After basic training he was ordered to Fort Leonard Wood, Mo., and trained as a combat engineer learning construction and demolition skills. "We'd build a bridge and then blow it up," Daligity said of the work. The men would even cut the logs to build the 40-to-60-foot-long bridges.

They also learned to construct steel 'bailey bridges' which were portable and prefabricated. Usually put together in 10-foot sections, the bridges were wide enough for a tank. "They were bridges we would carry from point A to point B and put together like a jigsaw puzzle," Dalgity said. For demolition work they used TNT and C-4 explosives.

Upon completion of this training, he was ordered to Germany and arrived by plane in Frankfurt in November 1960. Then he was taken to Hoechst, Germany, and McNair Army Base where he was assigned to the 317th Engineer battalion. Once again, the men constructed bridges where needed, learned how to lay out and destroy fields, and build double-apron fences.

Dalgity said there was still evidence of damage done during World War II in some of the areas he worked, and that for the most part the German people were friendly to the Americans. Unbeknownst to Dalgity and the unit, tensions were rising in Berlin and a crisis was about to begin.

Suddenly, in the middle of the night, the men were put on alert, told to load their gear in trucks and also to load plenty of ammunition. "I wasn't sure what was going on. I thought it was just another drill," said the unsuspecting engineer. The trucks rolled off and along the way more vehicles joined their convoy through the dark, suspense-filled night.

At daylight they piled out of the trucks and were told to fix bayonets and form a perimeter around their vehicles. "That's when we discovered it wasn't a drill. We looked out

War Stories

and there was a line of tanks, theirs, and ours, pointed at each other, face to face, no more than 60 feet apart," said Dalgity of his location within a few blocks of 'Checkpoint Charlie.'

As the day went on, they could hear occasional small arms and machine gun fire. Then near his area, behind an enemy tank, shots rang out and a man came running toward the American lines. He was defecting to the west and was grabbed by two U.S. servicemen.

During the day, Dalgity witnessed lines being painted on the streets, and wire being laid to create a no-mans-land. Dalgity was one of those chosen to patrol a portion of this line. A Russian soldier did the same on the other side.

As both sides patrolled, Dalgity said they would talk to each other as best they could. He learned the Russian soldiers also had no idea what was taking place. They even traded chewing gum.

The following day, tensions had eased so his unit was hauled back to McNair. Dalgity never returned to the Berlin Wall area again.

In 1963, after two years and nine months in Germany, he was sent home, discharged in New Jersey, and traveled back home to California. Eighty-seven days later he re-enlisted in the Army and was ordered to Fort Lewis, Wash. He was promoted and again made an engineer.

On March 27, 1964, a 9.2 magnitude earthquake struck Alaska. Known as the Great Alaskan Earthquake, it also resulted in tsunamis. In all it killed approximately 130 people. The worst area was Anchorage, but the tsunamis reached other areas in Alaska as well as Oregon, California, and Hawaii. Most deaths were caused by the tsunamis.

Engineer Dalgity was sent to Alaska for cleanup and recovery work where he ran a D-9 bulldozer with the 559th Engineer Company, 171st Infantry Brigade. As they cleaned up the debris and mud the men would occasionally come upon a dead body. "It was not a very good time. It was pretty devastating," said Dalgity of the experience.

Later he was again promoted and made a driver for an M-113 personnel carrier. His job was to haul troops, trailers, artillery and to assist infantry units as necessary. His final two weeks of service he trained officers on demolition work.

In 1966, at Fort Lewis, Dalgity was discharged again. In civilian life he worked for the Shell Oil Company until retiring in December 1993. In 2008 he and wife Betty moved to the Village from Houston. Dalgity has one son: Michael.

Looking back on his Army service Dalgity said the military set him on a straight path. "It taught me great discipline and gave me a focus in life."

War Stories

Mike Frantz served 26 years in the U.S. Navy

Mike Frantz grew up in Ohio, was born at home during a blizzard. His father wanted him to take over the family construction business, but Frantz had other ideas. Following his freshman year in high school a teacher got on his case about wasting a full year of school. She wanted him to return after summer vacation and tell her what he was going to do with himself after high school. He did just that, deciding to join the U.S. Navy as an electronics technician.

After graduation in June 1963, he enlisted and was sent to San Diego for basic. In September, after getting over a hand infection and finishing his training he went to Great Lakes in Illinois to attend electronics technician school. There Frantz learned at an accelerated pace about circuits, communication systems, how to do repairs and more.

In October 1964, he was off to Glynco in Georgia to train on air traffic control systems. Six months later he was sent to Naval Air Station (NAS) Oceana in Virginia as a ground control approach (GCA) technician. Frantz worked on radar systems there were in large trailers with nearby generators. Maintenance and aligning of the systems were part of his duties.

In March 1966, Frantz re-enlisted and went to advanced electronics technician school at Treasure Island, Calif. In April 1967, he reported to NAS Miramar, Calif., as a GCA tech, advanced to First Class Petty Officer and witnessed a terrible deadly accident at the airfield on Dec. 22, 1969.

Pilot Lieutent C.M. Riddell was coming in with his F-8J Crusader jet, lost hydraulics, then total power and safely ejected. Instead of dropping like a rock, the jet glided into a hanger and crashed into an F-4 jet. "There was a huge explosion when it hit that F-4 and a fireball came flying out those doors about 15 feet in diameter," said Frantz who was only a quarter of a mile away at the time. Fourteen were killed and 30 more injured in the incident.

Later, Frantz was moved again. This time to NAS Bermuda, again as a GCA tech at Kendley AB. There the USAF was moving out and converting to an NAS. Frantz spent four years there while the conversion took place, was promoted to Chief Petty Officer, and learned USAF systems and upgrades.

The purpose of the changeover was to get Navy planes over the Atlantic Ocean to monitor Russian subs. He didn't know this until approximately 10 years later when he saw a report on it on CBS's '60 Minutes.'

In June 1974, Frantz extended and went back to Glynco as a GCA maintenance instructor and course supervisor. Navy schools were moving to Memphis. In Memphis, he had additional duties involving curriculum development of radar systems and became Senior Training Specialist.

In October 1978, Frantz was assigned to the USS John Paul Jones in San Diego. Most of his time was spent on training in and out of port. He was promoted to Senior Chief Petty Officer and assigned the ship's '3-M' coordinator – maintenance, material and management – which meant providing maintenance on everything on the ship. "It was tons of paperwork which I really dreaded," said Frantz. "The ship was scored on the proficiency of reports." So, Frantz

War Stories

supervised all that important paperwork and documentation.

During his time on the JPJ they were in the Coral Sea when they were told to get to Pearl Harbor for fuel and supplies. Then came an order that they would be going to Iran. They were to station themselves off the coast because of a hostage situation. On the way, near Guam, they ran into a typhoon. For two days they suffered through the storm, then pulled into Guam. The ship had pitched so violently Frantz said one could see footprints on the bulkhead.

Next, they sailed to the Philippines for five days of repairs. Then their orders changed. There had been an assassination attempt on the president of South Korea so off they went, spending five days sitting of the country's coast, then returned to the Philippines for supplies.

Next, they headed for Iran. The JPJ spent months off the coast and a few times had scud missiles fired at them. When that would happen, the men got to the battle stations in just 45 seconds.

Finally, the ship headed back toward the U.S., but on the way had to do '3-M' inspections at sea with other ships. It was three weeks of intensive work, but eventually they arrived in Long Beach, Calif., where they underwent a major overhaul.

In May 1982, Frantz went to Newport, R.I., to the Senior Enlisted School for Senior Chiefs and Master Chiefs. It was an OCS-like school. Three months later he went to Pearl Harbor/Naval Communications-Eastern Pacific as Department Leading Chief where he was in charge of maintaining electronics equipment on the island of Oahu.

Jeffrey L. Meek

Some of what he did there is still classified so we couldn't talk about duties.

Three years later he was assigned to the USS Halsey, serving as Combat Systems Leading Chief, an assignment he called his best. Frantz's job was administrative, coordinating divisions, checking reports and taking care of problems that arose. Due to another person's illness, Frantz took on additional duties as Command Master Chief and Small Arms Gunnery Officer. They eventual deployed to the Persian Gulf, while his wife served the home front as ship's Ombudsman.

Eighteen-hour days were not uncommon during the cruise. The Halsey's main duty was to escort ships hauling oil. Frantz was also in charge of three boarding parties that had been trained back in San Diego.

Near the end of the deployment, they escorted the USS Enterprise through the Suez Canal. As they cleared the canal, they got world the USS Cole had been attacked. Up in Sicily, they took on fuel, made a five day stop in Spain and headed home.

Frantz talked about a maneuver ships made called 'Buckey Ball.' Outside their port in California, Russian ships would station themselves to monitor U.S. ship movements. An Admiral had an idea to have all the ships leave port at the same time for their pre-deployment exercises. Then at a designated time each ship would change direction. "We left (San Diego) at sunset and you could see the (Russian) trawler out there monitoring. Then the ships just exploded in all directions, and he had to figure out who he was going to follow," Frantz explained.

War Stories

Communications between ships ceased and the vessels would regroup at midnight to carry out their exercises. Doing all that reconnecting during radio silence was a bit scary, but Frantz mentioned no problems.

Later, the Admiral of his group invited all ship captains, wives, and ombudsmen aboard the USS Kitty Hawk to watch the ship in action. Frantz's wife and others gathered on the ship for lunch and observed as flights came in and out. It was an interesting, fun experience for all.

On June 5, 1989, 26 years to the day, Frantz was 'piped over the side,' a special retirement ceremony. Wife Chris was also honored for her work with the ship's crew.

On June 30, Frantz transferred from active duty to the Fleet Reserve. On July 1, 1993, he retired.

As a civilian Frantz worked on SDA Security Systems. They moved to Hot Springs Village in October 2004 from Chula Vista, Calif. The couple had two beautiful daughters, Lisa Ann, and Teresa Lynn, who have since died.

Jeffrey L. Meek

Pat Hagen served 20 years in U.S. Air Force

Hot Springs Village resident Pat Hagen grew up in Minneapolis, but finished his high school days in Houston, Texas. After attending the University of Houston for a time he decided to join the Air Force, applied, and was tested for flight training.

During the physical he learned he had an impacted tooth which would need to be taken care of before he could begin. Hagen got the tooth fixed, was then accepted, but learned the pilot cadet program was closed. Instead, he would attend navigation school.

At the school he studied math, shooting angles off stars, discipline and also attended a ground school. He then began flying in a Convair T-29 'Flying Classroom.' "There was a lot of pressure," said Hagen of those early flights as he learned about dead reckoning, drift, and the celestial Coriolis effect. Hagen graduated as a navigator in March 1961.

He was then assigned to the 431st Air Refueling Squadron flying with KB-50 aerial tankers that refueled fighter aircraft as they flew over the Pacific Ocean. Hagen said there were two operators in the plane to let out the hoses, at the end of which was a basket-like device called a drogue.

Later he signed up for the air commando program and was about to begin jump training when he was frozen in place. The Russians had placed offensive nuclear missiles in Cuba which caused the famous October 1962 Cuban Missile Crisis. He was instead ordered to Florida where U.S.

War Stories

fighter aircraft were being recalled from Korea and Japan for possible air assaults on Castro's Cuba.

After the crisis, Hagen was assigned to B-26 bombers saying he learned about bombs, rockets and how to keep down his 'lunch' during steep diving attacks. He was about to go with the plane to Vietnam in February 1964, but on the way the B-26s were grounded. There had been incidents of the wings tearing off upon diving. A month later they were cleared to leave and perform missions keeping the aircraft straight and level. He soon arrived in Bien Hoa where the crew began recon flights.

Later Hagen was put a C-47 Air Commando Squadron and flew as navigator on missions which resupplied Special Forces units, and at times, they would also drop flares at night to illuminate the enemy.

In November 1964, Hagen was sent to Ton Son Hut as part of the C-123 crew that was on duty to fly General William Westmoreland as needed. Hagen said they never once flew the General because he preferred a small Army airplane he could fly himself.

But Hagen did fly someone else that was pretty important – Bob Hope and his band of entertainers. From outpost to outpost, they flew with such celebrities as Hope and his son Tony, Miss World, Anita Bryant, Jill St. John, Jerry Cologna, and others.

When his tour in 'Nam was over he was ordered to Hickam AFB in Hawaii to fly in C-124 cargo planes in support of Pacific operations.

In 1966, Hagen volunteered to return to Vietnam to fly in B-26s, but his assignment was changed. Instead, he would be put with the Air rescue and Recovery Service out

Jeffrey L. Meek

of Da Nang flying in the UH-16 Albatross around the Gulf of Tonkin for pilots that went 'feet wet' as Hagen put it. In August 1967, he stayed on an extra six months to help get a new HC-130B outfit organized. Following this he returned stateside and was put in a C-141 unit that flew re-supply missions all over the world including Vietnam.

Next came an assignment in Hawaii with the 41st Air Rescue and Recovery Wing. As operations office Hagen planned the unit's missions. Following this he was put with the CTF-130 Joint Task Force which handled Apollo space flight recovery operations. While with the outfit he also was involved in three Sky Lab recoveries.

Hagen later moved on to California to learn to become a Flying Safety Officer but was switched to being a Plans Officer and flew with local C-130 crews. Next came a tour with the 13th Air Force in the Philippines as officer-in-charge of the Rescue Coordination Center. This was followed by an assignment in San Antonio, where he worked with logistics and life support obtaining necessary equipment. It was here that Hagen decided to end his career and retired in 1980.

As a civilian he worked in investments for a few years then later joined the Army-Air Force Exchange Service as an internal auditor, retiring from that position in December 2004. That same month he and wife Anne moved to Hot Springs Village. The couple has six children: Kevin, Christopher, Kathleen, Cindy, Jimmy, and Laura.

Our interview was concluding when Hagen mentioned two other Vietnam-related missions of note. "One day I was flying in a C-47, and it was cloudy, and we were trying to DR (dead reckon) where we were going. I was

War Stories

standing up between the (pilot) seats trying to figure out where we were," said Hagen. He told the pilots he needed to go back to his area to do some figuring. Just as he left where he was standing an enemy round came through the C-47 right where he had been.

On another flight they were in a C-130 heading for Laos where a crew had gone down. Helicopters were also on the way that would need refueling. Dodging enemy ground fire, the big tanker refueled the choppers which then successfully extracted the crew. Hagen's pilot received the Silver Star and him and the others received the Distinguished Flying Cross for that dangerous mission. "It was pucker time," smiled Hagen recalling the harrowing flight.

Hagen said the most fun he had in his 20 years of Air Force service was flying the Bob Hope troupe around. He has the navigation map he used at that time, and it's covered with autographs, including Bob Hope's. "Thanks for the good landings," Tony Hope wrote on the map. And we thank Pat Hagen for his many years of service to our nation.

Jeffrey L. Meek

Stormy Holden served for 22 years in the U.S. Army

Stormy Holden grew up in Midwest City, Okla. In school she enjoyed playing basketball and softball. When I asked her how it was that she joined the military Holden said, "I had my daughter and I had to take care of her."

Her first stop was Fort Jackson, S.C., for U.S. Army basic training. Holden said the training she received was the same as what the men had, lots of physical training, firing weapons and throwing grenades.

After nine weeks of basic she requested assignment to Fort Sam Houston for Basic Medical Lab School. Her request was granted. At the school she ran patient lab samples and more as part of the Medical Science Academy there on the base.

The days were long, and five months later Holden went to Fort Lee, Va., where she worked in a hospital drawing blood and processing samples as a medical technician on the night shift. "And I loved it. You're by yourself all night, kind of your own supervisor," Holden said of the job. Eighteen months later she did a 'stateside swap' to Fort Sill, Okla., doing the same work, again on the night shift. Additionally, she worked in microbiology.

Four years later she reenlisted and went to the 16th Medical Logistics Battalion at Camp Waegon in Korea in 1998 where she ran the frozen blood depot. Holden also organized blood drives on the post.

Ten months later she was back at Fort Sam Houston attending advanced medical lab school the first six months of which was in the classroom learning chemistry, anatomy, and physiology. Next, she put the knowledge to work in the hospital there.

Holden next went to Fort Bliss, Texas, where she trained to become a lab technician as she took the advanced training and also earned college credits. She did well and because of that was given a choice of assignments. She contacted husband Nathan who had earlier completed his Army service and the two decided to trek to Fort Eustis, Va., where she continued the lab work.

In January 2001, her Army career took a turn when she left the medical field to attend Nuclear-Biological-Chemical (NBC) School. She made the change in order to be promoted as part of another re-enlistment.

The training covered the necessary paper skills plus dealing with wind direction and other factors to determine how far and how fast an agent may travel if unleashed by the enemy.

Holden then was assigned to Fort Carson, Colo., to an ordnance company where she ran the NBC room and took the troops that were about to deploy through the gas chamber so they would know what to do in case of an attack.

Later Holden herself deployed and served during Operation Enduring Freedom in Kuwait and Operation Iraqi Freedom with the 60th Ordnance Company. In Kuwait she was the highest-ranking NBC person. As such, Holden worked with the 377th Theater Support Command. Eight months later she returned to Fort Carson.

Once again, her career changed when she became a recruiter. "I wanted to go to drill instructor school," she said, but that wasn't going to happen. The schooling took eight weeks. Thereafter she worked 14-hour days making phone calls, visiting schools, always busy. As a recruiter she was expected to put three people per month in the Army. If not, Holden said a recruiter would be much more 'micro-managed.' At this point Holden decided to end her Army career and got out on Nov. 3, 2005, but soon joined the Army Reserves at Fort Carson.

She got put on active duty orders to do strength management recruiting for a brigade, to keep the needed numbers up to the proper levels. And Holden also did some of the training. Next in her career came a job in the First Army Surgeon's office, moving from Carson to Fort Hood. "We scheduled all the medical deployment training," said Holden of the job.

Then she went back to Carson with the Fifth Armored Brigade as a lab technician running a portion of the lab and many clinics. In October 2012, Holden officially retired when she learned she had a kidney disease thus ending her military service.

She and husband Nathan moved to Hot Springs Village from Colorado in August 2012. They have four children: Josh, Lyndsey, Adriana, and Kaleb.

As our interview concluded Holden told of another assignment she once had working with wounded warriors, mostly as a counselor. She called it the toughest military job she had as she watched some healing and some attempt suicide. Holden still talks with the family of one of her terminally ill former patients.

Asked why military suicide rates are so high she offered an opinion. Holden said she felt that coming home with PTSD after deployment and changing into again being

War Stories

a civilian is a tall order and that spouses don't know how to help or cope. She then told of one case in which a civilian wife killed her husband, then killed herself. Holden said the Army now does a better job of getting the family involved to handle those with PTSD.

Jeffrey L. Meek

Bob Holder served with the 82nd Airborne Division

Few military units are better known than the U.S. Army's 82nd Airborne Division. Also known as The All – American Division, they fought at Saint – Mihiel and in the Meuse – Argonne offensives in World War I and in numerous campaigns in World War II, places like Normandy, France, Holland and in the Battle of the Bulge. They fought in Vietnam during Tet and continued to serve in the war on terror. With the 82nd in the 1950s was Bob Holder.

A native Arkansan, Holder loved sports, especially basketball and baseball which he played in high school. He earned a basketball scholarship to Henderson State and there joined the ROTC program. Upon completion, he received a regular Army commission as a Distinguished Military Graduate on May 28, 1956. Two weeks later he took the oath. "I went straight to Fort Benning (Georgia) for the basic infantry officer's course," said Holder of his first assignment.

There he learned all facets of combat and was placed with the 82nd at Fort Bragg. At Bragg he attended jump school with 462 other trainees, 22 of which were officers. "Of the 22 officers only two of us finished," Holder recalled.

At jump school they did a tough daily run which caused several men to drop out. They learned positioning and landing skills and how to get up in high wind. Jumps began from a 34-foot tower. "It looks a lot taller than 34

War Stories

feet. That (tower) and the runs are where most (men) were eliminated," Holder said. Five jumps were needed to earn those coveted jump wings and Holder said his first was the most memorable.

He was in the first group of planes, confident, yet nervous. He'd never been in an airplane let alone jump out of one. "The worst part of jumping is the prop blast. On our first jump it was January, and it was a cold, windy day. In fact, when we got to the drop zone the wind was about 35 knots, so we were supposed to get the red smoke (which cancels a jump), but the reason we didn't is because a group of about 75 senators had been bussed out there to watch the drop."

"The Major that was leading them out-ranked the drop zone safety officer. He told him to give us the green smoke instead of the red. We jumped and it dragged everybody into the tree line, so they cancelled the rest of the jumps that day," Holder said.

He successfully completed his five jumps, earned his jump wings, and joined the First Airborne Battle Group, 505th Infantry Regiment, 'C' Company. The men participated in many training exercises, some of them in large operations with thousands of men, as either the pretend aggressor troops or as a U.S. force.

"To me the most dangerous jumps are night jumps or when your drop zone is surrounded by water," Holder said, who added that on one occasion they had a man die during one of these dangerous jumps.

Holder said when over water they would get out of their harness one or two stories above the water, so the

Jeffrey L. Meek

parachute was not still attached to them and thus pull the jumper under water and drown.

Again, Holder always hit the drop zone and suffered no injuries. His only mishap involved broken straps on his helmet. During his time with the division there were no combat deployments, but the unit was put on alert during the September 1957 Little Rock High School integration crisis when nine Black students were denied entrance to the school in defiance of a 1954 U.S. Supreme Court ruling.

The 82nd ended up not going. Instead, the 101st Airborne Division's 327th Airborne Battle Group went in to help restore order. "The 101st went in because they were closer," Holder said.

During his time in uniform Holder attended schools, including Chemical-Biological-Radiological and Military Police School. He, as well as the entire division, had to qualify with several weapons – the M-1 rifle, the automatic rifle, the M-2 Carbine, .45 caliber pistol and .30 caliber machine gun.

He did so well he was in the top three percent in the entire division with all five weapons. Because of this he was selected to attend Third Army rifle and pistol matches representing his outfit. In one of the matches, he finished third.

As his three-year commitment neared its end, Holder decided to not extend, but before he got out he got a very interesting assignment. He was chosen to be the personal escort for famed World War II General James 'Slim Jim' Gavin during the General's weeklong retirement ceremonies at Fort Bragg.

War Stories

"It was a pretty busy week. His ceremonies were mostly parades and things like that," Holder said and added that receptions and other activities were also included that week. Holder spoke highly of the General saying, "He treated me fine. He was very professional." Holder drove Gavin to various activities. "It was a big deal because he was a pretty big deal in the 82nd," said Holder of the legendary commander.

Holder resigned his Army commission in June 1959 and was discharged at Fort Gordon after completing MP school, which he enjoyed.

As a civilian, Holder went to work for 10 years at 3M in Texas and Oklahoma, then worked 28 years as a southwest/southeast regional manager of a computer firm that developed software to automate research and development and medical facilities. He retired in 1995. With wife Ginger they moved to Hot Springs Village that same year from Atlanta.

Looking back at his Army days Holder said it taught him discipline, how to get along with others and how to command. "I never was much for the harassment way to command," he concluded.

Jeffrey L. Meek

Cy Holliday served 20-year U. S. Army career

Cy Holliday was born in West Virginia but moved around a lot because his family was in the carnival business. Asked how it is that he got into the Army, Holliday said, "Ever since I was first able to read a comic book, I wanted to join the Army." He'd even walk around the carnival midway with a copy of a G.I. Joe comic book in his pocket.

Holliday didn't enlist until age 27, at a time when he was in-between jobs. So he went to a Fort Lauderdale, Fla., recruiter and signed up in November 1975. He had a degree in journalism and started out as an E-3. As a result of his high testing scores, he was given a choice of jobs and picked intelligence, then left for Ft. Dix in New Jersey for basic training.

Then in March 1976, Holliday was ordered to Ft. Huachuca, Ariz., for Advanced Individual Training (AIT). "I was older than my drill sergeants," Holliday said with a smile. AIT taught him about land navigation, order of battle, weather impact, terrain, and enemy tactics. He did well, finishing first in his class.

Next came a trip to Ft. Bragg, N.C., for assignment to the 18th Airborne Division. He worked at headquarters, G-2 Department for plans and threat analysis. "I became their Middle East guy," he explained. "It was there we did the first field test of what became intelligence preparation of battlefield, which was a way to incorporate all the elements of weather, the enemy and terrain analysis into a procedure instead of being hit or miss, which was how they did it in the past."

War Stories

In May 1978, Holliday went to Ft. Ord, Calif., for duty with the Seventh Infantry Division as the Division G-2 Intelligence Sergeant, responsible for order of battle factors. He also prepared the boss's 'black book.'

He was just about to get out of the service, but ended up attending OCS at Ft. Benning, Ga. In August 1978, Holliday was ordered to Ft. Huachuca to attend the Intelligence Center and School. He said during this time he got an interesting assignment. He was told to report to Hollywood. Why, he asked?

To be a technical advisor for an Army intelligence training film called, 'Intelligence Preparation of the Battlefield.' During this time, he also taught foreign intelligence officers about intelligence collection, processing, and application.

In December 1980, he reported to Korea for duty with the Second Infantry Division at Camp Hovey. Holliday said the country was still under Marshall Law and war-related devastation from the 1950s was still evident. "I was the intelligence officer for the First Battalion, 38th Infantry," he said. That meant he was responsible for all intelligence matters.

Holliday spent several weeks working at the Demilitarized Zone (DMZ). "The rules of engagement were simple. If it's between the hours of dusk and dawn and it's moving to your front, shoot it. It was pretty easy because no one was supposed to be there," Holliday said.

From December 1981 through September 1987, Holliday worked on several classified assignments he could not talk about. "We got off into the black world," is all he would say.

Jeffrey L. Meek

Next, he went to the Joint Military Intelligence School in Washington, D.C. He earned a master's degree in Science and Strategic Intelligence. Then in September 1987, he was assigned to the First Infantry Division (Forward) in Germany. There he commanded a military intelligence battalion. It was the largest ground-based intelligence center at that time. Voice intercepts, interpreters, operations, jamming, you name it, and Holliday was in charge of it, as the U.S. kept their eye on Russian activities.

During this time the Berlin Wall came down. He had personnel in Berlin at the time and they brought him pieces of the wall which he still has today.

In 1990, Holliday attended graduate school at Georgia Tech for a PhD. In 1992, he went to the Combined Arms Center, Threat Directorate, in Ft. Leavenworth, Kan. "We did a lot of interesting things there. Primarily with the development of what's called World Class Opposing Forces, which are the people that our forces train against. "Our responsibility was to make sure, whatever scenario they came up with, the threat was acting as the threat should act," he explained.

In 1994, Holliday was assigned to Army Forces Command, Ft. McPherson, Ga. This command was basically the force provider for the entire U.S. Army. Later, Holliday was asked to teach at West Point, but in November 1995, decided to retire.

As a civilian he worked for a small defense contractor in Florida. "We did top attack weapons testing. We won a contract with the Missile Defense Agency in Colorado Springs, and I moved there in 2004. I assisted the government in planning and executing war games and

War Stories

exercises in the Pacific region," Holliday said. n May 2014, he and wife Debbie moved to the Hot Springs Village from Colorado Springs. They have a son, Cy.

Looking back on a very interesting Army career, Holliday said he learned a lot about himself, to never say never and that freedom is not free and it's also not inexpensive, that it costs a lot but is necessary. "The only regret that I have is that I didn't do it (join the Army) 10 years sooner. It's a young man's game," he concluded.

Jeffrey L. Meek

Joe Hoosty served 34 years in U. S. Coast Guard

Joe Hoosty grew up in Pennsylvania and after completing high school he attended the Coast Guard Academy beginning in 1962. Hoosty explained to me that the Academy is unique in that there are no Congressional appointments. To get in he went through two days of testing and a rigorous physical exam. Hoosty said 5,000 people applied, 800 made it past the physical and 400 were offered appointments, but by June of 1962, only 240 showed up. "Four years later that was down to 113," said Hoosty.

While at the Academy he played football for the legendary Otto Graham as a safety, running back and corner back during an undefeated season that sent the team to the Tangerine Bowl vs. Western Kentucky. Also, while at the Academy, Hoosty marched in President Kennedy's funeral procession.

After his 1966 graduation with a degree in engineering and being commissioned as an Ensign, he was offered a wish list. He applied for duty in Vietnam and put as his second choice naval flight school. His first duty assignment was aboard the Coast Guard Cutter Duane in Boston, where he was a deck watch officer, four hours on duty, eight hours off. It was during this time he applied for flight school.

He was accepted in 1967 and sent to Navy Flight School in Pensacola, Fla., for ground school and to get in top notch physical condition. He first flew the T-34, then instrument, formation and night flying at Whiting Field in Milton, Fla. Given another choice he chose to go with

War Stories

helicopters and flew the 'Bubble' Bell UH-1 and Sikorsky H-34.

In 1968, Hoosty was assigned to Coast Guard Air Station Astoria in Oregon on the Columbia River. There he transitioned to the H-52 which could land in the water and thus perform rescue missions, of which Hoosty eventually flew many.

In 1971, he attended Penn State University, earning a master's degree in electrical engineering, then went to the aircraft repair and supply center in Elizabeth City, N.C., in 1973. At the center Hoosty did C-130 modifications, installing new aviation electronics.

In 1974, he was off to Coast Guard Headquarters in Washington, D.C., to work on procuring new aircraft – medium range surveillance aircraft that could be used at times of oil spills, drug interdiction and search/rescue missions. Four companies were interested in providing these aircraft as Hoosty traveled all over the USA and Europe evaluating the candidate aircraft.

In 1977, he was sent to the Coast Guard Aircraft Program Office in Little Rock where 41 jet Falcon HU-25s were brought in. At the base, modifications in aviation electronic packages were made and Hoosty married the love of his life, Andreae Kay Grimmett of Little Rock.

Two years later he went to Coast Guard Air Station Miami in Opa Locka, Fla., operationally the busiest and most exciting of Hoosty's tours of duty. "The Miami air station is the busiest search and rescue station in the world," he said. While there he participated in what's referred to as the Mariel Boat Lift, in 1980, when Cuban Premier Fidel Castro allowed approximately 125,000 Cubans to leave Cuba, thus

Jeffrey L. Meek

flooding the Straits of Florida from Key West to Miami attempting to reach the USA in small boats.

By May 6, President Jimmy Carter declared a state of emergency in the areas where the refugees were coming in. Soon Haitian refugees were also granted temporary legal status in the U.S. Eventually Carter called for a blockade to be enforced by the Coast Guard and almost 1,400 boats were seized.

Countering drug operations was also a part of the Coast Guard. Hoosty flew many drug interdiction operations connected with the cartel transportation of drugs by sea and air into the country. He flew these missions in C-131 Convair aircraft and H-52 helicopter on ship deployments.

In 1983, still in Miami, he became operations officer in charge of the training, scheduling, and deployment of 52 pilots and 100 aircrew in executing CG missions involving law enforcement, search and rescue and maritime pollution. At that time, in his unit were two of the initial female pilots to operationally serve in the Coast Guard. "They were really screened. No women flew planes back then but these two were just amazing and were some of my best pilots," Hoosty said.

In 1985, he attended the Air Force Air War College in Montgomery, Ala. He was the only 'Coastie' in the class. Henry Kissinger was among the speakers at the college. There he studied military history, strategy, and world affairs.

The following year, Hoosty was assigned to the Air Station in Brooklyn, N.Y., as commanding officer of a helicopter unit. In 1989, he was part of the Coast Guard

War Stories

Maintenance and Logistic Command at Governor's Island, in New York, N.Y. There he worked on a centralized support concept for maintenance and engineers. He was also the head of personnel for the Coast Guard in the Atlantic area.

In 1990, he was assigned as the intelligence office for drug ops and counter terrorism and helped with the planning and support for Operation Desert Storm. He was once in a meeting with the later to be infamous CIA case officer Aldrich 'Rick' Ames, who was convicted in 1994 of espionage, providing CIA and other agency information to the Russian KGB.

In 1993, Hoosty went to what would be his final duty station – the National Drug Intelligence Center (NDIC) in D.C. and at Johnstown, Penn. He served as head of intelligence liaison with other agencies as well as head of the collections operations. On occasion he provided briefings for CIA Directors James Woolsey and John Deutch. Hoosty retired in 1996 having flown in nine different aircraft and logging over 3,000 flight hours during his decade's long career.

As a civilian, Hoosty's career included work at BETAC Corporation as a Systems Engineer and Technical Manager and as a teacher of math and computer programing at Northwest Area High School in Shickshinny, Penn. In 2017, the Hoostys moved to the Village from Benton, Penn.

Looking back on his service he said the experiences were exciting, it was a great education and an opportunity to serve the people of the United States.

Jeffrey L. Meek

Scott Hornbruch served in multiple roles during a 20-year Air Force career

Scott Hornbruch is from a military family and was born in a clinic at the Brooklyn Navy Yard. In 1966, he attended Rutgers University and later got a draft lottery number of 23. He was then in an ROTC program and was advised to complete the Armed Services Vocational Aptitude Battery (ASVAB) of tests, which he did.

He scored well, met with recruiters from each service branch and chose the U.S. Air Force. "The Air Force gave me what sounded like the best deal of the four, so I signed on with the Air Force and at that point entered what they called the POC, the Professional Officer Candidate program, which is reserve officer training commissioning program. That's where it started," said Hornbruch.

After his commissioning as a Second Lieutenant in the USAF reserves, he went to Detachment 1 of the 485th Air Commando unit where he was trained to do coastal water mapping. "I actually trained as a diver," he said. The premise was that he would be dropped offshore at a specific location, swim in and mark bombing targets.

At the same time Hornbruch was being encouraged to continue testing, which included pilot testing. Again, he scored well and was put in pilot training and sent to Moody AFB, Ga., in 1972.

Later his first solo didn't go so well. "I didn't keep my altitude up on final (approach) and I actually put the plane through the top couple feet of a willow tree," Hornbruch said. He successfully completed the training and went to Castle AFB, Calif., for combat crew training in the C-135

War Stories

aircraft. The C-135 was a real Air Force workhorse used in refueling and recon.

Hornbruch excelled in the receiver-refueling aircraft and was sent to Grisson AFB, Ind., and put with the Third Airborne Command and Control Squadron (ACCS) which is actually an airborne command post.

Soon he volunteered for duty in Alaska and went to Eielson AFB doing receiver-refueling and recon flying. Asked to talk about the delicate task of refueling from another aircraft at 20,000 feet Hornbruch said, "You go really slow. Initially it's all done by a navigator who arranges the rendezvous by radar, and it's done with turning angles so that you have an over-take on the tanker. I found that was something I thoroughly enjoyed doing. "Later he moved into the Standardization and Evaluation aspect of the program giving others their check rides.

Next, he was asked to go to Europe, an RAF base in Mildenhall, U.K., with the 10th ACCS. There he flew the C-135G doing the same work. This plane could also trail an antenna out the back for VLF radio transmissions, many times to submarines in the North Atlantic.

At Mildenhall he got involved in tactical deception missions and was also used in covert missions, some involved with flying, some just for observation.

In 1978, and now a Captain, Hornbruch was chosen to go to Moscow to pick up a scientific aircraft that had engine problems. In Moscow the crew was treated well, did not bring the plane back and was sent home with a British tour group. He was then made Chief of Safety for ease of movement all around Europe. In 1981, Hornbruch volunteered and was selected for flights with the 552nd

Jeffrey L. Meek

Airborne Warning and Control (AWAC) Wing at Tinker AFB, Okla. Flights from here were to locations all over the globe including Saudi Arabia, Libya, just to name a few.

He spent a total of one year in Saudi Arabia operating out of Riyadh. As an American, travel in the country was touchy. When he did travel it was with escorts called the King's Guards. One of those trips would be quite memorable while he was serving as senior instructor and was assigned as supervisor of flying.

One time an aircraft came in and needed to get out quickly, so flight information needed to be given quickly which involved the base's tower run by the British. To do so, Hornbruch went across several different sections of the base to the tower. When he left the tower, he was arrested and charged with espionage and smuggling by a Saudi Lieutenant and a squad of men. "They took me and held me in a transit facility," Hornbruch said.

He showed a Saudi Sergeant his King's pass and was then brought dates and tea by the Sergeant and was given an apology. "He made sure nobody interrogated me and about eight hours later an American liaison showed up, a full Colonel, and I was quickly released," said Hornbruch. At this point it was determined Hornbruch should leave the country the next day which he did, never to return to Saudi Arabia.

Then during an assignment out of Iceland, he was involved in the Falklands where U.S. AWAC planes flew support missions and intercepts of Russian aircraft which involved bringing in fighter aircraft to get Russian pilots to back off. Some didn't and "weapons had to be used," Hornbruch said. And Hornbruch was the first to land an AWAC in Norway during this timeframe.

War Stories

In the 1980s, he also served as coordinator of E-3 aircraft scheduling for the office of the vice president, U.S. Customs and the National Narcotics Border Interdiction System and as focal point for JSOC classified operations that are yet to be declassified. The AWAC planes helped with drug smuggling operations and sometime would carry DEA agents.

His next assignment was with the 15th Air Base Wing at Hickam AFB, Hawaii. There he flew EC-135s and served as Chief of Standardization and Evaluation. Later he was reassigned as Deputy Chief of Operations which involved hauling people throughout the Pacific to places like Johnson Island where chemical warfare testing was taking place and to Kwajelein where 'Star Wars' testing was being conducted with lasers.

Near the end of his career his aircraft came off alert and Hornbruch was selected to check out in a space shuttle simulator to be onsite commander for emergency space shuttle recovery should pilots on board become incapacitated. "I never got inside the shuttle but got close to it," Hornbruch said.

His final jobs were as air show coordinator for the famous Thunderbirds Pacific Tour and as a repatriation officer working to bring back the remains of those found in Vietnam. Hornbruch retired in 1992.

As a civilian he worked with the Hawaii Job Corps supervising academic and vocational training and high school diploma programs for Job Corps trainees. From 2000 to 2004 Hornbruch worked for the Department of Education as a teacher in Kakuku, Hawaii. In September 2005, he and wife Linda moved to Hot Springs Village. The Hornbruchs have two children: Lisa and Austin.

Jeffrey L. Meek

Dennis Horvath served 21-year Air Force career

Dennis Horvath comes from Barberton, Ohio and decided he'd join the U.S. Air Force right after his 1958 high school graduation. He was working in a grocery store, had no plans for college so he and a buddy signed up. "It seemed like the right thing to do," said Horvath of a decision that would lead to an interesting 21-year Air Force career. His basic training took place at Lackland AFB, Texas, then he was off to Amarillo, Texas, for training as an administrative clerk.

In January 1959, he was ordered to Laughlin AFB in Del Rio, Texas, and put with the 4080th Strategic Recon Wing in ground training at Wing HQ. One of his many duties was to keep track of all pilot hours.

Next, Horvath was assigned to the Standardization Division in early 1962 which meant he was involved in administrative testing of U-2 airmen. "My immediate boss was Major Rudolph Anderson. He was a wonderful guy to work for," said Horvath of the man who would later give his life in service to the United States during the Cuban Missile Crisis in October. Also in the outfit was Major Richard Heyser who would also play a very key role in the crisis.

In October 1962, Horvath had a sense something big was going on but didn't know what. Then suddenly he was told to get ready for deployment to another location. Later that day he ran into Heyser who told him they were headed for Florida. That night the two men flew to McCoy AFB – Orlando, Fla. "My job was to send all the messages of take-

War Stories

offs and landings," Horvath said. The information was sent to SAC Headquarters.

At McCoy the situation was chaotic, and it was obvious something big was in the works. It wasn't long until he knew there was serious trouble brewing in Cuba. Russia had placed offensive missiles there and Kennedy was determined to get them out. Horvath did his job in a hanger set up on the flight line. The work was hectic, constant, and important.

As he worked in Florida, back in Texas, his wife stayed with friends. "They scouted out caves where they could live during a nuclear war," Horvath said. "They pretty much knew where they were going to hide during the nuclear war. There were a lot of caves along the Rio Grande. We joke about it now, but that's how serious it was at that time."

In Florida, Horvath wondered if he'd ever see his family again. As the week developed, the crisis deepened as President John Kennedy debated what action would be taken. At McCoy, on October 26, Horvath borrowed $10 from Major Anderson, meaning to pay him back as soon as possible. But he wouldn't get the chance.

The following morning Anderson took off for a photo recon flight over Cuba in areas near Esmeralda, Camaguey, Manzanillo, Santiago and Banes, Cuba. Near Banes, a Russian surface-to-air (SAM) missile brought down the U-2 and killed Anderson. Electronic eavesdropping later that day picked up word that the Cubans had recovered the body and wreckage of the plane. Anderson was dead. "It was heart-wrenching. We all liked him, and it was tough on all of us," said Horvath of the loss.

Jeffrey L. Meek

Air Force RF-101s and Navy F-8U recon planes continued the overflights the next day as the Kennedy administration braced for nuclear war with Russia. Later that day, the U.S. heard a radio Moscow broadcast saying they would dismantle the missile sites. Had the Russians just blinked?

On October 29, Soviet First Deputy Minister Vasily Kuznetsov met with U.N. Secretary General U Thant to assure him the missiles were being dismantled. On November 5, Major Anderson's body was returned and the crisis eased.

Horvath was sent back to Del Rio, Texas, around this time and ran into Heyser who had been invited to and honored at the White House. It was Heyser, on October 14, that had taken the first overflight photos proving the missiles were indeed offensive in nature.

Later Horvath's 4080th unit was moved to Davis-Monthan AFB in Arizona. Horvath had re-enlisted and was sent to Osan Air Base in Korea in 1964 where he worked at Wing Maintenance doing maintenance and logistics reports.

In 1965, he was assigned to Bergstrom AFB, Texas; then, in 1966, to Grand Forks, N.D., working in Base Operations. In 1967, Horvath was assigned to the Strategic Recon Center at Offutt AFB, Neb., where he worked in the underground bunker. This job required numerous security clearances.

His work covered the scheduling of U-2 and SR-71 flights as well as C-130s, drones, and other electronic surveillance aircraft. "It was a very busy time and very satisfying work," said Horvath of the assignment.

War Stories

Three years later he and his family were sent to Lindsey Air Station in Wiesbaden, Germany, arriving in the summer of 1970. Horvath was put in the Recon Division of USAF – Europe. His job was mostly with managing the paperwork that came in each day. Even today he stays in touch with a few of the men he worked with there.

Horvath's next assignment took him to Shepard AFB, Texas, where he cross-trained and became a Personnel Superintendent. He spent a year there handling over 1,000 airmen transfers.

During this time, he finished work on a bachelor's degree in Education and was promoted to E-9, Chief Master Sergeant before being sent off again. This time it was to Hickam AFB, Hawaii, in the Quality Control Section of the Personnel Office of the headquarters at PACAF. During this three-year tour Horvath completed a master's degree in Public Administration and competed in the 1979 Honolulu Marathon.

He retired in 1979 and three days later was hired as the first Director of Parks and Recreation in North Richland, Texas. For the next 14 years he would serve as Director, Acting City Manager, Assistant City Manager and Deputy City Manager before retiring in 1993. That year he and wife Barbara moved to Hot Springs Village where for four years he sold annuities and real estate on a part-time basis. In 2001, Horvath felt another calling, this time to the ministry, serving in several area churches over the next few years. The couple had three children: Tammy, Jim and Tim, who unfortunately has died.

Looking back on his USAF service Horvath said his time in Germany was his favorite and best assignment of his 21-year career.

Jeffrey L. Meek

Larry Ketcham served 22 years with the U.S. Army

Larry Ketcham grew up on a farm in Shenandoah, Iowa, where he was a high school football and track athlete. After leaving school he got married and was working when some of his friends told them they were going to join the military. Ketcham had already joined the National Guard, had not told his draft board, and was later drafted in January 1960.

His first stop was a brief one in Omaha, Neb., then he was off to Ft. Collins, Colo., for processing, then sent to Ft. Riley, Kan., for basic training. At Ft. Riley the weather was bad with frequent days of cold temperatures.

While there Ketcham contracted pneumonia after being exposed to chlorine gas during a gas drill in which he removed his mask to help a struggling soldier better. After a few days in the hospital, he rejoined the group and continued his training.

Ketcham then received orders to report to Ft. Jackson, South Carolina for what was called AIT – advanced individual training. In his case this meant he'd be attending the Basic Army Administration Course. Ketcham was about to become a clerk.

After learning the clerk skills, he went to Ft. Lee, Va., where he was assigned to Headquarters (HQ) Company/Personnel. "That was my introduction to working on personnel records," said Ketcham of the duty.

Sometime later he volunteered to go to Germany where he again worked with personnel records. Three years

War Stories

later, in 1963, he returned to Omaha doing the same type of work, now as an E-5.

In 1966, Ketcham was ordered to Chicago to be an inspector with 5th Army HQ dealing with personnel matters. He also dealt with funds associated with National Guard units in 13 states as an inspector.

In 1968, he again volunteered, this time for Vietnam. He was told he'd be joining the First Cav at Pleiku; however, an IG inspector changed that order, sending him to a USARV-Inspector General office at Long Bin. "We traveled to units all over Vietnam," Ketcham said of the job of inspecting such things as NCO and officers' clubs at many different posts.

On some occasions Ketcham also ran into 'Charlie' (enemy Vietnamese troops). Asked if he was willing to share a few of those experiences, Ketcham told me about a night when he and others were watching a movie in a mess hall when enemy fire rained down on their position. Everyone scrambled for cover and fortunately no one was injured.

And there was a time in downtown Saigon in May 1968 when mortars came in, again close to his location. Ketcham took advantage of a truck in the area which he jumped upon and rode out safely to Ton Son Nut air base.

Another incident befell him while visiting with a Lieutenant Colonel in the Colonel's quarters. Once again, 'Charlie' hit them, but as was the case previously, no one was injured in the attack.

Following his Vietnam tour of duty, Ketcham was ordered to Ft. Sill, Okla., in March 1969 and became III Corps Personnel Sergeant. Here he maintained records and

Jeffrey L. Meek

was also the administrative flow for all correspondence coming through the battalions and brigades.

Then, in July 1970, he reported to Panama with HQ Company maintaining personnel records. Three years later he was promoted to First Sergeant (E-8) and took over the Company for the next two years. Ketcham said the Canal Zone was very interesting. When his parents or others would come for a visit, he would give them tours of the area.

In 1975, Ketcham was sent to Aberdeen proving ground in Maryland as a First Sergeant of the HQ Company.

In 1977, he volunteered to go to Okinawa where he would be the First Sergeant of a new area – the Resource Management Office (RMO). One year later he got some good news when, following up on a cryptic phone call he received, he learned he had made the list for promotion to Master Sergeant, but his orders to Chicago as an Army advisor to the reserve units slowed the process.

Then things changed a few more times as his assignment got switched to Minnesota, then Oklahoma as the Army Reserve advisor in Oklahoma City.

In 1982, he got wind of another change he was going to be asked to make – another tour in Germany as a Command Sergeant Major. The move didn't excite him seeing as his family had already moved several times. His children were in a new school and his daughter was planning a marriage. So Ketcham made the decision to end his Army career as of Dec. 31, 1981.

As a civilian he went to college, earned a political science degree, and worked at Tinker AFB, Okla., in logistics and maintenance. Later he became a civilian war planner

War Stories

with the U.S. Air Force, then a project manager and a program manager until retiring again on Jan. 1, 2003. That same month the Ketchams moved to Hot Springs Village. He and wife Nancy have three children: Jim, Debra, and Denise.

Looking back on his 22-year administrative Army career, Ketcham said the Army treated him very well and added that the overseas schools were really great.

Jeffrey L. Meek

Clara Nicolosi served in U. S. Coast Guard for 22 years

Clara Nicolosi was raised in Florida. Between her junior and senior year of high school, she decided she wasn't going to college. "I had decided to join the Navy," Nicolosi told me. "But my brother said why don't we talk to a recruiter first," she added.

While still in high school she chose the U.S. Coast Guard and in July 1981, was off to Cape May, N.J.,, for basic training. She enjoyed the experience, largely because she was in the band and got to travel to many events.

Then in September, Nicolosi received her first duty assignment. She was sent to St. Joseph, Mich. "I was the newbie, so I did whatever they wanted. Swabbing the deck, keeping the boat clean and anything we needed. I was a very good mess cook. As a matter of fact, I even took over for our actual cook. He had to leave for three weeks so I got to cook," she said.

In February 1982, Nicolosi attended her 'A' school in Yorktown, Va., to become a Boatswain's Mate. Boat driving, knot tying, advanced seamanship skills, deck maintenance, it was all part of the training.

After 12 weeks of schooling, Nicolosi was sent to Berwick, La., as Executive Petty Officer for an Aids to Navigation team. These teams worked with lights and buoys on the water to help mark the waterway channels and whatever else was necessary for safe travel.

I asked her what it was like for her working in a man's world. "I enjoyed it. I was truly blessed. I had great mentors and great people that would help me grow. And in

War Stories

most cases that was always men. There weren't many other women, just a few. It wasn't an issue. I was just another team member, another person on the deck and was treated with respect," said Nicolosi. Later, she told me one thing she loved about the Coast Guard was that it had no ceiling for her, so she was able to therefore accomplish much.

Soon, she met the man who would become her husband. Job related, they were on the radio with each other many times. That eventually led to dating and marriage about one year later.

In September 1983, both were transferred to New Orleans. She was assigned to the Captain of the Port, who supervised the safety of the entire port. "I worked in pollution response. I was a pollution investigator," Nicolosi said. Oil fields were all around so she was busy investigating leaks, spills, pipelines and more. To do those inspections she traveled by helicopter and boat to the sites.

In July 1985, Nicolosi went to Rio Vista, Calif., with another Aids to Navigation unit as Executive Petty Officer. Buoys and lights were again one of the responsibilities, with some duty on Lake Tahoe. Nicolosi drove the boat, fixed lights, trained others; you name, she did it.

In February 1987, she was put on the Coast Guard Cutter Fir in Seattle, as Boatswain Mate Second Class. On that buoy tender Nicolosi serviced buoys, eventually becoming deck supervisor, overseeing the entire operation. Boom operator, safety officer, once again, she was involved in everything. Later, she even drove the Fir through the different areas and passes.

In August 1988, Nicolosi was transferred again, this time to Station Neah Bay in Washington. Her husband was

Jeffrey L. Meek

now back in the Coast Guard and working on an ice breaker, while she made Search and Rescue Coxswain at the station, which was located on an Indian reservation. Upon arrival she had to do a 'swim to the beach call.' "That was an interesting time for me," she said of the experience of swimming through strong breaking waves. One way to get to shore through those big waves was to drive under them and swim, "I did it only out of necessity," Nicolosi said with a smile.

In October 1990, she was made Officer-In Charge of an Aids to Navigation team in Morgan City, La. Now a new mom, she oversaw operations of the five-man team and did duties such as driving the boat and learned all the other men's duties in case she had to sub in for someone.

Then, she went back to Michigan to Station Sault Ste. Marie for another stint in search and rescue. Here she was Second Officer-In-Charge. Nicolosi said there were many instances when they would have to go out on Lake Michigan or Superior to help with medical issues or for a boat that had broken down or for some other type of peril. At this station they also trained for ice rescue.

In June 1995, she headed south to Miami Beach to serve on the U.S. Coast Guard Cutter Hudson as Executive Petty Officer in charge of construction. The ship hauled building materials and even had a crane on it.

In June 1998, she was back in Aids to Navigation, this time in Buffalo, N.Y., as Third Officer-In-Charge, servicing buoys and monitoring a safety zone above Niagara Falls, making sure buoys were in the correct locations and lights working. "Those were some hairy times," she said. She also maintained lighthouses, which Nicolosi fell in love with.

War Stories

In June 1999, she was commissioned as a Warrant Officer in Aids to Navigation and made Weapons Officer too.

In 2003, Nicolosi retired from the Coast Guard, ending a 22-year exciting career. That year she and husband Michael moved to Hot Springs Village from Buffalo. They have a son Jonathan.

Looking back at more than two decades of service to her nation, she said the experiences enriched her life, she found a husband and learned more about herself, more about reaching for the stars. "If you work hard, put your mind to it and apply yourself, the sky is the limit. I really believe that. I'm grateful for the Coast Guard and the times I had."

Jeffrey L. Meek

Charles Sikes worked with Army Security Agency in Ethiopia

They were sometimes called 'shadow warriors.' Their unofficial motto was "In God We Trust, All Others We Monitor." The Army Security Agency (ASA) works on intelligence gathering and is responsible for the security of Army communications and electronic countermeasures.

In 1976, it was merged with the U.S. Army Intelligence and Security Command. It is composed of those with the highest scores on Army intelligence tests. Charles Sikes served with the ASA in Ethiopia monitoring events around the world.

Sikes said the Mississippi high school he attended was very patriotic. Many who attended the school wanted to join the military, including himself and several of his closest friends.

After completing high school, Sikes attended Mississippi State University and enrolled in their ROTC program. He enjoyed ROTC and in 1966 enlisted in the U.S. Army for a four-year tour of duty.

For Sikes, basic training took place at Fort Jackson, S.C. Once there, he was told about the ASA and wanted in. "The James Bond movies were out, and they said it (ASA) was a part of the CIA and NSA and I just knew I'd be a spy. So, I joined," said Sikes with a smile.

He went through a complete background check and then attended a communications school. The training began with learning Morse code. Sikes then went to electronics school to learn how to operate top secret

War Stories

communications equipment. "Today you can buy it in the local Radio Shack," said Sikes.

Suddenly one night he was taken from his barracks and sent to a forest at Fort Devons, Mass. He was being trained for service in Vietnam. The men learned infiltration and evasion skills. About this time, Sikes met a lady named Hillary. They were married three weeks later. Now married, his shipping out for overseas duty was postponed. In time, Sikes learned it was because the Army needed to do a complete background check on his wife.

Finally, he received his orders to go to Vietnam. At the last minute the orders were changed. Instead, Sikes was sent to Ethiopia to work at a listening post.

As the plane carrying Sikes and others approached their destination, they arrived in the middle of a war zone. It was June 1967 and Egypt, and Israel were at war. Sikes knew something was up when he saw Israeli jets flying by.

He landed safely and Sikes began a three-year tour at the post. He could not talk about several of the things he worked on but did share a few of his experiences.

He was on duty and became one of the first to learn that Russia had invaded Czechoslovakia. "I just happened to be copying Prague to Moscow. I picked up enough to know what was going on," said Sikes. He also intercepted information during the Jan. 23, 1968, attack on the USS Pueblo when the Navy ship was attacked off the coast of North Korea.

Many times, he would be searching several frequencies for any interesting traffic. Occasionally he would hear American soldiers in Vietnam calling for help. It

Jeffrey L. Meek

frustrated him being so far from them and not being able to do anything to help.

One night, Sikes was sent out on guard duty. He took up a position when he heard a .50 caliber machine gun going off in the distance. It kept getting closer and closer. Then a mortar round came in. Then nothing, all stayed quiet. Nothing happened, but it got Sikes' attention. Years later, back in the U.S., a doctor found a tiny piece of shrapnel in Sikes chest.

Sikes said the country was very dry. There was one stretch when it didn't rain for two years. As you might expect, water was at a premium. "We only had water (turned on) for about two hours a day," remembers Sikes. As for the people, he said they were nice, honest folks. "Dirt poor, but they walked with pride, heads up," Sikes added.

Sanitation was poor and everyone had to watch what they ate. Despite a warning, one day Sikes and his wife ate some ice cream. She was fine, but Sikes one taste of the stuff put him in the hospital.

After three years on duty, Sikes came home in 1970. After arriving, he was shocked at what he saw. In Ethiopia, the air was very clean. Upon arriving in New York, he immediately noticed the difference in air quality. "It almost made you gag," said Sikes.

Later he noticed the latest female fashion, the mini skirt. "Girls wore longer dresses when I left, but when I came back it was totally different," he recalled.

As Sikes settled into civilian life, he became uncomfortable around others. He was made to feel quite different than those around him. "I was some kind of monster, like I had done something wrong," Sikes said.

War Stories

Eventually, he returned to Mississippi State but was not allowed to attend classes until he went for psychological counseling. "I felt like they didn't trust me," is how Sikes put it. He got that behind him, graduated, and became a teacher in Mississippi. In 2004, he and his wife moved to Hot Springs Village.

He loves ancient history, and with his wife often travels to Italy for vacation. Sikes is the only one of four high school buddies to have lived through the era. The other three were killed in Vietnam. If there hadn't been a delay in his deployment, Sikes most likely would have ended up there too. He sometimes experiences guilt about being alive and his three good friends being killed. But he survived his four-year tour and the aftermath of the times.

Jeffrey L. Meek

Dan Turney served in both the Navy and Air Force

Dan Turney was born in Rhode Island but grew up in Harrison, Ark., where the family had a church pew business. Turney thought he'd try to be an artist, went to art school in Memphis, but soon changed his mind. He got his draft number - 85 – in 1972, which prompted him to enlist in the Navy.

After finishing boot camp and more training in Denver, he was sent to Guam as a photo intelligence specialist, serving in a VQ squadron. "They trained me to interpret photos taken from reconnaissance aircraft," Turney said. During this time, he did deployments to Korea, Japan and the Philippines.

Two years later, he returned to the U.S. for duty on the USS Saratoga (CV-60) in Jacksonville, Fla., again working in an intelligence center. In fact, Turney was the only qualified satellite imagery interpreter at the center. Sometimes he'd interpret top secret rolls of film.

There was a time when he picked the landing zones for helicopters for the evacuation of U.S. civilians during a crisis in Lebanon. Events cooled off and they weren't used, but he had them ready if needed. "It (the work) was so sensitive I was the only guy on the ship who had clearance to look at the film," Turney said.

In 1976, he left the Navy, went to school, got married and worked for Eastman Chemicals in Batesville, Ark. He also missed the service. After talking things over with his wife, he joined the Air Force to become a helicopter pilot. Why, I asked. "I thought it would be a lot of fun. I

War Stories

turned down fixed wing training twice to continue on with helicopter training," he explained.

After officer training school he went to Ft. Rucker in Alabama, an Army flight training school. Turney said, with helicopters, one is always doing something with their feet and their hands at the same time.

In 1980, he received his first assignment. It was at Indian Springs, Nev., with the 57th Fighter Weapons Wing. "Our job was to work the training site and the Nellis range, which supported fighters and search and rescue, but mostly supporting crashes that happened all the time out there," he said.

"We also supported the nuclear test site. I believe I flew overhead photographic support for five underground tests, which is pretty amazing to watch the bomb go off under your helicopter," he added. Turney told me they couldn't hear the blast and couldn't see it, but what was observable was a ripple across the ground, like the ripples on a pond when tossing in a stone. "You see the earth ripple and come back and then a little dust would rise up. Our job was to film in case something went wrong, which would be called a 'vent,' meaning the bomb had vented through the earth's surface.

In 1982, Turney was sent to Zaragoza, Spain, for duty with the 67th Aerospace Rescue and Recovery Squadron – Detachment 7. "We were a combat rescue squadron which meant we would train in case war broke out in Europe. We would do search and rescue for downed fighter pilots in our little Huey (UH-1N) helicopter," Turney said.

He did a few medivac flights, like the time when an older gentleman, a U.S. tourist, had a heart attack. "We took him to Barcelona but had to land twice in route for the doctor to do CPR. We got him there alive, but he died later," Turney said.

In 1985, he went to Edwards Air Force Base in California, to serve with the 40th Aerospace Rescue and Recovery Squadron – Detachment 5. Turney was operations and evaluation officer. There were a lot of test flights and some space shuttle landings during this time. His squadron would launch with a medical person on board in case a shuttle crashed. Turney said one could hear a double boom and then the shuttle would appear, coming in very steep and fast. Turney also deployed twice to Nassau, Bahamas, to support Operation BAT, a Drug Enforcement Agency drug interdiction. In their Huey's they'd chase drug smugglers.

And there were other missions as well, like the time they got a call during the night that a girl on a small island about 50 miles from Nassau needed a medivac. Through bad weather they found the island, but there was no space big enough to put the chopper on the ground and there was no hoist on the chopper. Sizing up the situation quickly and getting low on fuel, Turney put the craft down on a nearby seawall, balancing it there until the girl was on board, then took off for Nassau.

In 1987, at Hurlburt, Fla., he was assigned to the 55th Special Operations Squadron – First Special Operations Wing. There he flew MH-60G Blackhawk helicopters. The craft was new, so much was the learning was while doing. Turney was the special mission planner and a pilot for Operation Just Cause in Panama in 1989, when the U.S. invaded Panama to oust Dictator Manuel Noriega. He also filled the same role during Operation Desert Storm in 1990-

War Stories

1991. As such he coordinated rescue missions for special operations forces.

In 1992, Turney went to Osan, Korea, to serve with the 38th Rescue and Recovery Squadron. In 1993, he was back at Hurlburt as helicopter test manager and MH-60 test pilot. During this time, he interviewed for an Air Force One advance agent position and got the job. Over the next four years, Turney participated in 33 presidential missions, 22 stateside and 11 overseas. He was chosen Advance Agent of the Year in 1995. "That was a really interesting job. As advance agent you go five to 10 days ahead of the visit and you work with the White House advance team, the Secret Service advance team, and the White House communications advance team. You work on logistics, security and operations of the jet coming in. It's a military operation all the way," said Turney.

The team would figure out how the president's plane would be serviced, where it would park so as to be secure, how the motorcade would come in, and secure it for the night. When Air Force One was on the ground, Turney would go aboard to make sure the crew had whatever they needed. He said it was amazing to watch the public, that is, the crowd that was there to see their president. "The hope in their eyes, the pride, you could feel it in the air. It was just amazing." Turney's final trip was with President Clinton on a flight to Nashville. He got a handshake and a photo taken which he shared for this interview.

In 1998, Turney joined the Sixth Special Operations Squadron at Hurlburt. He was now chief helicopter pilot and senior combat aviation advisor for training and advising for

Jeffrey L. Meek

Central Asia and the Middle East allies in unconventional warfare, coalition support and foreign internal defense. "We would train their (allies) crews in tactics and procedures as well as crew coordination," Turney explained. "We would train to fly on their aircraft, so it was like retro-grading back from the Blackhawk to single engine Hueys."

Turney trained on the Russian Mi-17s and AS-332 French Pumas and flew with the Jordanian and Uzbekistan Air Force and Pakistani Army in support of Operation Enduring Freedom. "We were the first people to go to the old Russian flight academy in the Ukraine to learn how to fly the Mi-17," he said. They (the Russians) were certain we were spies."

And there was an incident in Pakistan that nearly turned into disaster. He was flying in a Puma, trying to teach others how to fly at night with night vision goggles. During a graduation exercise – a night insertion demonstration – the pilot almost crashed. I had to take the airplane away from him and he didn't give it up right away," he said. Turney recovered the plane and later got an Air Medal for his actions. "Thinking back, I was probably the only guy to get an Air Medal in a Pakistani Army, French helicopter with a mixed crew with a Paki General in the back seat," he said.

In 2003, now retired from active duty, Turney got with the Air Force Operation Command as a civil service program analyst in the requirements division. As such he'd set and validate requirements. He ended that service in 2010. After this, until 2012, at Ft. Rucker, Turney was a consultant for a Russian M-17 helicopter contractor and simulator instructor.

War Stories

He and wife Barbara moved to the Village in April 2017 from Ft. Walton Beach, Fla. Looking back on his service he said of his Navy time that it matured him and taught him discipline. In the Air Force he learned not to sweat the small stuff. As a planner he learned to analyze problems, to focus and get a job done.

In 2021, Turney was inducted into the Air Commando Hall of Fame. His citation reads in part: "The singular distinctive accomplishments of Major Turney reflect great credit upon himself, Air Force Special Operations Command and Air Force Commandos of every generation."

Jeffrey L. Meek

Chapter V: War on Terror Veterans

Damon Helton serves five deployments fighting the War on Terror

Damon Helton chased bad guys' through the urban areas of Iraq and the mountains of Afghanistan. He couldn't discuss some of the things I asked about because they are still classified, but he had much to share about his days in uniform with the 75th Ranger Regiment, 2nd Battalion, 'B' Company.

Helton grew up in Little Rock, went to UALR for a few years, then decided to enlist in the Army. "It's in my lineage. Dad was in Special Forces," said Helton. In February 2001 he signed up, seeking Ranger and Airborne schools. After basic training at Ft. Benning he completed Airborne school, making the five required jumps without injury. "So, I was a five-jump chump," Helton joked.

Next, he reported to Ranger school for the Regimental Indoctrination Program, known as R.I.P. The schooling was tough. "They tried to break you. In those three weeks they want to see who was going to stick around and who wasn't," said Helton. In R.I.P. they learned the Ranger Creed, how to patrol, land navigation and trained with different weapons. Helton said many men washed out. They called them 'world-wides' because they'd be sent off to Korea or some other assignment.

Helton made it through the grueling regimented training and was put with the 2nd battalion of the 75th Rangers, reporting to Ft. Lewis, Wash., in late August 2001. Weeks later came September 11. America was attacked,

War Stories

buildings collapsed, and thousands died. "It was all eight cylinders after that. We knew we'd be going somewhere. We just didn't know when," said Helton.

In late February 2002, he deployed to Afghanistan. They arrived right after the Battle of Takur Ghar, better known as Roberts Ridge, when atop Takur Ghar Mountain, several U.S. servicemen were killed, the first of which was Navy Seal Neil C. Roberts. Upon arrival Helton knew he was in the thick of it when he saw the bullet riddled helmets and body armor of another battalion's men.

Helton said the terrain was really difficult. "Our boots were being torn apart. We couldn't walk those mountains. That first deployment changed so many things about our gear and apparel the military was using. Oakley came out with better boots, and we needed better socks because it was so cold," Helton said. "We didn't have any experience with that terrain. Our gear was heavy and bulky, and we couldn't move through the mountains very well. We used to ditch our gear and leave it and chase bad guys up the mountains. We walked and walked and walked on little goat trails on the sides of sheer cliffs which were pretty wild. We'd go out on nightly missions; felt comfortable under night vision," he added.

These early missions were about gathering intelligence, images, and chatter, and, Helton said, the men learned a lot about themselves, walking for days at a time through the mountains. Did it freak you out, I asked. "It was definitely an experience. Some parts of it did. It's strange, we were so well trained for the fight, but we got freaked out about other things," said Helton as he described looking around the area with night vision and seeing eyes following them, which were wild animals.

Four months later, Helton returned to the U.S., trained, and went to Iraq in February 2003 as part of the initial invasion force. "We staged out of Saudi (Arabia)," said Helton, who also saw the U.S. missiles flying overhead heading for Baghdad.

Soon the unit flew into Baghdad and began their nightly missions. One of them was a raid on a prison, looking for POW Michael Scott Spicer, a Navy pilot shot down in January 1991. The unit had gotten a tip that he may be in a Baghdad prison, so his unit checked it out. "We found engraving in one of those cells, 'MS Was Here.' We assumed that was Spicer, but we didn't find anything else," Helton said. (Spicer's remains were found later in 2009. Tests showed he had not survived the crash).

This deployment to Iraq was completely different than the one to Afghanistan. This, in Iraq, was urban warfare, and there were IEDs (Improvised Explosive Devices) to deal with. "We were fortunate to never have any go off on us," Helton said. He explained that they modified their Humvees by removing doors and the top so they could quickly exit the vehicle if needed.

Many times, on patrol they would see Iraqis get on their cell phone as their vehicles approached. "There were eyes everywhere. We saw a lot of that, and we deemed them to be threats; and you handle those accordingly. You respond as you think you need to," said Helton. He added that the men in his unit where well trained, knew what they were doing and knew how to correctly access a situation.

War Stories

He also talked about hunting Saddam Hussain, his sons Uday and Qusay and other 'HVTs,' also known as High Value Targets. The urban environment meant busting down doors and clearing rooms, which at times had families and children in them. "Very easily something bad could happen," said Helton of these encounters. Helton said his experiences told him the Iraqi people wanted U.S. help and one reason why was the viciousness of Uday and Qusay. "They were monsters, evil, evil guys," Helton said as he described some of their acts told to them by an interpreter whose sister had been raped by one of them. The two were eventually killed in a July 22, 2003, shootout in Mosel.

Months later Helton returned to Ft. Lewis. He had met and married a girl named Jana after his first deployment. Now, months later Jana had come to Washington State and shortly after he's home he received a call at 1:30 a.m. Helton thought it was a training exercise, but it wasn't. He was going to Afghanistan again, right now. Jana didn't find out what happened for over a week. Because she had just arrived, no one knew to inform her that her husband was sent off on a mission. "She got a letter in the mail," said Helton.

Now on his third deployment he was part of a winter strike. It would be his shortest, but toughest assignment. Again, chasing HVTs through the mountains for two months in the cold heights of those mountains. They would be resupplied by air as they sought out targets and listened to chatter. Any chatter about Osama bin Laden I asked. "I can't really talk about any of the chatter, but definitely we got a lot of high value information," he answered.

Jeffrey L. Meek

The next deployment, his fourth, was to Afghanistan in early 2004 during what's known as 'The Spring Surge.' Now better equipped, the men spent a lot of time watching borders and checking border crossing points. Again, the terrain was difficult and driving trucks through riverbeds was extremely hard on them. Several trucks broke down which had to be destroyed so nothing was left for the enemy. With 'ground assault convoys' they'd drive up, engage the enemy, and move on, covering hundreds of miles.

IEDs were now everywhere. The men were told to never drive over anything out of place. "They knew our routes. The guys we brought in to find bombs, we'd pay them. Later we'd bust those same guys for planting bombs. It was ridiculous. Now, politics started getting involved. Those guys were enemy combatants and it winded up costing us lives. It was frustrating," said Helton.

This brave Ranger touched on a few other instances during this deployment, like finding poppy fields and the friendly-fire death of NFL player Pat Tillman. Helton said Tillman was in a nearby valley when the accident occurred, adding that it was a ;bad deal' when the Army was not at first honest about what happened. Tillman's brother, Kevin, was in the Headquarters Company and he was not even told the truth at first.

In the fall of 2004, Helton began his fifth deployment. He'd felt it would be his last. "I felt like five deployments was enough running the gauntlet," he said. Jana had told him that it was up to him whether or not he wanted to re-enlist, but if he wanted a family, it was time to

War Stories

get out, so he did and was discharged Feb. 22, 2005, at Fort Lewis.

As a civilian, he went to work for a tactical supply store called '511 Tactical,' first in Washington State, then in Arkansas. He helped grow the company exponentially, but the associated travel was not something he wanted. So, he walked away from a good paying job, bought a 165-acre farm in Lonsdale, and then the Olde Crow General Store.

Reflecting on his dangerous years of service, Helton said the war had really changed by the time he got out, tainted by politics. "Our rules of engagement on our first deployment were so different than our last deployment. It went from, if it had boots on, it's open game, shoot 'em, we're here to fight a war. It went from that to you cannot return fire until you receive accurate enemy fire. I was ready to get out at that point," he said.

He added that deployment cycles are important for people to understand. The four-month deployments seem like a year. The Rangers couldn't Skype, play X-Box or any of that stuff. They were high in the mountains doing serious business.

About service to the nation Helton said, "It was, by far and away, the most humbling and greatest time of my life. I met guys I'm still in touch with today. There's a bond that people just don't get. All of us have a level of PTSD to deal with, but I have a good wife, a good family and good training that allow me to cope with it better than most, unfortunately. What gets me and what brings the emotion out in me is service to this country. I get really fired up when

Jeffrey L. Meek

people start bringing her down and taking advantage of things. They have no idea of the guys who have sweat equity in this country and what they've done," he concluded.

War Stories

Jeffrey Lofgren becomes U.S. Air Force Lt. General

Jeffrey Lofgren grew up in Idaho where his father worked with the Indian Affairs Department. "We lived on an Indian reservation," Lofgren told me in an interview. After several moves, he ended up living in Oregon where he attended high school. After graduation, Lofgren attended the Air Force Academy, earning a mechanical engineering degree and graduating in 1984.

From there he became a student in a pilot training program at Columbus AFB , Miss. He finished at the top of his class and selected F-16 training, eventually doing so at MacDill AFB, Fla. His dream of becoming a fighter pilot was about to come true.

In 1986, Lofgren went to Nellis AFB, Nev., and became an F-16 instructor pilot as his first operational assignment. During this time, he also had deployments to Europe where they were on alert for the Cold War.

In 1989, Lofgren was an F-16 instructor, but also became the Chief of Training, and Weapons Officer at Luke AFB, Ariz. He was chosen as the Outstanding Graduate of the class at the Weapons School in the summer of 1991. "It's the Air Force version of 'Top Gun'," Lofgren said.

Now a Captain, he reported to Mt. Home AFB, Idaho as Squadron Weapons Officer and Flight Commander. This was a Composite Wing, all inclusive, with F-16s, F-15s, B-52s, KC-135s, AWACs and a ground-based radar unit. "I was part of the initial cadre there. It was a great time to be there. I learned a lot about those other airplanes," Lofgren said.

Jeffrey L. Meek

In 1994, he was assigned to the Pentagon as Staff Officer, Joint Requirements Oversight Council Coordinator. This was to build inter-operability, making sure the service branches and their equipment would work together for all. "So we could talk to each other," he explained.

In 1996, Lofgren was selected to attend Air Command and Staff College at Maxwell AFB, Ala., for professional military education. A year later he went to Osan Air Base, South Korea, as Wing Weapons and Tactics Officer. As such he worked with combat operations and to help the Wing put together the wartime materials that pilots need for war.

A year later, he was back in the U.S., but soon returned to Korea, with his family this time, as Director of Operations for the 36th Fighter Squadron, running all flight ops.

In 1999, Lofgren became Commander of the 14th Fighter Squadron at Misawa Air Base, Japan. Lofgren said this position was special. "I had the whole unit. I learned a lot about leadership and people," he said.

In 2001, he attended the National War College at Ft. McNair Army Base, Washington, D.C. In 2002, Lofgren graduated as a Distinguished Graduate and was sent to the Pentagon as Chief, Joint Studies Management Strategic Planning Branch – Joint Staff J-8 Directorate Force Structure, Resources and Assessment.

In 2004, he reported to Hill AFB, Utah, as Commander of the 388th Operations Group, 388th Fighter Wing. The squadrons there constantly deployed to Afghanistan and Iraq. Lofgren himself flew missions in the southern part of Iraq. He was then selected as Commander

War Stories

of the 8th Fighter Wing at Kunsan Air Base in Korea in 2005. This was a Wing that many wanted to have, said Lofgren, so he was excited to be selected for this prestigious Wing, known as the 'Wolfpack,' and he as 'The Wolf.' Tensions were high here when North Korea tested a nuclear weapon. Lofgren said the populace felt comfortable, but the military felt tension.

Next, he returned to D.C. and was assigned to the Institute for Defense Analysis where he was Director of the Joint Advanced War Fighting Program in 2007 – 2008. This was a small 'think tank' for the Joint Staff for the Secretary of Defense for Policy.

"Our primary focus while I was there was, are we winning in Iraq?" said Lofgren. "We worked a lot with folks in Iraq, a lot with Joint Forces Command and OSD policy on how to measure success, how to measure progress. I learned a lot about how you look at things through different lenses. You have a policy lens, you have a war fighter lens, an economic lens and when you start to put these lenses on a problem it gives you a different picture."

I asked him about their conclusions. Were we progressing in Iraq? "I would tell you at the time we had indicators of parts and pieces that were progressing very well. Translating them to a whole of government approach with our partners, the Iraqis, seemed to be a very difficult task to accomplish. Mainly because you had, in reality, competing interests. What we learned is, in some areas it would seem that the personality clashes that were going on were not going to be resolved without change," he explained.

Jeffrey L. Meek

In 2008, Lofgren went to Tyndall AFB, Fla., as Vice Commander, First Air Force and was promoted to a 1-Star Brigadier General. First Air Force was responsible for protection of the United States. All defense support to civil authorities ran through First Air Force. They also dealt with Mexico and Canada. Most of the First Air Force were Guardsmen from Florida, so Lofgren said he had to learn all about the National Guard and how it worked.

In 2009, he reported to Colorado Springs as Deputy Director of Operations, U.S. Northern Command Headquarters. He was responsible for all support to the U.S., Canada, and Mexico, with the biggest challenge relating to drug wars in Mexico. "There were more killings in Juarez, Mexico, than there was across the entire world in one month. So, we were extremely concerned about the spillover of violence in Mexico," Lofgren said.

In 2011, he went to Al Dhafra Air Base, United Arab Emirates, as commander of the 380th Air Expeditionary Wing. The Wing had several different aircraft, from fighters to tankers, to even the U-2 spy plane, flying from the Horn of Africa to daily flights to Afghanistan and Iraq. Lofgren himself flew F-16s, and the KC-10 tanker.

Next, he was again based at Nellis as Commander of the Air Force Warfare Center. Now a 2-Star Major General, Lofgren said it was a dream job. The center was responsible for all advanced training (weapons school, red flag exercises, support for the Army and much more.) and testing of all USAF weapons systems, from space to bombs to airplanes. Lofgren had 22,000 people under his command in 23 states.

War Stories

In 2014, he was selected to go to Al Udeid Air Base, Qatar, as Deputy Combined Forces Air Component Commander. That job was a culmination of all his previous experiences. "I was responsible for basically running the air war over everything in the Middle East," Lofgren said. That encompassed 20,000+ people in several nation/states wanting support. "We only had so many airplanes and so much fuel, so we had to balance that with our joint partners," he explained.

In 2015, Lofgen became a 3-Star, Lieutenant General and served in Norfolk, Va., as Deputy Chief of Staff, Capability Development, Headquarters Supreme, Allied Command Transformation, where he served until retirement on Dec. 1, 2018. In that final assignment, actually a NATO assignment, he was responsible for capabilities and development for all 29 NATO nations, looking for shortfalls and how to address needs and responsibilities.

Lofgren said the other big project then was to determine if they were fit for purpose, given the new security environment they were living in. The answer was not quite, so adjustments were made by Lofgren and his international staff to mitigate issues.

Just days after retirement, Lofgren was asked to return as a temporary Air Force Civilian, working as a highly qualified senior mentor.

Jeffrey L. Meek

Jason Temple served as a combat medic in Gulf War I

Jason Temple came to Arkansas from Illinois as a youngster. He had a goal to become an Air Force jet pilot, got an appointment to the USAF Academy and thought he was good to go. But the summer before he was to leave, the standards were raised and he was one point short, so cut loose. So, Temple went to Southern Arkansas University, then to Texas A & M for an aeronautical program, hoping for a NASA job someday. "Then the space shuttle blew up," said Temple. He thought the disaster would bring changes, plus he was getting more and more involved in Christian ministries, so he changed his focus to civil engineering.

Out-of-state tuition at A & M was proving to be really expensive so he joined the Texas Army Reserves to help qualify for in-state tuition costs. In June 1986, he entered the Reserves as a PFC and reported to Ft. Dix, N.J., for boot camp. In his platoon he was the only one to score expert rifleman, "but I could not hit a barn with a grenade," he added.

In September, he reported to the 273rd Medical Detachment in Tomball, Texas, for reserve duty, one weekend per month. Temple said the 273rd was a Huey helicopter Air Ambulance unit, earlier known as 'Dust-off' during the Vietnam War.

He began his training as a combat medic at Ft. Sam Houston, Texas, in June 1987, got married in 1990 and attempted to finish college, but instead went to work for Carter and Burgess Engineers as an 'engineer-in-training.' Then in November he was called up and got orders for

War Stories

active duty, additional training, and deployment. At Ft. Sam Houston he got squared away and left in a C-5 Galaxy in route to Saudi Arabia.

As the men settled in there were occasional 'Red Dragon' scares – missile attacks by Saddam Hussain. He was promoted to Sergeant by now as the 273rd deployed to their initial base next to Al Qaisumah Airport near Hafera Batin. There for two months they awaited supplies and the First Cavalry. While waiting Temple was sent on a 300-mile trip in an old two-and-a-half-ton truck, back to a Dhahran staging area to pick up medical supplies. Upon arrival he found the place in utter chaos and no supplies designated for the 273rd.

Supplies were randomly placed everywhere, so Temple went looking for what was needed, mostly air ambulance medical supplies. On the way back to his base the heavily loaded truck got stuck in the sand. Temple realized the truck had four-wheel drive, so he flipped a few switches and crawled the truck out, but in so doing lost third and fourth gear. So, at 25 miles an hour they crept across the desert for 300 long miles.

Soon Temple's unit began to go out on missions, usually to pick up wounded soldiers for transport to a hospital. Temple said the dust was incredible. "We had special dust control devices on the helicopters. We had plastic on the leading edge of our tail rotors that protected the end from the sand. Sometimes that stuff would fly off and it would shake the aircraft terribly, so we'd have to go down and cut it off and rebalance and take off again," said Temple.

Jeffrey L. Meek

Maintenance was important, especially when it came to what Temple called the 'Jesus Nut' – the one large nut that held down the main rotor. Temple said there was a safety pin through it that would always, always be checked. "If that main rotor comes off, you're yelling 'Oh Jesus'," he said with a smile.

Jan. 26, 1991, is a date Temple will not forget. The crew had a night mission; called out for a search and rescue assignment. A two-man crew on a surveillance chopper went down, so off they went looking for the crew and chopper. They searched with a LORAN system and as they neared the area, they listened for a radio transmission from the downed crew.

Flying in a circle as they got closer, Temple heard a faint transmission. Soon other crewmen heard it too and eventually they spotted the downed crewmen. They landed and were told to get in and out as soon as possible because their location was near the front lines.

Temple grabbed a crewman while his crew chief grabbed sensitive equipment and documents. As the sun rose, they took off. One crew member had an injured knee and the other was badly bruised. They took them to a nearby hospital for treatment and returned to base. More on this later, stay tuned.

Eventually, his unit was attached to the 217th Medical Battalion that moved forward into Iraq with the First Cavalry Division to provide medical support to combat elements. The outfit carried/helped not only U.S. personnel but Iraqi soldiers, children, and enemy POWs to field hospitals. Some of these Iraqis had been college educated in America, Temple said.

War Stories

One time Temple was putting a dressing on an injured child and the child grabbed his hand and bit him. "I guess he thought I was going to hurt him or was scared to death of me. It was really sad to see kids getting injured," he said.

In March 1991, they relocated to King Fahd Airport and slept in a parking lot, shopped in nearby Al Khobar and Damman and got to see a 300 A.D. Christian church down the road from Jubail. His unit also spent time cleaning aircraft before they were shrink-wrapped and sent home.

In April. Temple flew home. On the way he could barely see the famous Pyramids and saw something else that struck him as beautiful. As they were coming in for a stop in Ireland, Temple noted the tall, lush grasses and thought to himself he'd love to return there someday.

The plane landed in San Antonio and Temple reunited with family at a ceremony in a hanger. He stayed in the Reserves until 1994 and it was that year that something special happened.

He was again working for Carter and Burgess when one day his boss told him they needed to be downtown in Houston at 10:30 a.m. At 10:15 a.m., surprisingly, everyone was called into the break room. Temple looked around and saw a guy with a camera, "and then my family walked in and then I see one of the pilots I flew with in dress uniform, and he calls me to attention and awarded me an Air Medal with V device on it, in front of everybody," he exclaimed. The citation reads in part "for heroism while being observed by Iraqi Forces" and "denying the enemy the opportunity to capture" those downed airmen back in January 1991.

Jeffrey L. Meek

Temple and his wife have four children: Jessica, Mariah, Victoria, and Micaiah.

Reflecting on his Army service Temple said he is very proud to have served, learned a lot, and had a small taste of combat. He also said he remembers the look on the Iraqi people's faces, the fear of their government and all that was going on at that time. It gave him an appreciation for all the freedoms here at home.

"I think everybody should serve their country in some way, at some point in their life, someplace, because our country is so special in comparison to where you could be living in this world, afraid of things every day," he concluded.

War Stories

Photo Section

Soldiers climb aboard a C-47. (Photo courtesy of Sam Spurgeon)

USS Block Island. (Photo courtesy of Gene Andresen)

Jeffrey L. Meek

June 12, 1945 – Adolph Hitler's home, the Berghof. (Photo courtesy of Dr. Ken Seifert)

Author Jeff Meek at Hitler's Eagles Nest. (Jeanne Meek photo)

The entrance to Dachau Concentration camp. (Jeff Meek photo)

LeRoy Baird was a lookout on the USS Hornet during the Doolittle Raid. Here he holds a photo of Gen. Jimmy Doolittle, his wife and raider Davy Jones that was taken at a Raider reunion. (Jeff Meek

War Stories

During the evacuation of Saigon, helicopters land on the USS Kirk, only to be pushed overboard to make room for more helicopters. (Photo courtesy of Hugh Doyle)

A memorial in Belgium to the fallen members of the "Band of Brothers" near the Bois Jacques woods where "E" Company, 506 P.I.R., 101st Airborne Division fought during the Battle of the Bulge. (Jeff Meek photo)

Jeffrey L. Meek

A tank heads for Seoul, South Korea. (Photo courtesy of Bob Whipple)

From left, Korean War veteran Don Van Scotter, Vietnam War veteran Doug Beed and War on Terror veteran Damon Helton. (Jeff Meek photo)

War Stories

Conclusion

From these 85 military veteran stories I think you will get a better understanding of what they experienced, what they lived through, what remains in their memory to this day. In today's world we are detached, disconnected from those who serve. As author Andrew Bacevich wrote in his book, "Breach of Trust," "they fight, while we watch." There is no sacrifice on our part.

We are not with them in spirit like we were during World War II, when many Americans had maps of Europe or the Pacific on their walls, marking the advances of our troops. President Franklin D. Roosevelt, in his June 6, 1944, D-Day prayer with the nation, called them "the pride of our nation."

We in America need to always remember those who served, those who gave their lives to protect us and our way of life. Hopefully these stories will help you remember them always, not just on Veterans Day or Memorial Day, but instead remember them when you see our United States flag waving in the breeze, when you hear our National Anthem and when you sing "God Bless America." As I said in the introduction, "the greatest casualty is being forgotten."

Jeffrey L. Meek

OTHER BOOKS BY RAVEN'S INN PRESS

A LONE GUNMAN? – IT WAS SUPPOSED TO BE A WARM WELCOME IN PREPARATION FOR HIS SECOND RUN FOR THE WHITE HOUSE. NOT EVERYONE GATHERED IN DALLAS THAT FATAL DAY WANTED TO SEE JFK IN OFFICE FOR ANOTHER TERM. THE BIGGEST QUESTIONS ARE BY WHOM AND HOW WAS JOHN F. KENNEDY ASSASSINATED? WAS IT A DERANGED LEE HARVEY OSWALD AS STATED IN THE WARREN COMMISSION REPORT OR A CONSPIRACY? WAS IT REALLY…A LONE GUNMAN?

Years of cover-up now exposed. Read the book, decide for yourself -- Was it just A Lone Gunman? We give it 5-stars. -- Shadowlight Review. Rated 3 ½ Stars by Amazon.com.

MANIPULATION OF LEE HARVEY OSWALD – AND THE COVER-UP THAT FOLLOWED -- includes interviews with Dallas police officers and suspects, and explores the inner workings of the CIA. The author asks why Lee Harvey Oswald was used in Russia, New Orleans and Mexico City, and presents thoughts by former CIA officer Rolf Mowatt-Larssen on a possible assassination scenario. There is also a passage on missing and destroyed evidence in the case.

"This is a book of great detail that is thoroughly documented…a great resource for anyone wanting more information on the JFK assassination." Amazon review. Rated 4 Stars on Amazon.com.

SHADOWLIGHT.–.Ace reporter Rio Shannon searches for the girl of his dreams in a nightclub called The Silk Rose—a place where a woman can break his heart and government hit men can break his neck. But what's life without a little adventure?

"'A well told tale,'" according to MysteryFiction.net. Rated 4 Stars on Amazon.com.

WHILE THE ANGELS SLEPT – When Lydia Taylor's husband dies in an auto accident in Los Angeles, he leaves her so well off she becomes a target for scam artists. Lydia accepts an offer from close friends to stay at their villa in Carmel, but an international gang of art thieves has other plans for her.

Goodreads says, "'Del Garrett possesses the fantastic ability to spin a suspenseful tale, full of vivid imagery and a strong attention to the detail surrounding each scene.'" Rated 4 1/2 Stars on Amazon.com.

DEL GARRETT'S FLEA MARKET TALES – A collection of his award winning or previously published short stories, including *A Matter of Principal*, his Civil War story purchased and published by Louis L'Amour.

"'A recommended read,'" says Shadowlight Review. Rated 5 Stars on Amazon.com.

JAMES—A JOURNEY OF FAITH – An expositional and applicational walk through the text found in the book of James.

Rated 5 Stars on Amazon.com.

TEXAS JUSTICE – An old political enemy sends a killer bounty hunter after a retired Texas Ranger who killed a man in cold blood. The Ranger's adopted son has to track him down before the bounty hunter can find him.

Part I judged as finalist in international eBook competition for Best Historical Western Fiction; Part II won a 1st Place Westward Ho award from Dusty Richards. Rated 5 Stars on Amazon.com.

WHISPERS IN THE WIND (THE SEARCH FOR JACK THE RIPPER) – Late night danger lurks for the fallen angels in London's Whitechapel District. Chief Inspector Lionel Diggins. coping with his own personal demons, the death of his wife and his alcoholism, vows to track down the vile killer before Saucy Jack strikes again.

"'An intriguing look at the Jack the Ripper murders. Chief Inspector Diggins is a wonderfully noir character. Mr. Garrett does disturbing and icky very well.'" – Cam Robbins, Novelspot Reviews   Rated 5 Stars on Amazon.com.

THE EL DORADO TRAIL – A murderous outlaw kills a store-keeper and steals his money. U.S. Marshal Matthias Lawton rides The El Dorado Trail to bring his man to justice. Trouble is, there's three brothers and only one of him; that is until he gets help from an unlikely source—the cousin of the man who just tried to kill him.

A previously 1st Place winner at the White County Creative Writers conference.

THE BUCCANEER'S DAUGHTER – Lady Esther Crowley comes of age just as her father, Captain Robert, is crippled in battle by the evil Captain Diego de la Fuentes. Sharing her father's thirst for adventure, and vowing revenge, she sets out to make the Spanish pirate pay for his crimes against England and against her family. She soon discovers that being a buccaneer's daughter is not as easy as she thought but hiring a handsome thief to captain her father's ship might be more thrilling than finding the pirate's treasure chest…and just as deadly.

Rated 5 Stars on Amazon.com.

THE VAULT OF TERROR, VOLS. 1-2-3 – A collection of short stories designed to tantalize you and tickle your spine while making your blood run cold.

"Enjoyed it a lot. A wide variety of stories, ranging from the slightly weird to the really spooky. Some will keep you awake wondering, Could it really be...?" – Amazon review.

Rated 5 Stars on Amazon.com.

WHITE COUNTY CREATIVE WRITERS ANTHOLOGY 2018 – A collection of award-winning short stories, poems and essays from the member of the White County Creative Writers group in Searcy, Ark.

Made in the USA
Columbia, SC
13 April 2023

14791378R00202